# CINEMA IN BRITAIN:

## An Illustrated Survey

**IVAN BUTLER**

South Brunswick and New York: A. S. Barnes and Company
London: The Tantivy Press

© 1973 by A. S. Barnes and Co., Inc.

A. S. Barnes and Co., Inc.
Cranbury, New Jersey 08512

The Tantivy Press
108 New Bond Street
London W1Y OQX, England

Library of Congress Cataloging in Publication Data

Butler, Ivan.
    Cinema in Britain.

    1.    Moving-pictures—Great  Britain.    I.    Title.
PN1993.5.G7B8            791.43'0942            71-39836
ISBN  0-498-01133-X

SBN  90073060 9  (U.K.)
Printed in the United States of America

*For my wife*

# Contents

# Acknowledgments

I SHOULD LIKE to express my grateful thanks to the staff of the British Film Institute Information Department for their unfailingly cheerful help in research; to Tony Slide for access to valuable material dealing with the silent period; and to Peter Cowie for his many suggestions and his ever-watchful eye in editing the typescript.

Of books dealing solely with the British cinema, the four volumes of Rachael Low's *History of the British Film* published so far (George Allen and Unwin) are mines of information about the silent years; Charles Oakley's *Where We Came In* (George Allen and Unwin) is a succinct, clear account of the industrial side of film-making in Britain; and Denis Gifford's *British Cinema, An Illustrated Guide to the Leading Players and Directors* (Tantivy/Barnes), is a most handy and inexpensive reference book.

I am most grateful to the following for the loan of stills from their private collections:—Barrie Pattison, Peter Cowie, David Markham, Roger Manvell, Tony Slide and Maurice Speed: and to the following companies who have kindly supplied photographs, often going to considerable trouble to meet my requests—Bob Godfrey Films, British Lion, Children's Film Foundation, Columbia-Warner, Compton Films, Contemporary Films, Eagle Films, EMI Elstree Studios, London Screenplays, Michael Powell Productions, M-G-M—EMI Distributors, Paramount Pictures, Planet Film Distributors, Rank Film Distributors, Tigon Pictures, Twentieth Century-Fox, United Artists, West One Producers.

# Introduction

IN MAKING THIS SURVEY of over seventy years I have tried to keep two main considerations in mind: the necessity of including "important" films (good or not so good), and the desirability of including smaller scale productions which have been neglected or underrated, often disappearing from cinema screens almost as soon as they appeared. Many of the latter now stand a good chance of arriving on television, which thus (though not, perhaps, for wholly altruistic reasons) performs Good Samaritan work on films left to die shamefully by the wayside. In addition I have noted a number of productions which are interesting mainly from the historic angle, e.g. the first work of a now famous director, or an actor's early appearance: and no account of British Cinema would be complete without mention of regionally popular series such as *Old Mother Riley* or the George Formby comedies.

All these aims are, of course, limited by availability of space. Omissions are inevitable, and I apologise with bared head and without reservation to any empurpled reader whose most beloved masterpiece does not appear— and hope that perhaps the next most beloved one, happily, does.

During over forty years of film-going I have seen practically all the films discussed in the book (it is, I think, clear where I have included opinions other than my own), and in dealing with the earlier productions I have made every effort to view them in their period. It is absurd and unjust to criticise a film made, say, for the Thirties because it seems "dated" in the Seventies. No play has to undergo such biassed scrutiny, because any modern production is consciously or subconsciously adapted to the conventions and requirements of the present. Even a period novel is read with the modern mind's eye. A film, however, is seen exactly as originally made (probably with the added disadvantage of a poor copy), with all the trappings of its time for ever fixed upon it. If it "wears well," excellent— but in fairness alone the effort of adjustment should be made.

In general, and where ascertainable, films have been entered under the year of their release.

In the matter of stills, I have tried whenever possible to avoid those that have been frequently reproduced. With the large number of film books appearing nowadays it is becoming difficult sometimes to tell one from the other if the illustrations alone are glanced at. For this reason I have at times used stills from the less famous films of a particular year, rather than have the old, only-too-familiar faces reappear once more.

Finally there is the question of what exactly is a "British film." In the great majority of cases this is clear—but, particularly in more recent years, there are borderline cases. In these instances I have followed the listings of the British Board of Trade registrations (as does the *Monthly Film Bulletin* of the British Film Institute), which are based on financial rather than artistic considerations. It may be that in years to come, with the continuing increase of international productions, the division into nationalities will become increasingly arbitrary, and eventually almost meaningless.

# CINEMA IN BRITAIN

# 1895

Birt Acres films with his "Kinetic Lantern" the Derby, The Oxford and Cambridge Boat-race, and the Opening of the Kiel Canal—the latter claimed to be the first newsreel of an event of historic and international importance.

# 1896

THE SOLDIER'S COURTSHIP (R. W. Paul).
Slapstick comedy made an early appearance in this brief episode of a flirtation interrupted by an old woman, who ends beneath a park bench after being edged off it: perhaps the first example in Britain of a "plotted picture." "Extremely comic," says the catalogue, "and a fine film."

## 1896: Facts of Interest

The Lumière Brothers, with M. Trewey as their cameraman, give the first commercial film show (February) at the Polytechnic, Regent Street, London, under the auspices of Quintin Hogg. Films included one of workers leaving their factory, and a comedy, *Watering the Gardener*.

R. W. Paul becomes the first Englishman to give a public performance—at the Olympia, transferring to the Alhambra Music Hall. He also films the Derby and projects it the same evening.

William George Barker, later head of an important production company, starts work as an amateur photographer.

Cecil Hepworth opens an agency for cameras and dry plates in Cecil Court, London.

Michael Balcon and Mary Field are born.

# 1897

THE TWINS' TEA-PARTY (R. W. Paul).
   An early example of the use of close-ups, featuring two small children quarrelling and making-up over tea. 32 ft.

RAILWAY RIDE OVER TAY BRIDGE.
   One of the numerous early railway films, this illustrates a four-part journey across the Scottish bridge built to replace that blown down in one of the most famous of all train disasters. 292 ft.

QUEEN VICTORIA'S DIAMOND JUBILEE.
   Covered by R. W. Paul and others—an undoubted boost to news films, as Queen Elizabeth's Coronation would be to television sixty years later.

## 1897: Facts of Interest

An early glass studio is built by the Mutoscope and Biograph Company (E. B. Koopman, Managing Director).

Cecil Hepworth publishes his *ABC of Cinematography*.
   G. A. Smith begins to make films in Brighton of "Simple Actualities."
   "American Biograph" is installed in the Palace Theatre, London—invented by Herman Castor of Canastota, New York.
   A Mr. Lane attempts to establish a permanent home for movie shows in a shop in Kingston-on-Thames, Surrey, covering the windows with brown paper. The project is unsuccessful because people do not know what they are being asked inside to see.
   Walker & Turner, the first renting company in Great Britain, begin operations. Later, as Walturdaw, they enter the production side (1905).
   Alberto Cavalcanti and Victor Saville are born.

*1897: QUEEN VICTORIA'S DIAMOND JUBILEE,*
*"an undoubted boost to news films."*

# 1898

### THE DESERTER (R. W. Paul).

An early example of a "produced" drama, concerning a soldier who deserts, his mother who tries to hide him, and the military who come to arrest him and take him away. 80 ft.

### WAVES AND SPRAY (G. A. Smith).

A number of "moving seascapes" were made around this time. Others included *The Incoming Tide* (Prestwich, 1898), *Breaking Waves* and *Snapshots at the Seaside* (Hepworth, 1903). G. A. Smith was a Brighton photographer who became a pioneer British film-maker and lived to the age of ninety-six.

### GLASGOW FIRE ENGINE (R. W. Paul).

An example of another *genre* as popular as railways, seascapes and comedy incidents. Comedy in fact enters into this, for after the men have got the engine going a cart blocks the road "with amusing effect." 40 ft. In another fire film, *The Sensational Fire Engine Collision,* an engine dashes into the camera.

### 1898: Facts of Interest

Gaumont Company is set up in Britain by A. G. Bromhead and T. A. Welsh.

Charles Urban, an American managing the Edison film agency, founds the Warwick Trading Company.

Louis Le Prince, who was born in France but married an English girl and lived in Leeds, takes numerous films of the city with a single-lens camera which was also used as a projector. He later disappeared mysteriously on a train journey in France.

G. A. Smith uses double exposure in a number of fictional films. John Grierson, Richard Massingham and John Stuart are born.

# 1899

EXPRESS TRAIN IN A RAILWAY CUTTING (Hepworth).

The first film on the list of the famous pioneer producer. The date is given elsewhere as 1898, but Hepworth himself places it in 1899. The cutting is in Surrey. 50 ft.

## 1899: Facts of Interest

The first commercially successful cine-camera is constructed by Messrs. J. A. Prestwich.

The "Brighton School" of film-makers develops: G. A. Smith, Esme Collings, James Williamson.

John Bennett Stanford makes the first war news film. Joe Rosenthal becomes the first professional war cameraman, for Charles Urban. The newsreel develops rapidly through the Boer War, 1899–1902.

Alfred Hitchcock is born.

# 1900

### HOW IT FEELS TO BE RUN OVER (Hepworth).

An early motor comedy. Pursued by a cart, a car rushes along a road heading straight for the camera. The driver and occupants try frantically to stop it, but it apparently drives straight for the spectator—and he "sees stars." 50 ft.

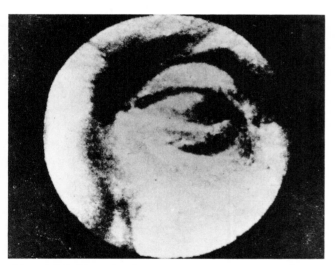

*1900: GRANDMA'S READING GLASS, an early example of extreme close-up.*

### THE ECCENTRIC DANCER (Hepworth).

A trick film in which, Hepworth claims, slow motion photography is used probably for the first time.

### ARMY LIFE, OR HOW SOLDIERS ARE MADE (R. W. Paul).

A series of short films depicting a soldier's career and various aspects of service activities.

### GRANDMA'S READING GLASS (G. A. Smith).

A trick film starting with Grandma using her magnifying glass, and then showing what she sees through it. 100 ft. The effect was used again a couple of years later to magnify a tooth which a man has extracted by means of a piece of string.

### 1900: Facts of Interest

G. A. Smith joins the Warwick Trading Company.

Waller Jeffs, of the West End Theatre, Birmingham, takes moving pictures of local workers leaving their factories and advertises "Come and See Yourselves on the Flickering Screen."

Will Barker Film Company is formed.

# 1901

**THE BIG SWALLOW** (Williamson).

A man approaches the camera until his mouth fills the whole frame, resulting in a dark space down which camera and cameraman seem to vanish. The man then moves backwards munching, with a look of satisfaction. An early example of a tracking shot, with the photographed object tracking, instead of the camera. 65 ft.

**FIRE!** (Williamson).

This film provides evidence of the growing complexity of the new medium. Five consecutive scenes tell the story of a house on fire, the alerting of the brigade, their arrival, and the rescue of the occupants. Portions of the film are stained red, and the whole shows the beginnings of editing in the combination of interior and exterior shots. 280 ft.

**THE HAUNTED CURIOSITY SHOP**
(R. W. Paul).

A quick succession of trick gags, including the top half of a woman crossing a room followed by her lower half; an Egyptian mummy dissolving into a skeleton; three gnomes becoming one; a large head looming through smoke issuing from a jar. 131 ft.

**FUNERAL OF QUEEN VICTORIA**
(Hepworth).

The film is taken from three positions, Hepworth himself being at Grosvenor Gardens opposite Victoria Station. "Everyone who takes part appears life-size," runs a contemporary report, "and has his portrait faithfully recorded."

**1901: Facts of Interest**

Cricks & Sharp Production Company starts up in Mitcham, Surrey. Charles Pathé establishes a British branch in London.

# 1902

**THE CALL TO ARMS** (Hepworth).

The film shows a dandified ladies' man who turns out a brave soldier—an interesting contrast to the pre-Boer War film showing sympathetic treatment of the deserter in 1898.

**HOW TO STOP A MOTOR-CAR** (Hepworth).

A trick film in which a police constable is broken into pieces by a car then joins himself up again, whereupon an inspector demonstrates that he should bend down with his back to the car so that it bounces off him. 89 ft.

**A RESERVIST BEFORE THE WAR, AND AFTER THE WAR** (Williamson).

An early example of social pleading. An army reservist is summoned from his wife and children to serve. After the war is over his home is bare and his family starving: he steals some bread, is followed home by a policeman, but the latter, seeing the man's conditions, takes pity on him. 286 ft.

**THE CORONATION OF EDWARD VII, AND THE DELHI DURBAR.**

Two more well-covered State Occasions which help build up interest in the newsreel. Filmed by Hepworth, Paul, Gaumont and others.

**1902: Facts of Interest**

Will Barker starts production at Ealing.

F. Ormiston-Smith takes films on Mont Blanc and the Alps.

Anthony Asquith and Brian Desmond Hurst are born.

# 1903

**ALICE IN WONDERLAND** (Hepworth).

One of the longest films of the period, done in sixteen scenes dissolving from one to the other, photographed in natural surroundings and based on the Tenniel drawings. The scenes were listed consecutively in the catalogue and could be purchased separately. Alice is played by May Clarke ("a little girl in the cutting room") and Mrs. Hepworth appears as the White Rabbit.

**A DARING DAYLIGHT ROBBERY** (Frank S. Mottershaw).

This first film by one of R. W. Paul's assistants encouraged, by its success, the growing vogue for crime-and-action stories. A straightforward account of a robbery, it featured local music hall actors. Five hundred copies were sold outright and the negative was eventually disposed of in America.

**WELSHED: A DERBY DAY INCIDENT** (Gaumont).

Directed by Alfred Collins, this contains an early example of a panning shot in the opening moments.

**A CHESS DISPUTE** (R. W. Paul).

Two men quarrel over a chess game. They fight and both fall out of sight on the ground. Clothing, arms and legs are seen flashing briefly into view, until a waiter arrives and hauls the battered antagonists upright. A pioneer example of the creation of suspense by what the camera does *not* show. 80 ft.

**1903: Facts of Interest**

Hepworth builds an indoor studio at Walton-on-Thames.

Urban leaves Warwick and founds his own trading company.

Betty Balfour is born.

# 1904

**HAMLET** (Barker).

This early and ambitious venture was completed in one day except for the drowning of Ophelia. The settings—over twenty of them—were erected one inside the other, onion-skin fashion, so that as each one was finished with it was dismantled and the action proceeded swiftly in the next. The actor chosen as Hamlet was a man already familiar with the part: the casting of the remainder was on the happy-go-lucky principles of the period.

**THE MISTLETOE BOUGH** (Clarendon).

One of the first horror films, based on the famous song (by Henry Bishop) about the bride who hides during a game at her wedding festivities and cannot be found. Years later her widower sees her ghost emerging from an old locked chest. Appalled, he forces it open and—finds a skeleton: an authentic horror film climax. 477 ft.

**THE JONAH MAN** (Hepworth).

A trick film making use of the camera's capability of causing things gradually to disappear and reappear: a man preparing to go on a journey finds everything—coat, case, transport—vanishing as he tries to make use of it. 246 ft.

**RUSSO-JAPANESE WAR.**

Reporting of death and destruction contributed to the expected impetus: covered by Gaumont, Pathé, Urban and others.

### 1904: Facts of Interest

Clarendon Film Company found studios in Croydon.

National Association of Theatrical Employees (now NATKE) starts to organise projectionists.

Ian Dalrymple is born.

# 1905

RESCUED BY ROVER. Director: Cecil Hepworth. Players: Sebastian Smith, Mrs. Smith, Cecil Hepworth, Mrs. Hepworth, "Baby" Hepworth, May Clark.

Holding somewhat the same position in British cinema as *The Great Train Robbery* (1903) in American, as the first major achievement in the fiction film. Making imaginative use of both ex-

*1905: RESCUED BY ROVER, the first canine star.*

26

terior and interior settings, using low-angle and panning shots, the film's main significance is its advanced editing and continuity technique. Dispensing with titles, the story (of a kidnapped child rescued by an intelligent dog) is told by cinematic, visual means. Re-made three times, the original cost was under £8, and it sold nearly 400 prints. Hepworth's wife wrote the story and played the mother, his eight-months old baby the heroine, his dog the hero. It is, in his own words, "a quaintly simple little film." 425 ft.

## THE LIFE OF CHARLES PEACE
(William Haggar).

One of the longest films of the period, it follows the career of the notorious murderer from the killing of Mr. Dyson to his execution in 1879. The Banner Cross crime and Peace's famous leap from the train after his arrest were filmed "on the exact spots." The execution is shown in grim detail. Though more elaborate than *Rescued by Rover,* it is technically less assured. It is also very much a family operation, William Haggar at the camera, four Haggar brothers taking part (Walter as Peace), one daughter playing Peace's mistress and another (twelve years old and dressed as a boy) his young burglar assistant. 735 ft. Another version of Peace's career was made by the Sheffield Photo Company, in twelve scenes. The execution was not shown, being regarded as "too ghastly and repulsive."

## FALSELY ACCUSED (Hepworth).

Another long film, depicting a robbery in the City of London: a clerk is accused, imprisoned; he escapes, and, helped by a priest, proves his innocence.

## A DEN OF THIEVES (Hepworth).

Yet another complex story of a crime from its preliminary plotting (a maidservant accomplice in a suburban house steals open a letter) through execution (disguised thieves follow their victim to a bank and rob him) to discovery and nemesis. 425 ft.

Films such as the above make 1905 a key year in early British cinema, though it is followed by periods of less interesting development. The strong interest in crime and retribution (canine or human) may be noted.

**1905: Facts of Interest**

Biograph Cinema, Wilton Road, London opens, with a claim to be the first building converted from a row of shops as a picture house: by an American, George Washington Grant. It survives to this day, flourishing gamely amid towering super-stores. Its original name was the Bioscope.

Walturdaw Company is formed.

Muriel Box and Michael Powell are born.

# 1906

**THE MOTORIST** (R. W. Paul).

This short trick film combines camera illusions with realistic treatment. Foreshadowing the first space satellite, it follows the journey of a motorist and his wife up the side of a building, over the roof, into the sky, through the stars to Saturn (circling the planet on its rings), back to earth, splashing down into a police court, changing into a pony trap and back, and rushing off. 190 ft.

**OUR NEW ERRAND BOY** (Williamson).

A Brighton School comedy with emphasis on the chase, featuring the slapstick mischief of a grocer's lad. A final close-up depicts the boy's pleasure at his havoc. 125 ft.

### 1906: Facts of Interest

G. A. Smith, with Charles Urban, patents Kinemacolor, the first commercially successful colour process.

Hale's Tours open in an Oxford Street shop—the audience sees travelogues while seated (and shaken) in a mock-up railway coach.

The first newsreel cinema opens in Bishopsgate, London—the Daily Bioscope. It runs continuously from twelve noon to nine p.m. Admission: 2d. and 4d.

Carol Reed and Harry Watt are born.

*1906: Early science fiction in THE MOTORIST.*

# 1907

THE SALMON POACHERS (William Haggar).
This very popular film perhaps owed its success to the fact that audience sympathy is directed towards the two poachers who, though caught by the police, manage to make their escape.

A SEASIDE GIRL (Hepworth).
Another advance in comedy from the plotless knockabout chase to a more "natural" situation and more recognisable characters. A girl reading on the beach is pestered by three men: after various attempts to escape them she hires a bathing machine, but they pursue her in a boat. Eventually one of them triumphs by overturning his two rivals into the water. 325 ft.

## 1907: Facts of Interest

William Haggar opens his first cinema in Aberdare, Wales.

Sound recording systems, Cinematophone (Walturdaw) and Vivaphone (Hepworth), are well established.

Will Barker builds a stage at his Ealing site, approximately on the spot of the later famous studios.

A programme of films only is shown for the first time at a regular theatre, the Balham Empire.

*Kinematograph Weekly,* trade paper, is launched.

Central Hall, Colne, Lancashire, opens—one of the first buildings erected *exclusively* for films.

Humphrey Jennings, Frank Launder, Edgar Anstey, Laurence Olivier, Paul Rotha and Basil Wright are born.

# 1908

JOHN GILPIN'S RIDE (Hepworth).

The story of the famous ride is used to bring in an authentic series of Georgian locations and country scenes. The technical feature of interest is a shot tracking the horse from a following car. 575 ft.

ROMEO AND JULIET (Gaumont). Players: Godfrey Tearle, Mary Malone.

The first major attempt at filming Shakespeare, recording a notable stage production with leading players, thus briefly anticipating the French *Film d'Art*, founded with much the same object. 1,240 ft.

THE GUARDIAN OF THE BANK (Cricks and Martin).

Another example of super-canine intelligence: in this instance the ancestor of Rin Tin Tin and descendant of Rover foils a bank robbery, and is awarded a final close-up all to himself. 570 ft.

## 1908: Facts of Interest

Two early British circuits are launched—Electric Theatres and Biograph. Both own cinemas in London.

Gaumont organises the first Trade Show.

The Alpha Picture House, St. Albans, Hertfordshire, is opened.

David Lean and Sidney Gilliat are born.

# 1909

**THE TILLY TOMBOYS** (Hepworth).

This pioneer short-film series started out as a single feature, *Tilly the Tomboy,* played by Unity More, a dancer. When a follow-up was needed she was not available, so Tilly was given a companion and the series continued their mischievous adventures, founding the careers of two leading players of the silent period—Alma Taylor and Chrissie White.

**THE AIRSHIP DESTROYER** (Charles Urban).
**AIR PIRATES OF 1920** (Cricks and Martin).

Two "wars of the future" features. The first depicts an air attack on England foiled by an aerial torpedo (the inventor spurred on by amatory rather than patriotic zeal); the second includes the bombing of a liner by an airship.

**1909: Facts of Interest**

The Cinematograph Act (1909) is passed, becoming law in January 1910.

Continuous performances become the general rule.

Provincial Cinematograph Theatres Ltd. is formed, with Ralph Jupp as Managing Director.

The Electric Theatre, first in Glasgow centre, opens.

American films predominate the British screen.

Charles Frend is born.

# 1910

FROM GYPSY HANDS (Cricks and Martin).

A messenger boy is robbed of some pearls by a gypsy, Scouts find the boy, trace the gypsy, retrieve the pearls, are pursued, but eventually obtain a reward. The film demonstrates the advances in technique during the last days of the one-reeler, such as the increase of camera set-ups (about thirty) and of panning shots. 570 ft.

BIRTH OF A FLOWER (Kineto Company—Percy Smith).

The first of Percy Smith's famous nature films, using time-lapse photography (a process invented by himself) to show the growth and development of flowers, plants, etc. through a long period.

**1910: Facts of Interest**

William Haggar builds his first *permanent* cinema, in Mountain Ash, Wales.

The Montagu Pyke circuit of small cinemas (about 450 seats) is built up.

Rover the Dog dies. (This is the date given by Hepworth: other authorities give 1914, and certainly Rover films appear in the catalogue after the earlier date. It is possible "Rover" became a generic term for Rover-type rescuers.)

# 1911

RACHEL'S SIN (Hepworth). Players: Hay Plumb, Gladys Sylvani.

A "strong domestic drama" of an unhappy marriage, a wife who accidentally kills her drunken husband, a lover who takes the blame on himself, serves a prison sentence, and on release finds the little widow waiting: this film was used as an attempt to lift British production out of the increasing monotony which was causing it to sink beneath the American influx. 900 ft.

HENRY VIII (Barker). Players: Sir Herbert Tree, Violet Vanbrugh, Arthur Bouchier, Edward O'Neill.

An ambitious version of the stage production by Tree and Louis N. Parker. Tree was paid £1,000 for one day's work. It was followed by versions of several of Sir Frank Benson's Stratford-on-Avon productions, such as *Richard III*, *Macbeth*, and *Julius Caesar*.

SCOTT'S ANTARCTIC EXPEDITION (Gaumont). Photography: Herbert G. Ponting.

The first part of the film covering the voyage, it caused a sensation on account of its beauty and realism. 3,000 ft.

SIDNEY STREET SIEGE (Gaumont).

Graphic newsreels include Winston Churchill directing operations at the scene of the battle with the Houndsditch anarchists. A Pathé film later shows the funeral of one of the policemen killed during the siege.

## 1911: Facts of Interest

*Today's Cinema*, trade paper, founded as the *Cinema News and Property Gazette*.

The Electric Cinema, South Kensington, opens: later re-named The Boltons, and now the Paris-Pullman.

The Picture House, Oxford Street, Manchester opens. It has now been re-built as the New Oxford, but parts of the original still remain.

Robert Hamer and Ronald Neame are born.

# 1912

SAVED BY FIRE (Clarendon). Player: Dorothy Bellew.

The first three-reel British drama also marks the entry of the vamp, in the person of Eulalie, an actress, who entices the hero from his "soft-eyed little wife," but is, with dramatic irony, burned to death when the latter upsets a lamp in the boudoir while watching—in understandable agitation—the adulterous pair at work. 3,000 ft.

OLIVER TWIST (Hepworth). Players: Harry Royston, Alma Taylor, Flora Morris, E. Rivarze, Willie West.

Hepworth's first film of over 3,000 ft. was commercially extremely successful, though not, as he says himself, "outstandingly good." It marks the beginning of a long series of adaptations from Dickens and other popular novelists. 3,700 ft.

OLD ST. PAUL'S (Clarendon).

The extraordinarily effective model work makes this large-scale version of Harrison Ainsworth's novel noteworthy. 3,000 ft.

MUSICAL MATCHES (Urban).

In this embryonic cartoon animation short, matches emerge from a silver box, form themselves into various shapes, and enact brief scenes. 330 ft.

### 1912: Facts of Interest

Merton Park Studios are opened by J. H. Martin, Ltd.

Bushey Studios are set up by the well-known painter Sir Hubert von Herkomer.

The Cinematograph Exhibitors' Association is formed.

The British Board of Film Censors is established, with G. A. Redford as President. Only two categories, U and A, are allotted.

Walpole Theatre, Ealing, London, opens.

1912: *Alma Taylor and Harry Royston in Cecil Hepworth's* OLIVER TWIST.

# 1913

HAMLET. Direction: E. Hay Plumb, based on the Drury Lane Theatre production. Players: Sir Johnston Forbes-Robertson, Walter Ringham, A. Scott-Gatty, S. A. Cookson, George Hayes, Eric Adeney, Robert Atkins, Gertrude Elliott, Adeline Bourne, Olive Richardson. Production: Cecil Hepworth. 3,100 ft.

*1913: A frame enlargement from Thomas Bentley's production of DAVID COPPERFIELD for Hepworth, showing the elopement of Emily (Amy Verity) and Steerforth (Cecil Mannering).*

*1913: Sir Johnston Forbes Robertson as HAMLET.*

Every care was lavished on the production, with Elsinore Castle built at Lulworth Cove, and the Hawes Craven (one-dimensional) scenery reproduced in solid form. In spite of all this effort, only the barest shadow of what was reputedly one of the greatest Hamlet performances remains—an example of the foolishness of making a silent record of a work created for circumstances where sound is all-important and scenery non-existent. A silent film of an orchestra playing a Beethoven symphony would convey almost as much of its original.

THE HOUSE OF TEMPERLEY. Players: Ben

Webster, Charles Rock, Charles Maude, Lillian Logan, Edward O'Neill. Production: London Film Company (Ralph Jupp).

The first production of the London Film Company is a version of Conan Doyle's Regency novel *Rodney Stone,* setting a high general standard and achieving considerable commercial success.

**THE FOOL.** Direction: George Pearson. Players: Godfrey Tearle, Mary Malone, James Carew. Production: Big Ben Films (George Pearson). 3,343 ft.

Pearson's first film is based on his own story—a society drama about a man who shields a woman charged with cheating at cards.

**PIMPLE.** Players: Fred Evans, Will Evans, Joe Evans. Production: Folly Films.

An enormously popular series of burlesque shorts, produced at the rate of one a week for some two years, mainly parodying current stage and film shows.

**SIXTY YEARS A QUEEN.** Production: Will Barker, Jack Smith, Ernest Shirley, in association with G. B. Samuelson. 6,000 ft.

A large-scale episodic reconstruction of somewhat arbitrarily selected events during the reign of Queen Victoria.

**THE DERBY** (Gaumont).

In one of the most famous newsreel scoops of all time, the Gaumont cameraman photographs the death of the suffragette Emily Davidson, who threw herself in front of the King's horse.

**1913: Facts of Interest**

Twickenham Film Studios, the largest in the country, are opened by the London Film Company.

Adrian Brunel starts to work in films.

Henry Cornelius, and John and Roy Boulting are born.

# 1914

A STUDY IN SCARLET. Script: Harry Engholm, from the novel by Arthur Conan Doyle. Direction: George Pearson. Players: Fred Paul, Agnes Glynne, Harry Paulo. Production: Samuelson. 5,800 ft.

Though Sherlock Holmes appears in the film, it is not until towards the end, and the greater part deals with revenge and murder among the Mormons—the Cheddar Gorge and Southport sands representing the Rockies and Salt Lake. The production—G. B. Samuelson's first under his own banner—is commendable for its fast, economical narrative power.

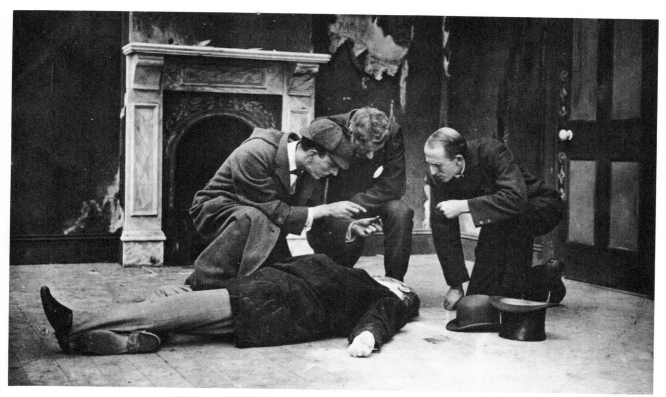

*1914: A STUDY IN SCARLET, directed by George Pearson.*

**KISMET.** Script: Leedham Bantock, from the play by Edward Knoblock. Direction: Leedham Bantock. Art Direction: Joseph Harker. Players: Oscar Asche, Lily Brayton, Caleb Porter, Herbert Grimwood. Production: Zenith. 4,000 ft.

For this production, yet another re-creation of a stage spectacle, Harker's sets were put up on the studio stage (Whetstone, Hertfordshire) and travelogues of Baghdad cut in with the action.

**THE SEVENTH DAY.** Script, direction and production: Arthur Finn, Charles Weston.

In a small manufacturing town the cinemas stay open on Sundays and everyone is happy—except the publicans. By scurrilous means, the latter manage to enforce closure of the picture houses. Result: universal drunkenness, and crime, culminating in a man's fatal fall over a cliff and the discovery of his battered body by his little daughter. A slight hint of a "commercial" in this film somewhere, perhaps, or even of special pleading—but the film-makers and exhibitors appear to have proved their point.

## 1914: Facts of Interest

Boreham Wood studios are built for the Neptune Film Company.

Worton Hall studios (Isleworth) are opened by Vesta Tilley for G. B. Samuelson, with George Pearson as producer/director.

British Actors' Film Company take over Bushey studios, with A. E. Matthews as managing director.

The first true animated cartoons in Britain appear, made by Lancelot Speed.

The Marble Arch Pavilion is opened.

J. Lee Thompson is born.

# 1915

JANE SHORE. Script: Rowland Talbot. Direction: Bert Haldane, F. Martin Thornton. Photography: Fred Bovill, Leslie Eveleigh. Art Direction: P. Mumford, F. Ambrose. Players: Blanche Forsythe, Roy Travers, Robert Purdie, Nelson Phillips, Dora de Winton, Tom Macdonald, Rolfe Leslie. Production: Will Barker. 5,500 ft.

Barker's best known film tells the story of King Edward IV's mistress and the struggle between the Lancastrians and the Yorkists on a vastly spectacular scale. The battle of Marston Moor was shot in three days in the Devil's Dyke, Sussex, by some five thousand extras. Technically the film is uninteresting, and the script demands some pre-

*1915: The Yorkists flock to Edward IV's Standard, from Will Barker's elaborate production JANE SHORE.*

knowledge of the intricate struggle for power to be comprehensible.

MY OLD DUTCH. Script: Albert Chevalier, Arthur Shirley. Direction: Larry Trimble. Photography: Tom White. Players: Albert Chevalier, Florence Turner ("The Vitagraph Girl"). Production: Turner. 5,600 ft.

The great commercial success of this film, which is merely a tenuous and sentimental story round the songs made famous by Chevalier, led to a fashion for similar treatment of other popular ditties.

SWEET LAVENDER. Script: Cecil Hepworth, from Arthur Pinero's play. Direction: Hepworth. Photography: Hepworth. Players: Alma Taylor, Chrissie White, Henry Ainley, Stewart Rome. Production: Hepworth. 5,000 ft.

One of Hepworth's most popular films of the period, it shows the stars of the *Tilly Tomboys* in very contrasting roles, and features, in Stewart Rome, one of his favourite actors.

A WELSH SINGER. Script: from a story by Allen Raine. Direction: Henry Edwards. Photography: Tom White. Players: Henry Edwards, Florence Turner, Campbell Gullan, Una Venning, Edith Evans. Production: Turner. 4,600 ft.

A fairly conventional romantic drama, this is notable as the first production of Henry Edwards —probably the earliest British actor to qualify for star status; and also as the first of Edith Evans's two appearances in silent films.

**NIPPER'S BANK HOLIDAY. Production: Lupino Lane.**

The first of Lupino Lane's series of *Nipper* one-reel comedies—relying mainly on his own personality, but somewhat short on general proficiency. In one of them, *Only Me,* he played all the parts (over twenty) himself.

## 1915: Facts of Interest

Ideal Films, formerly a renting company, enters production at Boreham Wood.

The Kinematograph Renters' Society is registered.

The Scala Theatre, London, is taken over for performances of Griffith's *Birth of a Nation*.

Terence Young is born.

# 1916

COMIN' THRO' THE RYE. Script: Cecil Hepworth, from the novel by Helen Mathers. Direction: Hepworth. Players: Alma Taylor, Stewart Rome, Lionelle Howard, Campbell Gullan. Production: Hepworth. 5,000 ft.

Hepworth's early version of the well-known tear-jerker is noteworthy mainly on account of its being the first film to receive a Royal Command performance before Queen Alexandra at Marlborough House. It was to be re-made in 1924.

ARSENE LUPIN. Script: George Loane Tucker, from the play by Leblanc and De Croisset. Direction: G. L. Tucker. Players: Gerald Ames, Manora Thew. Production: London Film Company.

The film contains an early example of the use of double exposure for dual roles.

SHE. Script: Nellie Lucoque, from H. Rider Haggard's novel. Direction: Will Barker. Art Direction: Lancelot Speed. Players: Alice Delysia, Henry Victor, Sidney Bland. Production: Barker, in association with C. B. Cochran, and H. Lisle Lucoque.

The first version of Rider Haggard's story, lavishly produced, makes full use of the opportunity of presenting the famous French actress in as little clothing as is (at the time) permissible, and packs out the New Gallery Cinema, Regent Street.

ULTUS, THE MAN FROM THE DEAD. Script: George Pearson. Direction: George Pearson. Players: Aurele Sydney, J. L. V. Leigh, A. Caton Woodville. Production: Gaumont. 6,000 ft.

This is the opening film of what was to become the most famous early series based on the adventures of a commanding mystery figure—Ultus the Avenger—replete with secret societies, hooded men, symbolic coffins—made in response to Leon Gaumont's request for a British partner to the French *Fantômas*. Future episodes, each complete in itself, comprise *Ultus and the Grey Lady, Ultus and the Secret of the Night,* and (finally) *Ultus and the Three Button Mystery,* involving—with prophetic vision—the kidnapping of a Cabinet Minister. Much of the mysterious strangeness of Feuillade is to be found in these Ultus productions.

BATTLE OF THE SOMME. Direction and photography: Geoffrey Malins, J. B. McDowell. 5 reels.

The earliest full-length documentary of the First World War, the propaganda value and the attunement to the mood of the moment of which account more for its enormous success than any intrinsic merits. However, though consisting mainly of unrelated shots interspersed with numerous and sometimes lurid titles, it contains some

*1916: Aurele Sidney as ULTUS, THE MAN FROM THE DEAD.*

striking scenes (e.g. of tanks in action), is authentic in detail and uncompromising—if naturally one-sided—in approach.

### 1916: Facts of Interest

Entertainment Tax is imposed on cinema seats. A typical price list of the period reads: "4d., 6d., 9d., and 1/− with tea."

Production of British films starts to show a decline under continuing war conditions.

*1916: Another scene from ULTUS.*

# 1917

MILESTONES. Script: Thomas Bentley, from the play by Arnold Bennett and Edward Knoblock. Direction: Thomas Bentley. Players: Campbell Gullan, Isobel Elsom, Owen Nares, Hubert Harben, Mary Lincoln. Production: Samuelson.

Though a straightforward adaptation, adventurous attempts are made to expand beyond the confines of the stage by relevant shots of the period, street scenes of old London, news items, and even a "modern" cinema.

THE LIFEGUARDSMAN. Script: Walter Howard, from his play. Direction: Frank Bayly. Players: A. E. Matthews, Annie Saker, Alfred Paumier, Alfred Bishop, Fred Kerr, Spencer Trevor, Fred Volpé, Leslie Carter, Leslie Henson, Sam Livesey, Cecil Humphreys, Charles Daly. Production: B.A.F.C.

A notable company of stage players came together to launch this first production of the B.A.F.C., somewhat delayed in its completion: a mythical-kingdom, uniform-and-tiaras melodramatic romance.

MASKS AND FACES. Script: Benedict James, from the play by Charles Reade and Tom Taylor. Direction: Fred Paul. Art Direction: Willie Davis. Players: Sir George Alexander, Sir Johnston Forbes-Robertson, Irene Vanbrugh, Gladys Cooper, Dennis Neilson-Terry, Winifred Emery, H. B. Irving, Matheson Lang, Gerald du Maurier, Lilian Braithwaite, Ellaline Terriss, Charles Hawtrey, Gertrude Elliott. Production: Ideal. 6,700 ft.

Possibly the starriest all-star cast of all time, cramped into the tiny Bushey studios, this film seems to have been somewhat overweighted by its own prestige—a result not unknown in later years also. Its purpose was to raise the reputation of British films and at the same time to raise funds, incongruously, for the Royal Academy of Dramatic Art.

BATTLE OF ARRAS, BATTLE OF ANCRE, BATTLE OF ST. QUENTIN. Direction and photography: Geoffrey Malins, J. B. McDowell.

The three follow-ups to the same team's *Battle of the Somme* did not prove as successful as their predecessor: but put together they conveyed some idea of what it meant to be at the front in the First World War.

## 1917: Facts of Interest

D. W. Griffith makes his *Hearts of the World* in agreement with the War Office Committee. His *Intolerance* is presented at Drury Lane Theatre.

T. P. O'Connor is appointed Film Censor.

Weekly attendance at the cinema in Great Britain is estimated at 20,000,000.

1917: Ben Webster, Lillah McCarthy, Dion Bouci-
cault, Irene Vanbrugh, Gladys Cooper and (in forefront) Dennis Neilson-Terry, in the all-star MASKS
AND FACES.

1917: High drama in ULTUS AND THE GREY
LADY.

# 1918

KIDDIES IN THE RUINS. Script: George Pearson, from a music hall sketch by Poubol and Paul Gull. Direction: George Pearson. Photography: M. Rollin. Players: Emmy Lynn, Hugh E. Wright, Georges Collin, M. Gouget and members of the Comédie Française. Production: Welsh-Pearson. 3 reels.

Despite the presence of a bereaved mother

1918: *KIDDIES IN THE RUINS, directed by George Pearson.*

46

*1918: Charles Rock, Hugh E. Wright and Arthur Cleave in Pearson's THE BETTER 'OLE.*

(played on the stage by Sybil Thorndike) the story is mainly one of comedy and thrills as a group of children play amid the ruins of French towns. It was filmed in a Paris suburb, Courneuve, and the Eclair studios.

**HINDLE WAKES.** Script: Eliot Stannard, from the play by Stanley Houghton. Direction: Maurice Elvey. Players: Norman McKinnell, Colette O'Neill, Edward O'Neill, Ada King, Margaret Bannerman. Production: Samuelson. 5,000 ft.

Maurice Elvey's span of over forty years in direction covers a consistently competent, and sometimes more than competent, volume of work. *Hindle Wakes* is a good example of his earlier years in its preservation of the realistic, unsentimental qualities of Houghton's play. Three more versions were to follow: by Elvey again in 1927, Victor Saville, 1931 and Arthur Crabtree, 1951.

**THE BETTER 'OLE.** Script: George Pearson, from the play by Bruce Bairnsfather and Arthur Eliot. Direction: Pearson. Photography: Lucien Egrot. Players: Charles Rock, Hugh E. Wright, Mary Dibley, Lillian Hall-Davis. Production: Welsh-Pearson. 6,600 ft.

The film opens with a scene of the Three Musketeers toasting "One for All and All for One," dissolves into the picture of the singing of the Marseillaise, and then into the three famous Bairnsfather soldiers in the trenches. It closes with them silhouetted as they go "over the top" at the end of their seven days' leave. Pearson's aim, he says, is to convey "the simple message of Carry On —and nothing more." Meggie Albanesi appears for a brief moment as a waitress, filling in for a small-part player who failed to turn up.

**THE LIFE OF KITCHENER.** Script: Rex Wilson.

Art Direction: M. Boella. Production: Windsor. 6,240 ft.

An elaborate series of episodes in Kitchener's career in Egypt, South Africa, India, and the First World War, presenting him as a military genius at the head of a great Empire. The desert (complete with Sphinx) was reproduced in the studio, this sequence alone costing £1,500.

## 1918: Facts of Interest

Stoll Film Company is founded.

Thomas Welsh and George Pearson form their own company, Welsh-Pearson, with a studio at Craven Park.

The Trade Benevolent Fund is set up.

Death of Birt Acres.

# 1919

THE GARDEN OF RESURRECTION. Script: Guy Newall, from the novel by Temple Thurston. Direction: A. H. Rooke. Photography: Joe Rosenthal, Jnr. Art Direction: Charles Dalmon. Players: Guy Newall, Ivy Duke, Humberston Wright, Franklin Dyall. Production: Lucky Cat (George Clark). 5,000 ft.

In a lean year, the arrival of Guy Newall to produce and act in a small London studio stands out, though the films themselves are unremarkable, and gain most from his pleasing personality as a player. This story of a man who nearly (but not quite) commits suicide for love of a girl of whom he knows practically nothing, is typical.

COMRADESHIP. Script: Jeffrey Bernard, from a story by Louis N. Parker. Direction: Maurice Elvey. Photography: Paul Burger. Players: Gerald Ames, Lily Elsie, Guy Newall, Peggy Carlisle. Production: Stoll. 6,064 ft.

The first production by the Stoll Picture Company, telling, somewhat tardily, the story of a pacifist who is persuaded to join the army during the war, saves the life of the man he thinks his own girl is really in love with, is blinded, marries the girl and—as a perhaps not altogether unearned bonus after all this—regains his sight.

## Short Films and Documentaries

South. Photography: Frank Hurley. Production: I.T.A. Film Syndicate. 4,494 ft.

A record of Ernest Shackleton's voyage to the Antarctic, vividly and excitingly photographed.

## 1919: Facts of Interest

Cecil Hepworth expands his company, forming Hepworth Picture Plays with a capital of £100,000.

Henry Edwards starts to work as Hepworth's producer, but with a large measure of independence.

British Lion, as a private company, operates at Boreham Wood.

*Alma Taylor*

*Violet Hopson*

# 1920

ALF'S BUTTON. Script: Blanche McIntosh, from the novel by W. A. Darlington. Direction: Cecil Hepworth. Players: Leslie Henson, Alma Taylor, James Carew, John MacAndrews, Gerald Ames, Jean Cadell. Production: Hepworth. 7 reels.

Hepworth describes this as perhaps the most successful film he made. The story—outside his usual type—of a soldier who found that one of his uniform buttons was made from the metal of Aladdin's Lamp and controlled a genie offers obvious possibilities for trick camerawork and these are fully exploited. Leslie Henson, kept firmly in check by his director, brings his own unique personality to the part of Alf.

NOTHING ELSE MATTERS. Script: George Pearson, Hugh E. Wright. Direction: George Pearson. Photography: Emile Lauste. Art Titles: Ernest Jones. Players: Hugh E. Wright, Moyna MacGill, Reginald Denham, Leal Douglas, Polly Emery, Betty Balfour, Mabel Poulton. Production: Welsh-Pearson. 6,400 ft.

A pleasant, sentimental little film about an old music hall comic who is brought to realise that Love Matters Most, this is noteworthy as marking the first appearances of both Betty Balfour and Mabel Poulton. The former plays a comedy servant. The film cost £7,000.

THE CALL OF THE ROAD. Script: A. E. Coleby. Direction: A. E. Coleby. Photography: D. P. Cooper. Players: Victor McLaglen, Phyllis Shannaw, Geoffrey Benstead, Warwick Ward. Production: I. B. Davidson. 6,000 ft.

Victor McLaglen makes a very successful *début* as highwayman Dick Turpin in this uncomplicated outdoor adventure story, based firmly on fiction.

### 1920: Facts of Interest

Minerva Film Company is set up, with Adrian Brunel as producer/director.

Michael Balcon enters the film industry as a renter.

Bruce Woolfe forms British Instructional Films at Elstree.

P.C.T. owns some seventy cinemas.

The first so-styled "super-cinema" is constructed at Dalston, London, E.

Alfred Hitchcock starts work at Islington with Famous Players, writing and designing titles.

Chrissie White

Betty Balfour

# 1921

SQUIBS. Script: Eliot Stannard, George Pearson, from a one-act play by Clifford Seyley. Direction: George Pearson. Photography: Emile Lauste. Players: Betty Balfour, Mary Brough, Fred Groves, Hugh E. Wright, Cronin Wilson, Annette Benson. Production: Welsh-Pearson. 5,750 ft.

All that remains of the original music hall sketch are the name and character of the roguish, chirpy,

*1921: Betty Balfour and Hugh E. Wright in SQUIBS*

*1921: Milton Rosmer climbing in the Lake District,
from Maurice Elvey's* A ROMANCE OF WAST-
DALE.

irrepressible little Cockney girl—now made into a Piccadilly flower-seller with a police-constable lover. The film launched Betty Balfour on her career as the most popular of silent British stars, and in the character to which she returns and is identified with as Mary Pickford with her curls. The films themselves are nothing remarkable, unadventurous in treatment and tailored to their leading player, who, however, is lively and endearing enough to satisfy all but the more sophisticated audiences of the day.

**KIPPS.** Script: Frank Miller, from the novel by H. G. Wells. Direction: Harold Shaw. Photography: Silvano Balboni. Players: George K. Arthur, Edna Flugrath, Edward Arundel, Annie Esmond, Christine Rayner. Production: Stoll. 6,139 ft.

The most notable aspect of this modest but pop-ular version is the performance of G. K. Arthur as the little draper's assistant. It was to lead him to Hollywood and stardom *via* Sternberg's *The Salvation Hunters*. The financial success of *Kipps* led to the filming of the companion novel *The Wheels of Chance*, also with Arthur, in 1922.

**A ROMANCE OF WASTDALE.** Script: from the novel by A. E. W. Mason. Direction: Maurice Elvey. Photography: J. J. Cox. Players: Milton Rosmer, Fred Raynham, Irene Rooke. Production: Stoll. 6,000 ft.

Though weakened by turning the events into a dream in the interest of the Happy Ending, this version of Mason's grim Lakeland story of jealousy and revenge among the mountains is photographed with a grey, gritty quality which admirably suits the circumstances. Enough tension is

*Eille Norwood as Holmes and Hubert Willis as Watson in an episode from THE ADVENTURES OF SHERLOCK HOLMES.*

generated between the small group of characters to make certain scenes stick in the memory long after worthier films have faded.

CARNIVAL. Script: Adrian Johnson, Rosina Henley, from the play by H. C. M. Hardinge and Matheson Lang. Direction: Harley Knoles. Photography: Philip Hatkin. Players: Matheson Lang, Hilda Bayley, Ivor Novello. Production: Alliance. 6,500 ft.

Though essentially a stage actor, Lang made a number of films, generally of his theatrical successes—and in a theatrical style. This one which has no connection with Compton Mackenzie's well-known novel of the same title—tells of a real-life Othello situation, and is probably his best-known part. Elaborately made, with spectacular scenes of Venetian carnival, it nevertheless remains theatre rather than cinema, with the titles, not the camera, telling the tale.

**Short Films and Documentaries**

THE ADVENTURES OF SHERLOCK HOLMES. A series of fifteen two-reel shorts. Script: W. J. Elliott, from Conan Doyle's stories. Direction: Maurice Elvey. Photography: Germaine Burger. Players: Eille Norwood (Sherlock Holmes), Hubert Willis (Doctor Watson). Production: Stoll.

Followed in 1922 by the *Further Adventures* and in 1923 by the *Last Adventures* (both adapted and directed by George Ridgewell), the three series cover nearly all the Holmes short stories then available. In the eyes of many, Eille Norwood,

though not greatly resembling the Sidney Paget drawings, is the greatest Sherlock of them all. He also made two long films, *The Hound of the Baskervilles* (1921) and *The Sign of Four* (1923), and played the part on the stage. The thoroughly enjoyable two-reelers, economically but intelligently and conscientiously made, represent an integral part of the early cinema programmes, the loss of which can only be deplored.

THE BATTLE OF JUTLAND. Script: Major-General Sir George Aston. Direction: H. Bruce Woolfe. Photography: Herbert Lomas. Production: British Instructional Films. 3 reels.

The first film from the B.I.F. studio, this relates the details of the great sea battle of the first World War by means of animated models, maps, "actual" film records and studio reconstructions.

**1921: Facts of Interest**

British Actors' Film Company is wound up.
The British National Film League is founded, to promote the interests of British films.
Michael Balcon makes his first film—a documentary about oil drilling.
William Friese-Greene collapses and dies after speaking at a meeting called at the Connaught Rooms, London, to discuss problems and differences in the industry. Long impoverished, he has in his pocket the sum of one shilling and tenpence —a common cinema admission price at the time.
Peter Ustinov and Jack Clayton are born.

# 1922

SQUIBS WINS THE CALCUTTA SWEEP. Script: Hugh E. Wright, George Pearson. Direction: George Pearson. Photography: Emile Lauste. Art Direction: Ernest Jones. Players: Betty Balfour, Hugh E. Wright, Fred Groves, Annette Benson, Bertram Burleigh, Mary Brough, Ambrose Manning. Production: Welsh-Pearson. 5,300 ft.

The second (and best-known today as it is one of the few Pearson films surviving) Squibs story is unusual in that it both opens and closes in an atmosphere of tragedy. Squibs's sister is married to a cat burglar who kills a householder and finally commits suicide. In between these two grim events Squibs wins the Calcutta Sweep through a ticket bought for her (with her own money) by her father. Much simple comedy is derived from her engagement to a policeman and its confining effect on her father's influence, and from her pretended airs and graces when, after receiving her winnings, she arrives in a chauffeur-driven car to visit her prospective in-laws. The hidden camera sequence of Squibs upsetting the peace of Piccadilly with her rejoicings, and the social comment implicit in other scenes, add to the liveliness and interest of this enjoyable, if minor, movie.

THE WONDERFUL STORY. Script: Graham Cutts, Herbert Wilcox, from the novel by I. A. R. Wylie. Direction: Graham Cutts. Photography: H. L. Egrot. Players: Lillian Hall-Davis, Herbert Langley, Olaf Hytten, Bernard Vaughan. Production: Graham-Wilcox. 5 reels.

This is the first film from Herbert Wilcox as producer, and the second from Graham Cutts as direc-tor. It is also the first to offer Lillian Hall-Davis a chance to rise to the prominent position she held during the rest of the silent period. Her death by suicide in 1933, when she failed to make the transition to sound pictures, was a tragic end to a successful career. The film itself is a gentle, quiet story of an English countryside now gone for ever.

THE GLORIOUS ADVENTURE. Script: Felix Orman. Direction: John Stuart Blackton. Photography: Nicholas Musuraca (Prizma Color). Art Direction: Walter Murton. Players: Lady Diana Manners, Gerald Lawrence, Cecil Humphreys, William Luff, Victor McLaglen, Flora le Breton, Tom Haselwood, Haidee Wright. Production: Stuart Blackton. 9 reels.

Stuart Blackton, vice-President of the American Vitagraph Company, came over to produce large-scale colour spectacles in Britain and to launch the Prizma Color process in which he was interested. *The Glorious Adventure*, the first result, is a massive, heavily-laden costume piece involving the Great Fire of London and the Plague, together with Society leader Lady Diana Manners. Even with such advantages, the outcome is disappointing. The story of two young lovers who, after falling victim to a wicked lawyer, narrowly (and uninterestingly) escape the Fire, is trite, the colour is blotchy, the action slow. Memory recalls a seat-squirming boredom, a rare bright spot being the glowing brazier on Tom Haselwood's head as he moves among the crowds—a ragged and skinny Solomon Eagle—crying the wrath to come.

*1922: A frame enlargement from THE WONDER-FUL STORY, with Herbert Langley and Olaf Hytten.*

*1922: Lady Diana Manners in THE GLORIOUS ADVENTURE.*

SECRETS OF NATURE. Production: B.I.F.

In this excellent series of shorts, photographers and naturalists such as Charles Head, Oliver Pike, Walter Higham, H. A. Gilbert, Edgar Chance and, in particular, Percy Smith, use time-lapse, microscopic and other special cine-cameras to record plant, animal and insect life, and present the results in a style which exhilaratingly combines popular entertainment with authoritative instruction. Each *Secret* deals with one particular subject (Edgar Chance's *The Cuckoo's Secret* being the first), and titles during the first year include *The Lair of the Spider, The Seashore, Story of the Buzzard, Spring, Frocks and Frills* and *Where Flies Go in the Winter*. Each film, costing some

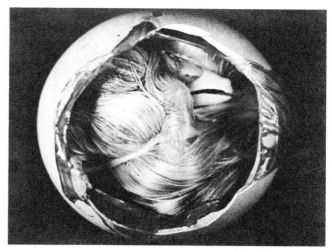

*A close-up of a hatching chick from the SECRETS OF NATURE series.*

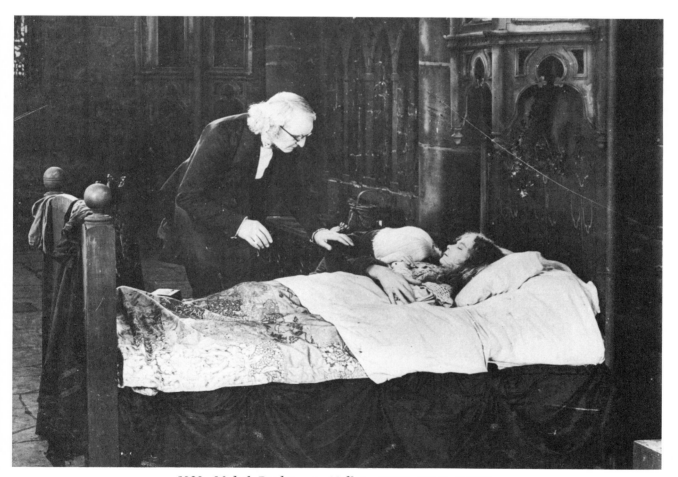

*1922: Mabel Poulton as Nell in THE OLD CURIOSITY SHOP, directed by Thomas Bentley for Welsh-Pearson.*

£500, lasts seven to eight minutes, and the series is one of the most significant contributions to British cinema in the Twenties. In 1927 Mary Field was to join the B.I.F. and bring a new and refreshing vision to the project which, though still unique, had become a little set in its mould.

### 1922: Facts of Interest

Graham-Wilcox starts production.

Beaconsfield studios are opened by Guy Newall and George Clark.

Gaumont Company becomes wholly British.

Michael Balcon, Victor Saville and John Freedman form an independent company at Islington. Famous Players-Lasky cease production at the studio.

Out of 420 British films, shorts and features, offered in America, only some half-a-dozen find buyers.

The Piccadilly Theatre, Manchester, first large-scale cinema in the North, opens its doors.

# 1923

WOMAN TO WOMAN. Script: Alfred Hitchcock, Graham Cutts, from the play by Michael Morton. Direction: Graham Cutts. Photography: Claude McDonnell. Editing: Alma Reville. Art Direction: Alfred Hitchcock. Players: Betty Compson, Clive Brook, Henry Vibart, Marie Ault, Josephine Earle. Production: Michael Balcon. 7,455 ft.

A film which brings together at the opening of their careers Michael Balcon, Victor Saville and Alfred Hitchcock would be noteworthy on that account alone. *Woman to Woman*, however, was one of the most commercially successful productions of the decade—partly because of the presence of Betty Compson, then at the height of her popularity in America and brought over by Graham Cutts (at £1,000 per week, good pay for those days) to give the British industry a much needed boost. The story, though, as Balcon says, naïve and melodramatic, was considered highly sophisticated and even daring. It concerns a British officer who has a love affair with a French girl, is ordered to the front before he can marry her, and loses his memory through a head wound. After the war he returns to England and marries an English society girl. The Frenchwoman, now a famous dancer, arrives in Britain—accompanied by child—to perform and, after a confrontation foretold in the film's title, dies after the convenient cinematic fashion of third parties in those days. In Boston the film was barred until a compromise was reached whereby, as Balcon says, "we arranged for our hero and heroine to be married for Sunday showings only." The film was also to lead to Hollywood stardom for Clive Brook, and

its editor became Hitchcock's scriptwriter and also his wife.

*1923: Betty Compson and Clive Brook in WOMAN TO WOMAN.*

LOVE, LIFE AND LAUGHTER (original title TIPTOES). Script: George Pearson. Direction: George Pearson. Photography: Percy Strong, A. H. Blake. Players: Betty Balfour, Harry Jonas, Frank Stanmore, Nancy Price, Sydney Fairbrother. Production: Welsh-Pearson. 6,300 ft.

Unfortunately this film, Pearson's own favourite, seems to have totally disappeared. Following the career of famous music hall comedienne Marie Lloyd, Pearson based a boy-loves-girl story on the old rags-to-riches theme, with Betty Balfour as the chorus girl who rises from the ranks. The film's historic importance, however, lies in the fact that here Pearson first starts to experiment in his search for a new method of story-telling, using, in place of the usual neatly plotted script, a series of more-or-less loosely connected scenes drawn together to illustrate a theme. Even in the present conventional story the change of approach was noted by contemporary criticism, with by no means unanimous approval. The film was reissued in 1927 in a slightly longer version.

COMIN' THRO' THE RYE. Script: from the novel by Helen Mathers. Direction: Cecil Hepworth. Photography: Geoffrey Faithfull. Players: Alma Taylor, James Carew, Shayle Gardner, Henry Vibart, Nancy Price, Ralph Forbes, Francis Lister. Production: Hepworth. 6 reels.

Of all his output, Hepworth's re-make of his earlier success was the one in which he felt most pride and affection but, sadly, time and technique had passed him by, and even when it appeared both story and treatment were considered old-fashioned. Little more than a year after its issue he was forced to close down his business. Even so, *Comin' Thro' the Rye* was one of the films listed for the British Film Weeks of 1924.

LILY OF THE ALLEY. Direction: Henry Edwards. Photography: Charles Bryce. Players: Henry Edwards, Chrissie White, Frank Stanmore, Mary Brough, Campbell Gullan. Production: Hepworth. 7,000 ft.

Though not the first film to be made without titles, this appears to be the first British feature to dispense with them. The experiment was not received with universal acclaim and complaints were made that the meaning of what was seen on the screen was often obscure—the difference between this case and the modern fashion for obfuscation being that Henry Edwards wanted to be understood. It was even suggested that lack of titles might cause eye-strain.

ROYAL OAK. Script: from a play by W. Dimond. Direction: Maurice Elvey. Players: Betty Compson, Clive Brook, Henry Ainley, Henry Victor, Peter Dear, Thurston Hall. Production: Stoll. 6,170 ft.

The American star Betty Compson and Clive Brook appear together again in this costume drama

*1923: Betty Compson and Clive Brook together again in Maurice Elvey's ROYAL OAK.*

built round Charles II's escape from Cromwell after the battle of Worcester and his concealment in the oak tree at Boscobel. Betty Compson portrays Lady Mary Cholmondeley who, by impersonating the king, enables him to reach the sea. Technically unremarkable, it is nevertheless a good example of effective use of period locations and the English countryside. The child, Peter Dear, was to grow up as Peter Dearing, to become well-known as a theatrical producer—brother to Basil Dearden.

FIRES OF FATE. Script: Alicia Ramsey, from Conan Doyle's play and his novel *The Tragedy of the Korosko*. Direction: Tom Terriss. Photography: St. Aubyn Brown, H. W. Bishop. Players: Wanda Hawley, Nigel Barrie, Stewart Rome, Edith Craig, L. de Cordova. Production: Gaumont. 7,200 ft.

Another entry for the British Films Week 1924, directed by an American and with an American star. The script neatly combines a double adapta-

*1923: A location scene from ROYAL OAK.*

tion, from novel and play, into cinematic form. The film is notable for a daring moment of ugly-head-rearing sex, 1923 style: the raging but concealed lust with which the villain gazes down at Miss Hawley as she sits chatting with her back to him, is indicated by the dissolve of the gauze wrap on her shoulder to reveal bare skin, shoulder-blade and all, for a brief moment of vicarious satisfaction.

## 1923: Facts of Interest

The Tivoli Theatre, Strand, London, is opened. Lindsay Anderson and Richard Attenborough are born.

# 1924

**REVEILLE.** Script: George Pearson. Direction: George Pearson. Photography: Percy Strong. Art Direction: Leslie Dawson, Harry Jones. Players: Betty Balfour, Frank Stanmore, Stewart Rome, Ralph Forbes, Sydney Fairbrother. Production: Welsh-Pearson. 8,000 ft.

The idea for this film, probably Pearson's best-known after the Squibs series, was given to him by the critic George Atkinson who happened to mention a "poor old widow who lost three sons in the war." From this he constructed an episodic story of ordinary people who suffered loss from the Great War, following up his belief that a great film needed to expound a theme (in this case the Victory of Courage) rather than follow a neatly constructed plot. Its simple, slow, quiet emotion-alism matched the mood of its day and it was enormously successful. Most famous is the scene depicting the Two Minutes' Silence where, with considerable daring, Pearson leaves the screen without movement except for a brief brushing of a lace curtain against the face of the mother as she stands looking out through her window. During the first presentation the conductor of the orchestra, Louis Levy, laid down his baton so that the stillness of sound and vision was complete.

**THE PASSIONATE ADVENTURE.** Script: Michael Morton, Alfred Hitchcock, from the novel by Frank Stayton. Direction: Graham Cutts. Photography: Claude McDonnell. Art Direction: Alfred Hitchcock. Players: Alice Joyce, Clive Brook, Marjorie Daw, Victor McLaglen, Lilliam Hall-Davis. Production: Gainsborough (Michael Balcon) 8,000 ft.

*1924: Betty Balfour and Stewart Rome in George Pearson's REVEILLE.*

The first Gainsborough picture is an unremarkable, one might almost say unbelievable, story of a man who attempts to escape from his marital frustrations by disguising himself as a tramp in East London. Locations include Waterloo Station, and the American actress Alice Joyce was brought over to push the film's chances and sharpen the hero's miseries. In the former she was successful,

*Mabel Poulton, a leading actress of the Twenties.*

for the film did well.

**OWD BOB.** Script: Hugh MacLean, from the novel by Alfred Oliphant. Direction: Henry Edwards. Photography: Charles Bryce, Bert Ford. Players: J. Fisher White, James Carew, Ralph Forbes, Frank Stanmore. Production: Atlantic Union. 6,300 ft.

A film of great charm and originality, concerning shepherds and their dogs, shot mainly on location with photography of high quality preserving a memory of the English Lake District at a time when the voice of the tourist was heard not so stridently in the land.

### Short Films and Documentaries

**BONZO.** Cartoon series by G. E. Studdy.

Bonzo is one of the most inventive and imaginative of the earlier British animated films. An extremely likeable and inquisitive dog who began life in illustrated papers and postcards, he transfers well to the screen, developing a considerable depth of canine/human character and proving eminently graphogenic.

### 1924: Facts of Interest

The Hepworth Company is wound up and his studios bought by Archibald Nettlefold. His negatives of twenty-four years were, shamefully, sold to a man who re-sold them to be melted down for "dope" for aeroplane wings. Cecil Hepworth himself was eventually to join National Screen Services, makers of film trailers, etc.

Gainsborough Pictures starts production.

British Films Week is inaugurated in an attempt to bolster up a sinking industry.

Entertainment Tax reductions come into force.

A *Daily News* poll registers Betty Balfour and Alma Taylor as favourite British stars.

Death of William Haggar.

# 1925

THE RAT. Script: Graham Cutts, based on the play by David L'Estrange (i.e. Ivor Novello, Constance Collier). Direction: Graham Cutts. Photography: Hal Young. Art Direction: Charles W. Arnold. Players: Ivor Novello, Mae Marsh, Isabel Jeans, James Lindsay, Robert Scholtz, Marie Ault, Julie Suedo. Production: Gainsborough. 7,323 ft.

Despite its (to put it mildly) improbable story of a handsome Parisian apache, a demi-mondaine, her evil protector who casts a lustful eye towards a young innocent girl who loves the apache, and all the mayhem, self-sacrifice and happy ending (young innocent/apache) that ensues, this enormously popular film is commendable for direction and photography that far transcend its material. It marks the first real attempts in Britain to develop the mobility of the camera, even if it amounts to little more than trundling around after the characters, acting as substitute for straight cuts from medium to close shots, etc. Camera angles are also used imaginatively. The story was originally written as a film script by Novello, who was persuaded by Constance Collier to turn it into a play: following the success of the latter, he re-wrote the movie version. It helped to establish his position as a matinee idol, though his film career was to be confined mainly to the silent era. Two Rat films were to follow: *Triumph of the Rat* (1926) and *Return of the Rat* (1929). *The Rat* was remade in sound (1937) by Jack Raymond, with Anton Walbrook, Rene Ray and Ruth Chatterton.

SHE. Script: Walter Summers, from the novel by Rider Haggard. Direction: Leander de Cordova.

Photography: Sydney Blythe. Art Direction: Heinrich Richter. Players: Betty Blythe, Carlyle Blackwell, Tom Reynolds, Mary Odette, Heinrich George. Production: G. B. Samuelson. 8,250 ft.

Though this version of Rider Haggard's story of Whitest Africa and its eternally youthful queen has since been declared a total disaster, its critical reception at the time was, if not rapturous, at the very least respectful. Imagination, sense of spectacle, excellent quality of softly-lighted interiors, gripping entertainment, good camerawork, artistic mounting—are some of the phrases used. "Good for any class of hall," is *The Bioscope's* enthusiastic, if somewhat ambiguous conclusion, adding cautiously that Betty Blythe is at her best in scenes which make the least demand on her emotions. Brought over from America after her success as the Queen of Sheba, Miss Blythe glitters in costumes which caused some difficulties during production, to be followed by greater troubles and litigation between Samuelson, Betty Blythe and the studios, from which the former seems to have emerged with most satisfaction. The film was made in splendidly equipped studios in Berlin, but even so (and despite the above paean of praise) many of the sets look as artificial as the posturing going on in front of them.

THE PLEASURE GARDEN. Script: Eliot Stannard, from the novel by Oliver Sandys. Direction: Alfred Hitchcock. Photography: Baron Ventimiglia. Art Direction: C. W. Arnold, Ludwig Reiber. Players: Virginia Valli, Carmelita Geraghty, Miles Mander, John Stuart, Nita Naldi. Produc-

*1925: Betty Blythe as SHE, with Carlyle Blackwell.*

tion: Gainsborough-Emelka. 7,508 ft.

Hitchcock's first feature as a director (he started a two-reeler previously, but it was never completed) was filmed entirely in Munich as a joint production with a German company. It tells a closely-knit story of two chorus girls who each become engaged. One jilts her *fiancé*, the other marries and finds her husband is worthless. The jilted man and the disillusioned wife come together. Before this symmetrically satisfying solution, however, the door has already opened silghtly on the Hitchcock world of murder (made to appear as suicide), and a threatened second killing averted at the last moment by the death of the murderer. This final scene caused one of the German producers to say that it was too brutal to be shown. Already in this pioneer effort the director shows his skill in keeping the audience's attention alert and stimulated, conveying neces-

sary narrative information while simultaneously indicating character by seemingly irrelevant details and sly clue-dropping. Already, too, we have the theatre settings which were to reappear so often with such good effect. Seeing this film without knowing the director's name, it is doubtful whether anyone would be moved to exclaim "Ah, Hitchcock!", but on being told, he might well, as the action proceeds, mutter "Ah, yes!"

THE ONLY WAY. Script: Freeman Wills, from Charles Dickens's *A Tale of Two Cities* and the play by Wills and Frederick Langbridge. Direction: Herbert Wilcox. Photography: Claude McDonnell. Art Direction: Norman J. Arnold. Players: Sir John Martin-Harvey, Ben Webster, J. Fisher White, Madge Stuart, Gibb McLaughlin, Mary Brough, Michael Martin-Harvey. Production: Graham Wilcox. 10,075 ft.

1925: *THE PLEASURE GARDEN, Hitchcock's first completed feature film, with Virginia Valli and John Stuart.*

Martin-Harvey's most famous role as Sydney Carton is brought to the screen in a mammoth spectacular (cost £24,000), with enormous sets and milling crowds. Though inevitably theatrical in conception and performance it is not merely an overweighted prestige production. Wilcox received, and deserved, high praise for his handling of vast numbers of extras, and Norman Arnold for his imposingly realistic settings. Titles abound, but are sometimes used with imagination. A leading contemporary critic said of the far-far-better-thing climax, "at this point the film ceased to be great—it became sublime." What producer could ask for more—from a contemporary critic?

## 1925: Facts of Interest

The (London) Film Society is founded, and a Kinema Club is started at Cambridge University, with provincial Societies quick to follow.

Oscar Deutsch enters the industry as exhibitor.

It is estimated that ninety-five per cent of British screen time is given over to American movies.

The Capitol Cinema, Haymarket, London, is opened, and the New Gallery, Regent Street, London, re-opened after extensive reconstruction.

# 1926

THE LODGER. Script: Eliot Stannard and Alfred Hitchcock, from the novel by Mrs. Belloc Lowndes. Direction: Alfred Hitchcock. Photography: Baron Ventimiglia. Editing and subtitles: Ivor Montagu. Art Direction: C. W. Arnold, Bertram Evans. Players: Ivor Novello, June, Marie Ault, Malcolm Keen, Arthur Chesney. Production: Gainsborough. 7,685 ft.

The first "real" Hitchcock, and a landmark in the British silent period. The story is based on a mysterious character suspected of being a Jack the Ripper murderer, haunting the foggy London streets in search of golden-haired girls to kill, and it is weakened by the fact that, after somewhat dishonest hints to the contrary, he is found to be innocent. It is, in fact, the treatment rather than the story which is memorable. The atmosphere is heavily Germanic, full of heavily symbolic shadows and chiaroscuro lighting effects. "Hitchcock touches" are already in evidence: the screaming girl's face filling the frame at the opening, the close-up of a hand descending the banisters, the first appearance of the lodger from the fog, his feet as he paces his room photographed through the ceiling of the floor below (actually through plate glass), the martyr-like figure hanging from the railings. Already, too, are present the problems of innocence and guilt which are to exercise Hitchcock to such an extent in later years. The film encountered some resistance from renters on its first appearance, and now seems tame, but there is no denying its historical importance.

THE LITTLE PEOPLE. Script: George Pearson,

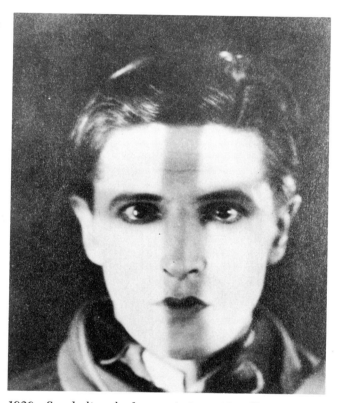

*1926: Symbolic shadows of Ivor Novello as THE LODGER.*

Thorold Dickinson. Direction: George Pearson. Photography: Percy Strong. Editing: Fred Pullin. Art Direction: Cavalcanti. Players: Mona Maris, Frank Stanmore, Gerald Ames, Randle Ayrton, Barbara Gott. Production: Welsh-Pearson. 7,500 ft.

One of Pearson's most endearing pictures, telling the story of a family of puppeteers in a small

71

Italian village. Two Englishmen on tour see possibilities for the old puppeteer's adopted daughter as a dancer and persuade her to leave the troupe and be trained. Her *début* is a disaster and, disillusioned but not embittered, she returns to her old life in the village. Through this simple, modestly made story (the film cost £9,000) Pearson develops an equally simple theme: we are all puppets activated by invisible wires of chance and whim. The film had a mixed reception and was later revised—not, it appears, by Pearson himself. It marks the first appearance on the credits of an English film of Alberto Cavalcanti.

## MADEMOISELLE FROM ARMENTIÈRES.

Script: Victor Saville, V. G. Gundrey. Direction: Maurice Elvey. Photography: W. Shenton. Art Direction: A. L. Mazzei. Players: Estelle Brody, John Stuart, Marie Ault, Alf Goddard, Humberston Wright, Clifford Heatherley. Production: Gaumont. 7,900 ft.

Maurice Elvey's first film for the Gaumont

*1926: Estelle Brodie as MADEMOISELLE FROM ARMENTIÈRES.*

Company was a big commercial success and a step forward in his industrious career. Without the pretensions of even *The Big Parade* (King Vidor, 1925) to investigate the grim realities of war, it treats the whole thing as an exciting thriller in which the heroine of the famous song works (in the nicest way) on the bad Germans to help the good British, and has in the Canadian star Estelle Brodie a young actress of exceptional charm and vivacity. It is competently made throughout, and hit off a mood of the moment, a sort of incongruous nostalgia for a disaster survived. A sequel, *Mademoiselle Parley-Voo*, came out in 1928.

## THE FLAG LIEUTENANT.

Script: P. L. Mannock. Direction: Maurice Elvey. Photography: W. Shenton, Leslie Eveleigh, F. Young. Art Direction: A. L. Mazzei. Players: Henry Edwards, Lilian Oldland, Fred Raynham, Fewlass Llewellyn, Humberston Wright, Dorothy Seacombe. Production: Astra-National. 8,900 ft.

The success of this war-time adventure spectacle led Maurice Elvey to Gaumont and Henry Edwards to the formation of his own company with Julius Hagen. Though described in the esoteric magazine *Close-Up* as "dither," the story of the young naval officer who wins the Admiral's daughter by bravery amid shot, shell, seaplane, battleship, desert fort and multiple encounters, pleased those audiences out for adventure, and added to the already great popularity of its likeable and capable star, Henry Edwards.

## BOADICEA.

Sinclair Hill in collaboration with Anthony Asquith. Direction: Sinclair Hill. Photography: Jack Parker. Art Direction: W. Murton. Players: Phyllis Neilson-Terry, Lillian Hall-Davis, Sybil Rhoda, Humberston Wright, Clifford McLaglen, Cyril McLaglen, Clifford Heatherley. Production: B.I.F. (Bruce Woolfe). 8,000 ft.

A workmanlike rather than an inspired director, Sinclair Hill nevertheless made a not inconsiderable contribution to the British screen of the Twenties and early Thirties. His range was wide and his direction unobtrusive and unadventurous, but in general sympathetic. *Boadicea*—anti-ancient-Roman propaganda depicting the unhappy plight of the oppressed Britons and the rising of the Iceni under their Queen—suffers

*1926: BOADICEA, Phyllis Neilson Terry, right fore-
ground, as the Queen, Humberston Wright as the
King, Sybil Rhoda and Lillian Hall-Davis as the
daughters.*

from inadequate resources, particularly in battle and spectacle scenes. Its strong narrative line and unfussy acting are, however, effective: it has a splendidly regal Queen in Phyllis Neilson-Terry, and in Lillian Hall-Davis and Sybil Rhoda two ancient Britons who would grace any Icenian household. Apart from collaborating on the script, Anthony Asquith doubled for Miss Neilson-Terry as Boadicea, in a long blond wig, on a chariot.

NELL GWYN. Script: Herbert Wilcox, from a story by Marjorie Bowen. Direction: Herbert Wilcox. Photography: Roy Overbaugh. Art Direction: N. G. Arnold. Players: Dorothy Gish, Randle Ayrton, Sydney Fairbrother, Juliette Compton, Gibb McLaughlin. Production: British National. 7,760 ft.

Chosen to open the magnificent new Plaza Theatre, Piccadilly, this version of Sweet Nell of Old Drury, overshadowed by Wilcox's later version in sound, has not much sense of period, despite Randle Ayrton's dignified monarch. The antics of the Restoration Court are glossed over, and the true relationship between a kittenish Nell and her Sovereign remain in discreet doubt. The film does, however contain a pioneer nude scene, with Nell teasing the censor and the audience in a barrel. It was a financial success.

## 1926: Facts of Interest

British National builds new studios at Elstree.
Piccadilly Pictures Company is formed.
The Plaza Cinema, Lower Regent Street, London, is opened, and also the Kensington, W.14, claimed to be the largest in England.

Karel Reisz, John Schlesinger and Bryan Forbes are born.

# 1927

THE RING. Script: Alfred Hitchcock, Eliot Stan-
nard. Direction: Alfred Hitchcock. Photography:
Jack Cox. Art Direction: C. W. Arnold. Players:
Carl Brisson, Lillian Hall-Davis, Ian Hunter, Gor-
don Harker, Forrester Harvey. Production: British
International Pictures (John Maxwell) 8,400 ft.

Hitchcock's first picture for B.I.P.—*Downhill*
and *Easy Virtue* for Gainsborough preceded it. A
young boxer marries the cashier in his boxing
booth, becomes successful, loses his wife to the
champion, fights the latter at the Albert Hall, appears to be losing, is encouraged by his repentant
wife, and wins. On this not very promising material Hitchcock constructs an entertainment by ingenious symbolisms and visual narrative points
which aroused widely conflicting opinions at the
time. "It *is* treated visually, but there the merit
ends": "He has invested his picture with an element of continual surprise—a triumph for British
films and for Hitchcock in particular." Typical
"touches" include champagne bubbles going flat
at a celebration party when the boxer realises his
wife has been unfaithful; the film's title referring
not only to the boxing ring but the serpent brace-
let given to the wife by her lover; the clean "2"
card contrasting with the worn "1," indicating the
first time a challenger has lasted more than one
round in the ring with Brisson. Despite its not
wholly favourable reception at the time, the film
wears well and Hitchcock has expressed his personal liking for it. The art direction includes early
use of the Schuftan process, an ingenious, time-
and-money-saving combination of mirrors and real
backgrounds.

*1927: Carl Brisson as the boxer in THE RING. Gordon
Harker displays the sign.*

BLIGHTY. Script: Eliot Stannard, from a story by
Ivor Montagu. Direction: Adrian Brunel. Photog-
raphy: J. J. Cox. Editing: Ivor Montagu. Art Di-
rection: Bertram Evans. Players: Ellaline Terriss,
Godfrey Winn, Nadia Sibirskaia, Jameson Thomas,
Lillian Hall-Davis, Seymour Hicks, Renee and

Billie Houston. Production: Gainsborough. 8,603 ft.

Adrian Brunel entered the industry through the scenario department of the British Actors' Film Company at Bushey, after which he formed one or two short-lived concerns and produced a number of films, including a series of short burlesques of current pictures and newsreels. *Blighty* was his first film for Gainsborough and his most popular success, starting him on a modest but regular career which lasted until the Second World War. A somewhat sentimental story of the Lady's son and the chauffeur enlisting together, the son having a child by a French girl and losing his life, the chauffeur bringing the child to England and eventually marrying the French widow—it caught the curious mood of war-nostalgia as did *Madem-* *oiselle from Armentières* the year before. Actual shots of fighting in France and of the Armistice celebrations are used to inject reality into the proceedings (and to save money), but simply by that reality make one aware of the artificial aspects—for neither the first nor last time in the cinema. The French girl is played with quiet effectiveness by Nadia Sibirskaia, star of the French *Menilmontant* (1924).

THE LUCK OF THE NAVY. Script: from the play by Mrs. Clifford Mills. Direction: Fred Paul. Photography: Claude McDonnell. Players: Evelyn Laye, Henry Victor, William Freshman, Robert Cunningham, Wally Patch. Production: Graham-Wilcox. 8,000 ft.

More naval heroics, with spy complications,

*1927: Godfrey Winn greets Jameson Thomas in*
BLIGHTY.

*1927: Carlyle Blackwell seems uncertain what to do next with Flora le Breton in THE ROLLING ROAD, a romantic desert island story from Gainsborough Pictures, directed by Graham Cutts. Blackwell, a popular American silent star, appeared in a number of British pictures, including BULLDOG DRUMMOND (1922, directed by Oscar Apfel) and THE GLORIOUS ADVENTURE (1922). He also formed Piccadilly Pictures with C. M. Woolf and Michael Balcon.*

notable mainly for one of the rare early appearances of Evelyn Laye in the cinema. It is one of the last Graham-Wilcox productions.

## Short Films and Documentaries

THE BATTLES OF THE CORONEL AND FALKLAND ISLANDS. Script: Harry Engholme, Captain Frank C. Bowen. Direction: Walter Summers. Photography: Jack Parker, Stanley Rodwell. Production: B.I.F. (Bruce Woolfe). 8,300 ft.

This most famous, and best, of the re-created battles of the First World War can be faulted only on its failure to integrate successfully studio shots with actual settings and battleships loaned by the Admiralty. The Coronel disaster was judged at the time to be more grippingly reproduced than the Falkland victory, the final sequences of which suffered from "comic relief" in the shape of the Island Defence Forces. The film as a whole was also accused of romanticising war, but in general its integrity and accuracy was acclaimed.

### 1927: Facts of Interest

Cinematograph Films Act (1927) is passed, stipulating that a quota of British films must be screened. It encounters considerable opposition, and is to result later in the cheap and nasty quota quickie: but it does inject some much needed capital into the industry.

Gaumont-British Picture Corporation is formed: Provincial Cinematograph Theatres becomes associated with it, but retains its own identity.

The Film Artists' Guild is founded.

British International Pictures is launched as a public company with John Maxwell, and takes over the British National Studios at Elstree.

Herbert Wilcox also opens new studios at Elstree, for his British and Dominions Film Corporation.

British Lion Corporation is formed with Edgar Wallace as chairman: first film is his *The Squeaker*.

Granada Theatres organise the first regular children's matinees, using films in regular distribution.

Mary Field joins British Instructional Films.

John Grierson joins the Empire Marketing Board as Films Officer.

The Astoria, Charing Cross Road, London, opens (with *The Rat*).

The Avenue Pavilion, Shaftesbury Avenue, London, starts a policy of screening continental and "unusual" films.

# 1928

SHOOTING STARS. Script: Anthony Asquith, J.O.C. Orton. Direction: A. V. Bramble: Assistant Direction: Anthony Asquith. Photography: Stanley Rodwell, Henry Harris. Art Direction: Walter Murton, Ian Campbell-Gray. Players: Annette Benson, Brian Aherne, Donald Calthrop, Chili Bouchier, Wally Patch. Production: B.I.F. (H. Bruce Woolfe). 7,200 ft.

Although the name of A. V. Bramble appears on the credits, *Shooting Stars* is very much the work of the young Anthony Asquith, and the older director is rarely remembered in connection with it. He left the company, in fact, before the film was trade shown. The story, involving few characters, is simple and not particularly original, but the direction shows a virtuosity and subtlety which places the film high among the decade's best. A film actor discovers his wife's infidelity with another actor (a Mack Sennett type comedian) and threatens to divorce her. She, a star, knows that the scandal would finish her career and decides to kill him by substituting a real bullet for a blank in a gun to be used in one of his scenes. By chance a blank is used after all, the gun is taken to an adjoining set, fired at the comedian as part of the knockabout action, and kills him. The irony of the plot is reflected in the ironical view of studio drudgery; Sennett high jinks on the grey, dreary seashore, small-scale Western villainy on the cold, enormous stage. Titles are cut to a minimum and at times superimposed, cutting and camera angles are daringly original. Four justly famed scenes may be noted: the comedian's transformation from jolly clown to mean little man as he re-moves his make-up; his death while swinging on the chandelier (producing the same effect of horrible incongruity as the death of Fritz Lang's *Spy*); the sequence where the wife prays in a huge church setting as it is dismantled around her; and the often quoted closing shot as, told by her unrecognising husband (now a director) that he has no work for her, she slowly crosses the enormous wastes of the empty studio floor and goes out through a little door in the far distance.

UNDERGROUND. Script: Anthony Asquith. Direction: Anthony Asquith. Photography: Stanley Rodwell. Art Direction: Ian Campbell-Gray. Players: Elissa Landi, Norah Baring, Brian Aherne, Cyril McLaglen. Production: B.I.F. 7,282 ft.

Following the success of *Shooting Stars* Asquith was given a free hand to direct his own script—employing once again a small cast in a tightly-knit plot. Set in actual locations on the London Underground and surrounding streets, it concerns the love and hate relationships of a porter, an electrician at the power station, a shop girl, and the electrician's drab little ex-mistress. The picture was not very well received. Asquith was accused, with some reason, of indulging in heavy Germanic lighting effects to an extent that overloaded the story. As an attempt to tell an admittedly melodramatic tale in terms of everyday, ordinary people, however, it holds considerable interest, and the cutting and angled shooting of numerous sequences such as the plot on the circular stairs and the final chase are imaginatively

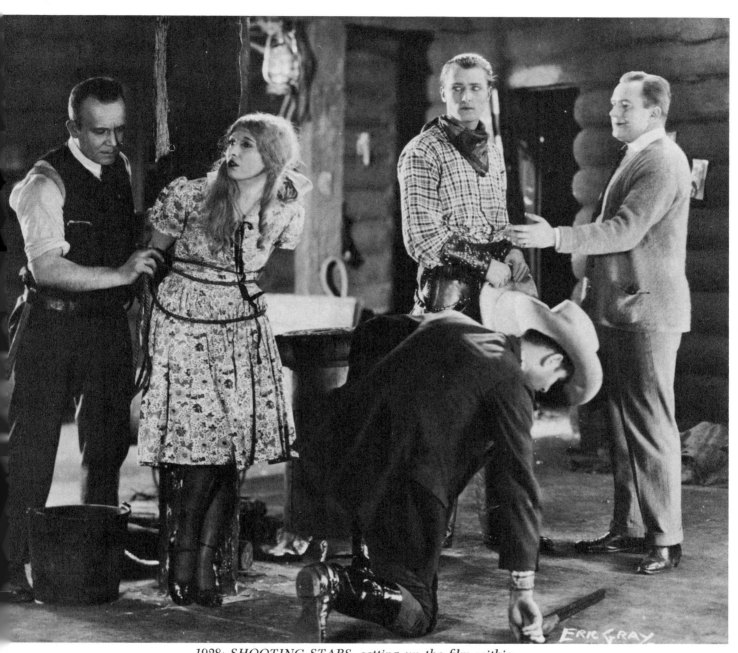

1928: SHOOTING STARS, *setting up the film within
a film, with Annette Benson and Brian Aherne.*

and excitingly done. The film marks the first appearance of Elissa Landi, an actress whose unusual beauty and personality altogether outweigh the question whether she is really an actress.

1928: *Elissa Landi and Cyril McLaglen in UNDERGROUND.*

THE CONSTANT NYMPH. Script: Adrian Brunel, Alma Reville and Margaret Kennedy, from the latter's novel, and the play with Basil Dean. Direction: Adrian Brunel. Photography: Dave Gobbett. Players: Mabel Poulton, Ivor Novello, Benita Hume, Frances Doble, Mary Clare, J. H. Roberts. Production: Gainsborough (Basil Dean). 10,600 ft.

Basil Dean's production was followed five years later by the talking version which he directed himself, but Brunel's film (which marked Dean's first connection with picture-making) is notable for a most delightful performance by Mabel Poulton, an actress of great charm whose career was to be so shortly terminated by the advent of sound, for which her accent was unsuitable. Novello, oppo-

site her, is also at his best as the conventionally tempestuous musician: his big moment is when, after careful coaching, he conducts a full-scale orchestra at the Queen's Hall in a totally soundless symphony. Though the film was accused of sticking too closely to the stage play, there is some beautiful location work in the Austrian Tyrol and the action—unlike that of many such transfers—is never slow. The leading parts in the sound version are played by Victoria Hopper and Brian Aherne.

BOLIBAR. Script: Walter Summers, J. O. C. Orton, from the novel by Leo Perutz. Direction: Walter Summers. Photography: Jack Parker. Editing and titles: Adrian Brunel, Ivor Montagu. Art Direction: Arthur Woods. Players: Elissa Landi, Jerrold Robertshaw, Cecil Barry, Carl Harbord, Peter Dear. Production: B.I.F. 8,000 ft.

This strange and apparently little remembered film deserved, despite certain melodramatic extravagances, a better fate than oblivion. Set in the time of the Peninsular War with the town of Bolibar in the hands of Napoleonic troops and the garrison beseiged by Spanish guerillas, it deals with the attempted strategies to take the town—and also with admittedly rather too many romantic interludes of the Napoleonic staff. Imaginatively directed and visually beautiful, it could have become a collector's piece, but with attention being drawn increasingly to the advent of sound, this was a luckless time for originality in the silent medium.

DAWN. Script: Reginald Berkeley. Direction: Herbert Wilcox. Photography: Bernard Knowles. Players: Sybil Thorndike, Mary Brough, Marie Ault, Dacia Deane, Haddon Mason, Gordon Craig. Production: British & Dominions. 7,300 ft.

*Dawn* marks a change in Wilcox's productions from costume spectacular to quicker moving, smaller scaled and more strongly characterized pictures. It is a straightforward and mainly unbiassed account of events still alive in the memory of most audiences, and Wilcox is content to record rather than comment and to let those events, fairly presented, speak for themselves. The film is illuminated by Sybil Thorndike's nobly moving and unmannered performance. The production encountered some foolish opposition on the grounds

*1928: THE CONSTANT NYMPH, Ivor Novello and Mabel Poulton.*

*1928: Estelle Brodie in MADEMOISELLE PARLEY-VOO, sequel to MADEMOISELLE FROM ARMENTIÈRES (1926).*

that it might offend the Germans—largely from people who had never seen it and even refused to do so. The result was, of course, much useful publicity for all financially concerned.

## 1928: Facts of Interest

The industry braces itself for the advent of sound.

British Instructional Films opens new studios at Welwyn.

Associated British Cinemas is registered, with John Maxwell as chairman and a circuit of twenty-nine cinemas.

The Gaumont Studios at Lime Grove become the home of Gainsborough Pictures.

The Carlton, Haymarket, London, opened in 1927 as a "live" theatre, turns to films.

The Empire, Leicester Square, and the Regal, Marble Arch, open.

The Alexandra, Aldershot, is reconstructed to become the first "atmospheric" cinema in England.

Tony Richardson is born.

# 1929

BLACKMAIL. Script: Alfred Hitchcock, Benn Levy, Charles Bennett, from the novel and play by Charles Bennett. Direction: Alfred Hitchcock. Photography: J. J. Cox. Editing: Emile de Ruelle. Music: Campbell and Connely. Art Direction: N. G. Arnold, Wilfred Arnold. Players: Anny Ondra [with voice of Joan Barry], John Longden, Donald Calthrop, Sara Allgood, Cyril Ritchard, Hannah Jones. Production: B.I.P. 7,136 ft.

*Blackmail* was begun as a silent and converted, when partially completed, into a full-length talking picture, the first to come from a British studio. For its time it is an astonishing *tour-de-force*, particularly in its use of subjective sound. Moments such as the doorbell which swells into a knell of doom in the girl's ears, or the neighbour's idle chatter dwindling into an indistinguishable murmur until only the word "knife" is heard, climaxed by the father's demand for the bread-knife, are quoted to this day as examples of Hitchcock's virtuosity in so new a medium. It even contains the first use of voice substitution—Joan Barry speaking lines into a separate microphone as Anny Ondra mouths them (this has been inaccurately referred to as dubbing. It is, in fact, simultaneous synchronisation). The final chase over the roof of the British Museum involved the use of the Schuftan process. In general, however, the film is a fairly commonplace suspense story, deprived for box-office reasons of the ironic ending Hitchcock wanted. In his original script the girl is arrested for the killing, and her detective *fiancé*, on being asked if he is going out with her that evening, replies "No, not tonight." Two names do not appear on the general credits list: Ronald Neame as clapper-boy and Michael Powell as stills photographer.

PICCADILLY. Script: Arnold Bennett. Direction: E. A. Dupont. Photography: Werner Brandes. Editing: J. N. McConaughty. Music: Engene Contie. Players: Gilda Gray, Jameson Thomas, Anna May Wong, Cyril Ritchard, Charles Laughton. Production: B.I.P. 9,763 ft.

E. A. Dupont, well-known as a German director, came over and made a small number of films in Britain before moving on to Hollywood. *Piccadilly*, a (silent) mystery-thriller, concerns a night club proprietor, a soon-to-be-discarded mistress, and a young Chinese girl whom he promotes from work in the kitchen to replace the woman in her dance act—as a result of which she is, not altogether surprisingly, done to death. At the time of its release it was described by one critic—perhaps influenced by the illustrious name of its script-writer—as the best film to be made by B.I.P. Unremarkable in general, and lacking any particular connection with its topographical title, it is nevertheless notable for sets and camerawork, and for a brief glimpse of Charles Laughton as a disgruntled diner.

WOULD YOU BELIEVE IT? Script: Walter Forde, H. Fowler Mear. Direction: Walter Forde. Photography: Geoffrey Faithfull. Editing: Adeline Culley. Art Direction: W. G. Saunders. Music: Paul Mulden. Players: Walter Forde, Pauline Johnson, Arthur Stratton. Production: Archibald Nettlefold.

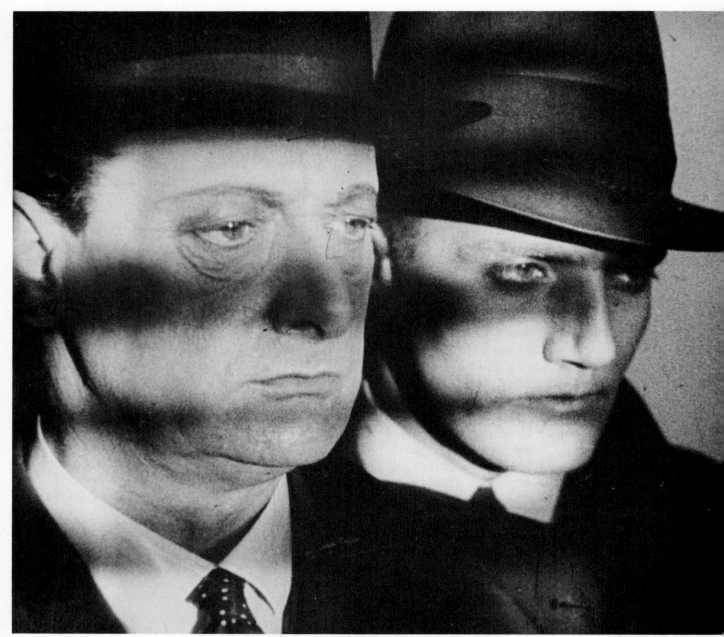

*1929: BLACKMAIL, the first British talking feature film. John Longden on the right.*

*1929: Anna May Wong, as the promoted dancer in
PICCADILLY, is sternly reprimanded by King Ho
Chang.*

5,015 ft.

Walter Forde was probably the best of the
British silent comedians. After a childhood stage
training in tumbling, dancing, juggling and piano-
playing, he made his film *début* in a series of
shorts in 1921. He soon became known for his hall-
mark, a Harrow School broad-brimmed straw hat,
and for his character of a normal, well-meaning
young man who landed in endless difficulties. He
may have been influenced by Harold Lloyd, but
his style was distinctive. In the late Twenties he
appeared in several feature-length comedies, of
which *Would You Believe It?* (which had a record
run of twenty-two weeks at the Tivoli) is both
the best-known and the best. In it he plays the

mild young inventor of a wireless-controlled army
tank, an achievement which involves him with
foreign spies, Whitehall bureaucrats and general
excitement, with a girl waiting at the end of it
all. Directed with great liveliness, with several
hilarious sequences, it can stand up to many a
better-known American comedy of the period. A
Vocalion music recording accompanied the film
which, unfortunately for possible future Forde
comedies, arrived on the very threshold of sound.
Forde went on to a distinguished career as director through the Thirties and Forties.

**KITTY.** Script: V. S. Powell, from the novel by
Warwick Deeping. Direction: Victor Saville. Pho-

*1929: Walter Forde in* WOULD YOU BELIEVE IT.

tography: Karl Püth. Art Direction: Hugh Gee. Players: John Stuart, Estelle Brody, Marie Ault, Moore Marriott, Gibb McLaughlin, Jerrold Robertshaw. Production: B.I.P. 8,100 ft.

A wartime story of an upper-class young man who makes an "unsuitable" marriage with a shop-girl, leaves for the front, and is told by his mother that his wife is being unfaithful to him. He loses the use of his legs and returns home in a wheel-chair, but through Kitty's love all ends satisfactorily. This potentially sentimental subject is saved from an excess of cloy by its sincerity and pleasantly natural surroundings and performances. Made as sound was becoming obligatory, it is interesting in its ingenious handling of the hybrid part-talkie problem. Synchronized for sound but without dialogue for much of its length, its first words are spoken just before the hero recovers the use of his legs—in the middle of a scene. The mo-

ment is ingeniously chosen to minimise the grotesque break from silence to speech. The dialogue scenes were made in New York. In a long shot (at Elstree) Estelle Brodie is seen running to her husband, in the following close-up (New York) he speaks to her. The shots are so well integrated that the difference of the Atlantic between the couple passes unnoticed.

ATLANTIC. Script: from the play by Ernest Raymond. Direction: E. A. Dupont. Photography: Charles Rosher. Players: John Longden, Madeleine Carroll, Ellaline Terris, Franklin Dyall, Monty Banks, John Stuart, Donald Calthrop, Joan Barry, Francis Lister. Production: B.I.P. 8,213 ft.

The first spectacular talking film to be made in Britain, the first multi-lingual talking film to be made in Britain, the first by a famous foreign director to be made in Britain, and one of the biggest failures, silent or sound, to be made in Britain. The reverent awe with which audiences were ushered into the super-cinema to see the great super-production of courage, sacrifice, tragedy, irony, etc., etc., seems incredible when extracts are presented today. A few shots of struggling passengers and flooding lounges are all that remain. The film can claim one record—the longest dramatic pauses in cinematic history. "Sir," says the officer to the tycoon in the lounge as the water washes the decks, "I ----- have something ---- to ---- tell you --- something I ---- feel --- you should know." Slowly, slowly, the tycoon turns his head. "The ship," continues the tight-lipped naval type, "has ----- one hour ---------- to --- live." The words may not be exact; sleep is apt to intervene before the final syllables are dragged out.

**HIGH TREASON.** Script: from the play by Pemberton Billing. Direction: Maurice Elvey. Players: Benita Hume, Jameson Thomas, Humberston Wright, Basil Gill. Production: Gaumont. 8,263 ft.

Gaumont's first sound feature, an attempt to forecast the world in 1940, with futuristic sets, spies in high places, and bombs on Peace Missions, was generally derided, despite its intention as a grim warning of what was in store for us; but it is to be noted for two technical reasons—the introduction of the British Accoustic system in a full-length feature, and an early use of split matte shots.

**Short Films and Documentaries**

**DRIFTERS.** Direction and editing: John Grierson. Photography: Basil Emmott. Production: New Era, for the Empire Marketing Board. 3,631 ft.

This famous silent film about the herring fishing industry is regarded as having pioneered the true documentary film in Britain. Applying to some extent the editing technique of the Russians, Grierson brings to the screen the life and work of the people in a form which combines information, entertainment, and a carefully constructed aesthetic balance. Sequences include trawlers leaving the harbour, storms at sea, the catch, the fish auction, the herring gutting, and the transport to market. As is inevitable with a trail-blazer, the film was later said to have been overpraised, but there is no denying either its intrinsic merit or its importance in the history of British documentary.

*1929: DRIFTERS, a pioneer British documentary.*

**1929: Facts of Interest**

British & Dominions (Herbert Wilcox) equips a sound studio at Boreham Wood, Hertfordshire.

Associated Talking Pictures Company is set up, with a studio at Ealing.

C. M. Woolf becomes joint managing director of Gaumont-British, taken over by the Ostrer brothers.

The Empire Marketing Board Film Unit is established by John Grierson.

In a terrible fire on New Year's Eve at the Glen Cinema, Paisley, seventy out of some five hundred children are killed when panic breaks out.

The first Astoria opens, at Brixton, South London.

The Commodore Super-Cinema, Hammersmith, London, opens.

Peter Yates is born.

# 1930

A COTTAGE ON DARTMOOR. Script: Anthony Asquith, from a story by Herbert Price. Direction: Anthony Asquith. Photography: Stanley Rodwell, M. Lindholm. Art Direction: Arthur Woods. Players: Norah Baring, Hans Schlettow, Uno Henning. Production: B.I.F. 7,528 ft.

In this, the first B.I.F. sound film (with a short dialogue sequence) Asquith is again concerned with an enclosed tale of love, jealousy and death among "ordinary people"—a hairdresser, a pretty manicurist, a farmer. Opening with a highly dramatic prison escape, the film throughout maintains a high degree of tension. There are, once again, only the most essential titles—a cut to an important flashback, for instance, is made without any such explanation, still a daring procedure at the time. Cross-cutting, use of the subjective camera (as when the man in the barber's chair sees the hairdresser's intention to murder him with the razor), and the general method of suspense building, all demonstrate Asquith's developing control of the medium. His production was cut in half by the arrival of sound, and he gets his own back with a mischievous in-joke, set in a cinema, in which he himself participates.

MURDER. Script: Alma Reville, Alfred Hitchcock, Walter Mycroft, from the novel *Enter Sir John* by Winifred Ashton (Clemence Dane) and Helen Simpson. Direction: Alfred Hitchcock. Photography: Jack Cox. Editing: René Harrison. Art Direction: John Mead. Players: Herbert Marshall, Norah Baring, Phyllis Konstam, Edward Chapman, Donald Calthrop, Esmé Percy, Miles Mander. Production: B.I.P. (John Maxwell). 92 mins.

Hitchcock's third sound film (following *Blackmail* he made *Juno and the Paycock,* a competent, straightforward recording of O'Casey's tragedy), does not contain the technical fireworks of his first, but even so he employs innovations such as the "voice-over" (in a scene where Marshall is heard thinking aloud as he shaves) and a distortion effect of a chattering jury. During the former a radio is playing the prelude from *Tristan and Isolde*—in reality a thirty-piece orchestra out of camera range. The story is a true Hitchcock subject: a murder thriller with a touch of the grotesque when the killer turns out to be a transvestite trapeze acrobat—though Hitchcock has stated that he does not really like a "whodunit." A German version was made simultaneously, with Alfred Abel in the Marshall part of the juror who believes in an accused girl's innocence.

TELL ENGLAND. Script: Anthony Asquith, from Ernest Raymond's novel. Direction: Anthony Asquith. Photography: Jack Parker, Stanley Rodwell, James Rogers. Editing: Mary Field. Art Direction: Arthur Woods. Players: Carl Harbord, Tony Bruce, Fay Compton, Dennis Hoey, C. M. Hallard, Wally Patch, Frederick Lloyd. Production: B.I.F. (H. Bruce Woolfe). 7,850 ft.

Asquith follows closely the spirit as well as the letter of Raymond's story of the Gallipoli campaign—omitting neither the disillusionment and bitterness which overtakes the two young officers who enlist in the zeal of public school patriotism, nor the sentimentality which at times softens the

*1930: Norah Baring and Uno Henning in Anthony Asquith's A COTTAGE ON DARTMOOR.*

book's attack, nor the upper-class approach which leaves the rank and file to be depicted as a sort of supporting cast of comic relief and loyal serving-men. It thus lacks the impact of the American *All Quiet on the Western Front* of the same year. However, though the characters may be paste-board, the background is not. The spectacular beach landing in particular is handled with hor-rific power and, though he has himself stated that he did not welcome the advent of sound, Asquith proves that when it came he was able to use it in masterly fashion. In the end, despite softening, one is left with a sense of the infamous futility of the whole botched campaign.

**THE W PLAN.** Script: Victor Saville, Miles Malle-

*1930: Herbert Marshall and Norah Baring in the Hitch-cock mystery-thriller MURDER.*

*1930: The landing at Gallipoli, from TELL ENG-*
*LAND.*

son, Frank Launder, from the novel by Graham Seton. Direction: Victor Saville. Photography: René Guissart, Fred Young. Editing: P. Maclean Rogers. Art Direction: Hugh Gee. Music: John Reynders. Players: Brian Aherne, Madeleine Carroll, Milton Rosmer, Clifford Heatherley, Austin Trevor, George Merritt. Production: B.I.P. 9,347 ft.

A spy story of the First World War, developing from the discovery on the body of a dead German of a plan based on the letter W. Though uneven, and dwindling in its later part, the picture as a whole is taken at a pace sufficient to cover up, at least for its duration, the coincidences and improbabilities. Two spectacular sequences stand out; the shooting down of a British plane, and a lengthy series of scenes in tunnels under the British lines, concluding in their destruction.

### 1930: Facts of Interest

New Ealing studios are opened by Stephen and Jack Courtauld and Basil Dean.

The Leicester Square Theatre turns to films.

The first Odeon Cinema opens at Perry Bar, Birmingham.

The Cameo-Moulin, Piccadilly, opens as the first modern-style news theatre.

The Granada, Dover, first cinema built in Theodore Komisarjevsky's "Moorish" style, opens; also the enormous "Italian Renaissance" Trocadero, at Elephant and Castle, South London.

# 1931

**DANCE, PRETTY LADY.** Script: Anthony Asquith, from Compton Mackenzie's novel *Carnival*. Direction: Anthony Asquith. Photography: Jack Parker. Choreography: Frederick Ashton. Art Direction: Ian Campbell-Gray. Players: Ann Casson, Carl Harbord, Michael Logan, Flora Robson, Moore Marriott, René Ray, Hermione Gingold, Marie Rambert Corps de Ballet. Production: B.I.P. 5,786 ft.

In a poor year, Asquith's re-creation of Edwardian ballet-dancing life stands out for its charm and period atmosphere. The bitter taste of Mackenzie's fine novel is sweetened, particularly the ending—despite the wonderful closing shot the original final sentence could have made. On its own terms, however, there is much to be admired. The ballet scenes of Tchaikovsky's *Swan Lake* are the most imaginatively handled to date, and the world of gas-lit London streets, gaudy cafés, hot glowing stages, cabs, smoke, glitter and gloom is lovingly captured; the whole crowned by Ann Casson's beautifully poised performance.

**SALLY IN OUR ALLEY.** Script: Miles Malleson, from Charles McEvoy's play *The Likes of 'er*. Direction: Maurice Elvey. Photography: Bob Martin, Alex Bryce. Art Direction: Norman Arnold. Players: Gracie Field, Ian Hunter, Florence Desmond, Fred Groves, Gibbs McLaughlin, Ben Field. Production: Associated Radio Pictures (Basil Dean). 77 mins.

This modest adaptation of a well-known low-life play marks the first appearance of Gracie Fields, soon to become Britain's most popular actress. Though unremarkable in every other sense, and as static as a telephone booth, the picture is carried along by the personality of "Our Gracie" and became a triumphant financial success.

**DREYFUS.** Script: Reginald Berkeley, Walter Mycroft, from the play *The Dreyfus Case* by Herzog and Rehfisch. Direction: F. W. Kraemer, Milton Rosmer. Photography: W. Winterstein, J. Harvey, M. Wheddon. Editing: Langford Reed, Betty Spiers. Players: Cedric Hardwicke, Charles Carson, George Merritt, Sam Livesey, Beatrix Thomson, Garry Marsh, Henry Caine, George Skillan, Leonard Shepherd, Arthur Hardy, Abraham Sofaer. Production: B.I.P. 7,800 ft.

Making a virtue of necessity, this tight-budgeted production presents the most impressive account of the famous Case to be found on film. The very sparseness of the simple, plain sets permits the dramatic events to come across in all their stark and bitter truth. With all respect to Joseph Schildkraut's fine performance in *The Life of Emile Zola*, Hardwicke's Dreyfus in this modest film is unsurpassed, and he is greatly helped by unfussy, unobtrusive direction. By emphasising the coldness of the strange man at the centre of the scandal, Hardwicke is able, in brief moments of contrast, to underline the pathos and tragedy of his suffering. There is a moment when, as he sits alone in the steaming heat of his Devil's Island hut, he bows his head slowly and his *pince-nez* slips from his nose to the table: impossible to convey in words the emotional impact of this tiny, incongruous

91

1931: Carl Harbord and Ann Casson in DANCE, PRETTY LADY.

movement. The fact that by it his despair is so movingly conveyed is a measure of the greatness of both performance and direction. The story is not brought to its end. On a blacked-out screen a voice tells of the months of waiting and frustration still to come before restitution, as far as such a thing is possible, will be made—a novel use of sound at this time.

**THE GHOST TRAIN.** Script: from Arnold Ridley's play. Direction: Walter Forde. Players: Jack Hulbert, Cicely Courtneidge, Ann Todd, Cyril Raymond, Donald Calthrop, Angela Baddeley, Allan Jeayes. Production: Gainsborough. 6,425 ft.

This version (the second) of the well-known railway thriller brings Jack Hulbert and Cicely Courtneidge together for the first time in straight roles. As a thriller, neither this version nor the later one (in 1941, when the leading character is split in two and divided between Arthur Askey and Richard Murdoch) is as effective with real trains as the original stage play with its thunder-sheets, garden roller over wooden slats, and oxygen cylinders to represent them. But as the *début* of two leading players of the decade it is worthy of note, and it has the advantage of Walter Forde's proficient handling of the comic possibilities—such as they are.

**THE SKIN GAME.** Script: Alfred Hitchcock, Alma Reville, from John Galsworthy's play. Direction: Alfred Hitchcock. Photography: Jack Cox. Editing: René Harrison, A. Gobbett. Players: Edmund Gwenn, Jill Esmond, John Longden, C. V. France,

*1931: DREYFUS (Cedric Hardwicke) in the dock, is accused by Colonel Henry (Henry Caine).*

Helen Haye, Phyllis Konstam, Frank Lawton. Production: B.I.P. 85 mins.

This very untypical Hitchcock subject—an adaptation of a play dealing with the conflict between landed gentry and belligerent self-made tycoons—is redeemed from utter flatness by the powerful playing of Edmund Gwenn and other principals, and by the director's skill in setting the action against the English countryside without a too obvious "opening-out" of the play.

SUNSHINE SUSIE. Script: from the German musical comedy *The Private Secretary*. Direction: Victor Saville. Editing: Ian Dalrymple. Music: Paul Abrahams. Players: Renate Müller, Jack Hulbert, Owen Nares, Morris Harvey, Sybil Grove. Production: Gainsborough. 87 mins.

Great hopes were entertained of this film as opening a new world for the British musical and capturing some of the spirit and effervescence which, it was considered, had already been achieved in America. The original play (with a conventional secretary-weds-boss theme) had already been made into a German film, which Michael Balcon saw and decided to adapt into English: it was actually made in Germany. Renate Müller, an attractive German actress with a sprightly personality and an appealing accent, scores a considerable success, as does Jack Hulbert as an endearing old janitor. The result, however, remains oddly isolated. The hopes that went with it remained unrealised, and the famous theme song, *Today I Feel So Happy*, charmingly put over by Miss Müller, has a somewhat forced gaiety at variance with the grim realities of life in an England where slumps and unemployment darkly loom. Renate Müller's end was a tragic one. After becoming closely and publicly involved with the Nazi *régime*, she committed suicide.

*1931: Jack Hulbert, Renate Muller and Owen Nares in* SUNSHINE SUSIE, *the British musical directed by Victor Saville on which high hopes were based.*

### 1931: Facts of Interest

Alexander Korda founds London Films, and starts work on his first English production, *Service for Ladies*, with Leslie Howard.

Michael Balcon begins his five years as Director of Production at both Islington (Gainsborough) and Shepherd's Bush (Gaumont-British).

Herbert Wilcox starts production of film versions of the famous Aldwych farces.

# 1932

ROME EXPRESS. Script: Clifford Grey. Direction: Walter Forde. Photography: Gunther Krampf. Editing: Ian Dalrymple. Music: Louis Levy. Art Direction: A. Mazzei. Players: Conrad Veidt, Cedric Hardwicke, Esther Ralston, Eliot Makeham, Hugh Williams, Donald Calthrop. Production: Gaumont British. 93 mins.

The first film to be made at the rebuilt Gaumont studios, and still one of the best train thrillers, involving murder and theft on a journey from Paris to Rome. Forde establishes himself as equally competent with suspense as with comedy, and his studio train and railway (interspersed with documentary footage) is satisfactorily convincing except for the model bridge crash. Throughout he manages to convey both the claustrophobia of a railway carriage and the sense that we are on something which is moving, and vibrating as it moves—an effect which the mere recording of a rat-a-tat-tat and the showing of process shots of passing scenery through the windows often fail to achieve. The constant sense of being on something which you could dangerously fall off adds greatly to the climax when it arrives. Conrad Veidt makes an impressive English *début* (he appears also in *Congress Dances*, made in Berlin the same year), though it cannot be said that either he or any of the other characters are much more than chessmen.

JACK'S THE BOY. Script: Jack Hulbert, Douglas Furber. Direction: Walter Forde. Photography: Leslie Rowson. Editing: Ian Dalrymple. Music: Vivian Ellis. Art Direction: Andrew Mazzei. Play-

*1932: ROME EXPRESS, directed by Walter Forde, with Conrad Veidt.*

ers: Jack Hulbert, Cicely Courtneidge, Winifred Shotter, Francis Lister, Peter Gawthorne. Production: Gainsborough. 90 mins.

Hulbert and Courtneidge did much to brighten the often gloomy British screen of the thirties and, directed with the requisite lightness of touch by Forde, this joint effort is one of their best. Hulbert is at his most genial as the convivial son of a stern Scotland Yard officer who, stung by his father's taunts, determines to become a policeman himself. His singing of *The Flies Crawl up the Window*, and Cicely Courtneidge's ditty as she prepares a banquet are high spots, and the final chase in Madame Tussaud's is an excellent example of well-handled knockabout comedy.

**RICH AND STRANGE** (East of Shanghai). Script: Alma Reville, Val Valentine, from a story by Dale Collins. Direction: Alfred Hitchcock. Editing: Winifred Cooper, René Harrison. Music: Hal Dolphe. Art Direction: C. W. Arnold. Players: Henry Kendall, Joan Barry, Percy Marmont, Betty Amann, Elsie Randolph. Production: B.I.P. 83 mins.

One of Hitchcock's most underrated films, the subtleties of which seem to have escaped those who looked forward to more *Blackmail*-type suspense. A suburban young couple who come into a lot of money go on a world cruise. The girl falls for an older man, and the husband for a fake princess to whom he loses what is left of the legacy. They start for home in a cargo boat which sinks, and are rescued by Chinese who horrify the couple by their impassive acceptance of cruelty and their total "foreignness." Eventually the couple arrive safely back home. Superficially a story of two people who are made sadder and wiser through experience, the underlying question is asked: are they in fact any wiser (happier or not)—or are their neat little lives already putting up a self-protecting wall of forgetfulness? The uneasy ambiguities which are to lie beneath the suspense-thriller surface of later Hitchcock are already in evidence. The dichotomy of the film is noticeable in the contrast between the light (rich) first part and the dark (strange) second part. Having shown what he can do with sound when he likes, in this case he uses it sparingly; much of the film is, in fact, shot silent.

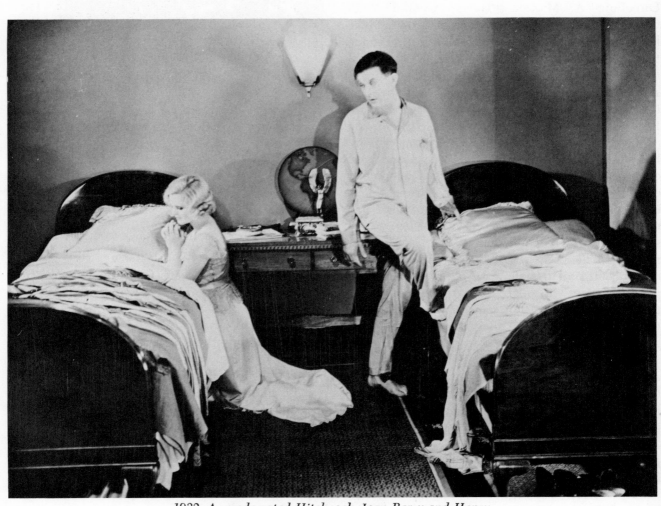

*1932: An underrated Hitchcock, Joan Barry and Henry Kendall in RICH AND STRANGE.*

1932: *John Stuart and Ann Casson in NUMBER SEVENTEEN.*

GOODNIGHT VIENNA. Script: Erich Maschwitz, Holt Marvel, George Posford. Direction: Herbert Wilcox. Editing: E. Aldridge. Music: Erich Maschwitz, George Posford. Art Direction: L. P. Williams. Players: Jack Buchanan, Clive Currie, William Kendall, Gibb McLaughlin, Clifford Heatherley, O. B. Clarence, Gina Malo, Anna Neagle. Production: British & Dominions. 75 mins.

This light and cheerful version of a typical "Viennese" musical comedy has, apart from its entertainment value which is undoubted and proven, three noteworthy points: it was the company's biggest financial success to date when financial successes of any kind were few and far between; it established Jack Buchanan as a leading box-office attraction in the cinema, as he already was in the theatre; by bringing Anna Neagle and Herbert Wilcox together it started what is probably the most famous and longest lasting partnership in the British cinema.

NUMBER SEVENTEEN. Script: Alma Reville, Alfred Hitchcock, Rodney Ackland, from the play by J. Jefferson Farjeon. Direction: Alfred Hitchcock. Photography: J. Cox, Bryan Langley. Editing: A. C. Hammond. Music: A. Hallis. Art Direction: Wilfred Arnold. Players: Leon M. Lion, Ann Casson, Anne Grey, John Stuart, Barry Jones, Donald Calthrop. Production: B.I.P. 60 mins. approx.

Minor Hitchcock, but an amiable burlesque thriller, set in a fog-enshrouded house and having something to do with jewel robbers. Leon M. Lion repeats his stage performance of the old tramp who discovers the hiding-place of the thieves, and various events of increasing unlikeliness cheerfully multiply, culminating in some blandly unconvincing model work of different types of transport. Hitchcock describes it as a disaster, but it's really rather fun.

### 1932: Facts of Interest

London Films opens a studio at Denham.

The Sunday Entertainments Act is passed, giving local authorities the right to license Sunday openings.

Jacey Cinemas opens its first house, the Oxford, Birmingham.

*The Film in National Life*, report of a Commission on Education and Cultural Films, is published.

# 1933

THE PRIVATE LIFE OF HENRY VIII. Script: Lajos Biro, Arthur Wimperis. Direction: Alexander Korda. Photography: Georges Périnal. Editing: Stephen Harrison. Music: Kurt Schroeder. Art Direction: Vincent Korda. Players: Charles Laughton, Robert Donat, Merle Oberon, Binnie Barnes, Wendy Barrie, Elsa Lanchester, Lady Tree, Franklin Dyall, James Mason, Miles Mander, Sam Livesey, Judy Kelly. Production: London Films. 95 mins.

This famous landmark in British cinema (directed and produced by a Hungarian, photographed by a Frenchman, half scripted by another Hungarian, art directed by a third Hungarian, with music by a German), has probably had more written about it than any other, at least up to the post-war period. It was the first British production to achieve financial success outside its own country, not only in America but elsewhere. It loosened the strings of big business purses, enabling Korda —principally through the Prudential Assurance Company—to enlarge the Denham studios until they were as good as any in the world. The film sticks firmly to its title (which some of its more solemn critics forgot) and makes no pretence at teaching history. The story that Korda was in a taxi and heard the driver singing "I'm 'Enery the Eighth, hI am," and so got the idea is probably apocryphal, but possibly true. Arguments as to whether Henry really carried on like that are as irrelevant as they are pointless. The film is about jolly fat Charles Laughton dressed up in Tudor costume and playing at being a king with six wives and amusingly bad table manners such as throwing meat-bones over his shoulder. The film has no exciting directorial innovations to offer, but is written, shot, played and edited with plenty of sparkle. "An enjoyable historical romp," was one critic's verdict. Remove the penultimate word and you have it. Henry VIII as an influential figure in the world has little to do with the film: and after all, he *did* have six wives, *did* want a son, *was* fond of music, *was* fat, and wore flat hats. And the film *was* the (temporary) salvation of the British industry.

*1933: Charles Laughton in the epoch-making PRIVATE LIVES OF HENRY VIII.*

THE GOOD COMPANIONS. Script: W. P. Lipscomb, from the novel by J. B. Priestley. Direction: Victor Saville. Photography: Bernard Knowles. Editing: Ian Dalrymple. Music: George Posford. Art Direction: Alfred Junge. Players: Jessie Matthews, Edmund Gwenn, John Gielgud, Mary Glynne, Percy Parsons, Dennis Hoey, Viola Compton, Finlay Currie, Jack Hawkins, Frank Pettingell. Production: Gaumont British/Welsh-Pearson. 113 mins.

Priestley's immensely long picaresque novel is skillfully compressed into a lively and pleasant film. The story of three oddly assorted people who came together, and toured depression-ridden England as a concert party deserved and achieved considerable success, with Jessie Matthews as the little soubrette giving a delightful performance in what might be called, cinematically, "her year"— though her greatest single success came in 1934. Under Victor Saville's unobtrusive but competent guidance a vast cast and a multiplicity of scenes and locations were blended together with economy and clarity: no technical fireworks, but the skill

1933: Jessie Matthews finds Donald Calthrop's attentions a little pressing in FRIDAY THE 13TH.

which conceals skill, and puts the subject matter first. Work started with Henry Ainley as Jess Oakroyd, but he was unable to complete it and his scenes had to be shot again with Edmund Gwenn excellently replacing him. King George V and Queen Mary saw this as their first talking picture, as a Charity Matinee at the New Victoria cinema. Assistant to Michael Balcon on the production side was Pen Tennyson, later to be regarded as a director of considerable promise before his tragically early death during the war.

FRIDAY THE THIRTEENTH. Script: Emlyn Williams, from a story by C. H. Moresby-White and Sidney Gilliat. Direction: Victor Saville. Editing: Ian Dalrymple. Music: Louis Levy. Art Direction: Alex Vetchinsky. Players: Jessie Matthews, Edmund Gwenn, Sonnie Hale, Robertson Hare, Gordon Harker, Frank Lawton, Elizabeth Allan, Ursula Jeans, Max Miller, Emlyn Williams. Production: Gainsborough. 84 mins.

Jessie Matthews scored another success in this episodic or portmanteau film, which traces the early stories of a number of different characters who all assemble on the same bus by chance on the reputedly unlucky date of the title.

I WAS A SPY. Script: W. P. Lipscomb, Ian Hay, from the book by Martha McKenna. Direction: Victor Saville. Photography: C. van Enger. Players: Conrad Veidt, Madeleine Carroll, Herbert

1933: One of the brightest lights of the Thirties, Jessie Matthews, in THE GOOD COMPANIONS.

*1933: A finely composed still from I WAS A SPY, depicting the arrivals of German troops in a Belgian village.*

Marshall, Gerald du Maurier, Edmund Gwenn, Donald Calthrop. Production: Gaumont British. 85 mins.

Saville's third picture in a hat-trick year is based on a series of newspaper articles, later published in book form, by Martha McKenna, a Belgian woman who had worked for the Allies in the First World War. Set in Flanders, it concerns a German officer who hunts down a spy, only to find it is the girl with whom he has fallen in love. Balcon describes it as the most ambitious film he had yet attempted. During production, the libel case against M-G-M's all-Barrymore Rasputin film came up, and, fearful lest Mrs. McKenna might consider certain episodes in his own film libellous, he sent his production manager, Herbert Mason, to seek her approval. On arrival in Belgium, Mason found her married to a former member of his own regiment. After a suitable reunion, in which Mrs. McKenna joined, Mason returned with full permission to proceed. The film set the seal of stardom on Veidt, whose performance is the most memorable thing in the production.

*1933: Conrad Veidt and Madeleine Carroll in I WAS A SPY.*

SOLDIERS OF THE KING. Script: W. P. Lipscomb, J. O. C. Orton, Jack Hulbert, from a story by Douglas Furber. Direction: Maurice Elvey. Photography: Leslie Rowson. Editing: Ian Dalrymple. Music: Louis Levy. Art Direction: Alex Vetchinsky. Players: Cicely Courtneidge, Edward Everett Horton, Dorothy Hyson, Anthony Bushell, Frank Cellier. Production: Gainsborough. 80 mins.

On her own, Cicely Courtneidge proves less effective than when teamed with Hulbert, despite the welcome presence of Edward Everett Horton, and the Walter Forde touch is missing. Her rendering of the title song, however, is in the genuine, unbeatable music hall tradition.

### Short Films and Documentaries

INDUSTRIAL BRITAIN. Direction and photography: Robert Flaherty. Editing: John Grierson. Production John Grierson.

This interesting film was the result of an invitation from Grierson to Flaherty to photograph the British industrial scene and demonstrate the lasting importance of craftsmanship in a mass-producing machine age. Eventually Basil Wright, Arthur Elton and Edgar Anstey, all leading documentary film-makers, became involved, the final editing being done by Grierson himself.

90 DEGREES SOUTH.
A sound version of Herbert Ponting's film of Scott's last voyage.

### 1933: Facts of Interest

Shepperton Studios are opened at Littlewood Park and John Baxter starts a series of inexpensive realistic films such as *Doss House, Song of the Plough* and *Flood Tide.*

J. Arthur Rank becomes interested in films.

General Post Office Film Unit is formed.

The Curzon cinema, Mayfair, then the last word in luxury houses, opens.

Everyman Theatre, Hampstead, turns from plays to films, with a policy of special programmes which has lasted until this day.

The first specially designed provincial news theatre opens, in Birmingham; and the Victoria News Theatre in London.

The H (Horrific) category is added to the British Board of Film Censors certification.

The British Film Institute is established. A three-year boom in British production starts, sparked off by *The Private Life of Henry VIII*. Death of James Williamson.

# 1934

**THE MAN WHO KNEW TOO MUCH.** Script: A. R. Rawlinson, Charles Bennett, D. B. Wyndham Lewis, Edwin Greenwood, Emlyn Williams. Direction: Alfred Hitchcock. Photography: Curt Courant. Editing: H. St.C. Courant. Music: Arthur Benjamin. Art Direction: Alfred Junge, Peter Proud. Players: Leslie Banks, Edna Best, Peter Lorre, Frank Vosper, Nova Pilbeam, Henry Oscar, Hugh Wakefield. Production: Gaumont British. 84 mins.

Generally regarded as the first "real Hitchcock," this contains most of the elements to be found throughout his work—the slow build-up to the sudden shock, the incongruous and/or sinister lurking just beneath the commonplace surface, the potential menace in the everyday object, the quirky characterisation, the arousal of an emotion and its unexpected displacement by a climax in complete reversal from that which was apparently developing. The fast pace and quick changes of setting in *The Man Who Knew Too Much* conceal the improbabilities in the script. The climax at the Royal Albert Hall, where the diplomat is to be shot at a certain point in an orchestral performance—the views of the audience, the victim moving and settling in his chair, the enormous close-up of the slowly moving gun barrel—is a famous set piece, as is the final shooting match, based on the 1911 Sidney Street siege. Scarcity of funds caused the exercise of technical ingenuity such as the use of a reflected painting to represent part of the audience. Already, too, Hitchcock is demonstrating his lack of concern over the obvious falsity of backcloths or studio sets.

The Hollywood re-make (1955) is undoubtedly superior in script and production quality, but the 1934 version has a sort of naïve attractiveness all of its own: it also has the advantage of Peter Lorre, and of two superbly sinister villains in Frank Vosper and Henry Oscar.

**EVERGREEN.** Script: Emlyn Williams, Benn Levy, from the play by Benn Levy. Direction: Victor Saville. Photography: Glen MacWilliams. Editing: Ian Dalrymple. Music: Harry Woods; songs by Richard Rodgers and Lorenz Hart. Art Direction: Alfred Junge. Players: Jessie Matthews, Sonnie Hale, Betty Balfour, Barry MacKay, Ivor McLaren, Hartley Power, Betty Shale. Production: Gaumont British. 94 mins.

Regarded for many years as Britain's best musical (not in itself a superlative recommendation), *Evergreen* is mainly of interest as a vehicle for Jessie Matthews, whose featherweight dancing and honeyed if somewhat refined singing exactly suit the romantic, nostalgic story. She even copes creditably enough with doubling up as her own mother. The picture, pleasing to the eye and undemanding on the mind, proved immensely popular. Saville is not content merely to record the stage production: new numbers are added, and Emlyn Williams widens the proscenium arch with unobtrusive skill. Its purpose as a rival to the brasher but livelier American musical was thwarted, as is well known, by the arrival of Fred Astaire and Ginger Rogers. However, even taken out of period, it has much to please the indulgent viewer.

1934: *THE MAN WHO KNEW TOO MUCH, Leslie
Banks becomes suspicious of his dentist (Henry Oscar).*

**NELL GWYN.** Script: Miles Malleson. Direction: Herbert Wilcox. Photography: F. A. Young. Editing: Melville White. Music: Edward German. Art Direction: L. P. Williams. Players: Anna Neagle, Cedric Hardwicke, Jeanne de Casilis, Muriel George, Miles Malleson, Esmé Percy. Production: British and Dominions. 85 mins.

The most remarkable thing about Wilcox's remake of Charles and Nell is that thirty-five cuts were demanded by the American censorship, including a complaint about the extent of Anna Neagle's "cleavage" (according to Wilcox, the first use of the word in a mammary connection). Two suggestions were made: Charles must marry Nell; and she must not move on into the bed of James II on the former's death. In the event, a totally false epilogue was tacked on, with Nell shivering in the gutter, and the film was a failure. In Britain, however, with all its immoralities large upon it, it broke box-office records. Hardwicke was then at the height of his powers as an actor and his portrait of Charles II is memorable, as is the restraint, dignity and feeling for period with which most of the film is handled, in particular the King's death. Much of the dialogue is taken from Pepys. Anna Neagle may not be history's Nell Gwyn, but might very well have been her rival had Charles come across her at the time.

**BOYS WILL BE BOYS.** Script: Will Hay. Direction: William Beaudine. Photography: Charles Van Enger. Editing: A. Roome. Music: Louis Levy. Art Direction: A. Vetchinsky. Players: Will Hay, Gordon Harker, Jimmy Hanley, Davy Burnaby,

*1934: Jessie Matthews toasted at the Café Royale in*
*EVERGREEN.*

*1934: Anna Neagle (with "cleavage"), and Cedric Hardwicke in NELL GWYN.*

Claude Dampier, Percy Walsh. Production: Gainsborough. 6,867 ft.

Will Hay was the leading comic of the Thirties in British cinema. While more limited in range and less universal in appeal than the Hollywood greats, more closely tied to the music hall tradition from which he came, he is in the true clown category and his best films, though sometimes slow, still stand revival today. His first film was an adaptation of Pinero's old farce *Dandy Dick* (*Those Were the Days*), but in *Boys Will Be Boys* he appears in his most familiar guise—the incompetent, rascally, cunning but foolable schoolmaster. Both films are directed by the American William Beaudine, maker of several Mary Pickford features.

Hay never plays for pathos. He is a rogue—selfish, amoral, righteously indignant when done himself but always willing to do others. Decidedly one would steer clear of him in real life. He does not attain the universal humanity of the great comedians: nor, on the other hand, does he fall into the bathos and sentimentality that sometimes entraps them.

SING AS WE GO. Script: Gordon Wellesley. Direction: Basil Dean. Photography: Robert Martin. Editing: Thorold Dickinson. Art Direction: Edward Carrick. Players: Gracie Fields, John Loder, Dorothy Hyson, Stanley Holloway, Frank Pettingell. Production: Associated Talking Pictures. 80 mins.

Coming in the middle of the Depression, Gracie Fields's film has an all-pull-together-now and keep-on-keeping-cheerful atmosphere about it that stimulated rather than irritated contemporary audiences, which presumably casts some kind of light on the national character. It follows the usual good-hearted mill girl formula, was shot in Bolton and Blackpool, Lancashire, and made enough money to pay for vastly increasing the space of Ealing studios. Owing to an emergency, the film was shot complete without cutting and Thorold Dickinson was called in at the last moment to complete a mammoth job in record time. The production marks the end of a partnership between director and star which began with *Sally in Our Alley* and included the latter's most popular roles.

**JEW SUSS.** Script: Dorothy Farnum, from Leon Feuchtwanger's novel. Direction: Lothar Mendes. Photography: Gunther Krampf. Editing: Otto Ludwig. Art Direction: Alfred Junge. Players: Conrad Veidt, Frank Vosper, Paul Graetz, Benita Hume, Gerald du Maurier, Joan Maude, Cedric Hardwicke. Production: Gaumont British. 107 mins.

A rather over-weighty adaptation of a best-selling novel, the outstanding merits of which are Conrad Veidt's powerful performance as the Jew and Frank Vosper's coarse, overbearing Count. The theme of the film is tolerance, and it deals with one man's struggle to attain power for the good of his persecuted people and his ultimate discovery that he is not, in fact, Jewish himself, but an illegitimate child. The period atmosphere (Wurtemberg in the early Eighteenth century) is painstakingly and convincingly captured. The production encountered difficulties both from Nazi Germany (who apparently brought pressure on Veidt not to play the part), and paradoxically from fears that the Jews in New York might not approve of it. It also encountered, in this country, a gem of irrelevant criticism for being a film about the suppressed Jews instead of about shipbuilding, farming, fishing, railways or unemployment in Britain: which is about as meaningful as criticising a Wagnerian opera for not being a treatise on office management.

**Short Films and Documentaries**

**MAN OF ARAN.** Script, direction and photography: Robert Flaherty. Editing: John Goldman. Music: John Greenwood. Production: Gaumont British. 75 mins.

Three years in the making, *Man of Aran* tells of the life of the lonely islanders off the West Coast of Ireland, their struggle to wring from an un-

*1934: JACK AHOY, directed by Walter Forde, shows Jack Hulbert and nymphs in a typical musical of the period.*

ceasingly hostile environment the bare necessities of existence, their fortitude, their stubbornness, but above all their common humanity. It is the sort of subject done almost to death these days in television documentaries, but Flaherty achieved during his long sojourn a sense of personal involvement which makes the result far more than a record of fact and comment, despite criticisms that the film as a whole is too slight and affords little more than a cursory glimpse. As a crowning glory the film was awarded the Mussolini Gold Cup at the Venice Festival—it has since proved to be not gold at all, but very inferior plating, and is used by Michael Balcon as "quite an impressive ashtray."

**1934: Facts of Interest**

J. A. Rank forms British International Films.

The London Pavilion, Piccadilly Circus, becomes a cinema.

The Cinema House, Oxford Circus, one of the earliest, becomes The Studio, later divided into Studios One and Two.

The Ritz, Leicester Square, small sister of the adjoining Empire, opens.

Len Lye joins the G.P.O. Film Unit and makes a number of animated colour films using his own technique of drawing and painting direct on the frame. (First: *Colour Box*, 1935)

It is estimated that there are some 4,300 cinemas in Britain, of which 20 per cent have under 500 seats and 3.5 per cent over 2,000.

# 1935

THE THIRTY-NINE STEPS. Script: Alma Reville, Charles Bennett, from John Buchan's novel. Direction: Alfred Hitchcock. Photography: Bernard Knowles. Editing: Derek Twist. Music: Louis Levy. Art Direction: Otto Werndorff, Albert Jullion. Players: Madeleine Carroll, Robert Donat, Lucie Mannheim, Godfrey Tearle, Peggy Ashcroft, John Laurie, Frank Cellier, Wylie Watson. Production: Gaumont British. 81 mins.

With this picture Hitchcock's reputation became international. In it for the first time he develops the kind of sex-relationship between two of his leading players which is to become a marked characteristic of much of his later work. Comedy has an increasing part, serving when necessary to tighten rather than loosen suspense. The increasing complexity and subtlety of brief encounters is shown in the scene in the farmer's cottage. His brilliant use of anti-climax occurs in such incidents as Donat's being forced to deliver a political speech at a hall into which he blunders while escaping from his pursuers, or when his imminent murder is prevented by the announcement that dinner is served. Once again the theatre as a setting is present: the music hall climax provides Hitchcock with a double audience, "them" and "us," on whom to work. The film differs considerably from the book—to the extent of rendering the title almost meaningless. Buchan was at first annoyed, later appreciative. In his interview with Truffaut, Hitchcock agrees that it is with this film that he begins to trouble less about the intrinsic plausibility than about the emotion it may arouse. What matters is not what the "secret papers" contain, but what happens to the people involved in connection with them.

SANDERS OF THE RIVER. Script: Lajos Biro, Jeffrey Dell. Direction: Zoltan Korda. Photography: Georges Périnal, Osmond Borrodaile, Louis Page. Editing: Charles Crichton. Music: Michael Spolianski. Players: Paul Robeson, Leslie Banks, Nina Mae McKinney. Production: London Films. 96 mins.

Robeson's *début* in British films was accused even at the time of paternalism and imperialism, though it is only fair to add that it was also praised for its integrity and its dignified treatment of its subject. The script is a combination of a number of African adventure stories by Edgar Wallace, told against finely photographed backgrounds, spoilt by studio settings, and accompanied by some well-recorded (for the period) singing. Robeson's voice lives in the memory, though at least one contemporary critic chose the performance of Leslie Banks as the film's most enduring asset. It was widely distributed, made a lot of money, and contributed a good share to the mid-Thirties boom in British production.

THE SCARLET PIMPERNEL. Script: Arthur Wimperis, Robert E. Sherwood, Sam Berman, from the novel by Baroness Orczy. Direction: Harold Young. Photography: Harold Rosson. Editing: Stephen Harrison. Art Direction: Vincent Korda. Players: Leslie Howard, Merle Oberon, Raymond Massey, Nigel Bruce, Bramwell Fletcher. Production: London Films. 98 mins.

This amiable piece of stap-me fustian is the best adaptation of the adventures of Baroness

*1935: Godfrey Tearle reveals his amputated finger, and his true nature, to Robert Donat in THE THIRTY-NINE STEPS.*

Orczy's dandified, aristocrat-rescuing hero, largely owing to Howard's beautifully underplayed, humorous, circumspectly tongue-in-cheek performance. (Other portrayals have been by Barry K. Barnes, 1938, and David Niven, 1950.) Howard is aided by a sturdily reliable supporting cast led by Raymond Massey. Little more direction is called for than presenting the characters against a reasonably convincing background, and little more is provided. Settings suit the romanticised period atmosphere, and the photography warmly records some charming landscape exteriors. Howard is to present a modernised Pimpernel, in less gracious settings, in 1941.

**BROWN ON RESOLUTION** (Forever England).

Script: J. O. C. Orton, from C. S. Forester's novel Direction: Walter Forde. Photography: Bernard Knowles. Players: John Mills, Betty Balfour, Barry Mackay, H. Marion-Crawford, Jimmy Hanley, H. G. Stoker. Production: Gaumont British. 79 mins.

In his first starring role Mills portrays a young able-seaman whose ship is sunk in action in the First World War, and who is rescued by the Germans: when their ship puts into an island port for repairs, Brown manages to secure a rifle and ammunition and by sniping at the men working on the ship manages to delay its departure until it can be sunk by the British. The moral would appear to be: if you leave your enemies to drown instead of rescuing them, you will probably save the lives of your own countrymen and your ship

*1935: THE SCARLET PIMPERNEL, Leslie Howard in one of his most famous roles, with Merle Oberon.*

but this seems to have passed unnoticed. Mills gives an extremely likeable performance of a young man bravely and unquestioningly doing what he thinks is expected of him in time of war and the battle scenes (done by a unit under the direction of Anthony Asquith) are mildly, if not wildly, exciting. Made "with the full co-operation of the Admiralty," the film was one selected for showing to the Civil Defense personnel during their periods of idleness in the 1939–40 period of the "phoney" war—presumably to teach them some sort of lesson.

**THE OLD CURIOSITY SHOP.** Script: Margaret Kennedy, Ralph Neale, from the novel by Charles Dickens. Direction: Thomas Bentley. Photography: Claude Friese-Greene. Editing: Leslie Norman. Music: Eric Coates. Art Direction: Cedric Dawe. Players: Ben Webster, Elaine Benson, Hay Petrie, Beatrix Thomson, Gibb McLaughlin. B. I. P. 105 mins.

With a little more imagination and attack in the direction, this could have ranked alongside David Lean's two great films of the Forties, *Oliver Twist* and *Great Expectations*. Bentley was at one time a Dickens impersonator and had already made several silent Dickens films, including one of this very book with Mabel Poulton. He obviously knows and loves his author. The spirit of Dickensian rural England with its coaches and village hostelries is accurately caught, and the wonderful grotesques which surround the sentimental centre of the story—Jarley's Waxworks, the Punch and Judy Men, and above all Quilp (done to the life by Hay Petrie)—are given their full value. In Quilp's sudden shock entrances, for instance, Bentley's direction has a sharp edge which is lacking in much of the film. Ben Webster, though allowed to overdramatise, prevents the old grandfather from becoming too great a bore. It is probably impossible to clothe Little Nell in flesh and blood (though Dickens's portrayal of her is much less slobbery than mockers who have not looked at the book for years like to pretend): Elaine Benson has a stab at her, but does not penetrate very far.

**THE IRON DUKE.** Script: H. M. Harwood. Direction: Victor Saville. Photography: C. Courant. Editing: Ian Dalrymple. Players: George Arliss, Ellaline Terriss, Gladys Cooper, A. E. Matthews, Allan Aynesworth. Production: Gaumont British. 80 mins.

George Arliss, untouchable eminence of the American Thirties "historical" reconstructions, was persuaded to come to Britain (at considerable expense) to make three or four prestige films. The experience does not seem to have been an altogether happy one. *The Iron Duke* is the best of the bunch, but with Arliss as usual turning a historical character into an Arliss characterisation rather than the reverse, the result is hardly worth the trouble, or the expense.

**THE TURN OF THE TIDE.** Script: based on the novel *Three Fevers*, by Leo Walmsley. Direction: Norman Walker. Players: John Garrick, Wilfrid Lawson, Geraldine Fitzgerald, Sam Livesey, J. Fisher White. Production: British National. 80 mins.

Inexpensively produced, this semi-documentary story of two rival families in a Yorkshire fishing village is notable for its photography of sea and

*1935: THE TURN OF THE TIDE, the film that brought J. Arthur Rank into the industry.*

shore. The antagonism between the adherents of older, traditional methods of fishing and the newcomers with more up-to-date equipment is paralleled by the rivalry between youth and age—the younger members of each family combining to try out the modern way together. The real importance of this film, however, lies outside its intrinsic merit. It delighted J. Arthur Rank by its moral content and its combination of entertainment with instruction. On finding that it was receiving scarcely any bookings on account of its supposed lack of box-office appeal, he decided to remedy the state of affairs by entering the industry itself. Symbol-hunters may note the title: from such small incidents is history made.

### Short Films and Documentaries

SONG OF CEYLON. Direction: Basil Wright. Photography: Basil Wright. Music: Walter Leigh. Production: John Grierson, for the Ceylon Tea Production Board. 40 mins.

This exquisitely photographed film is concerned with the lives and customs of the inhabitants of Ceylon and the impact of Western commerce upon them. Constructed on the basis of a musical composition, it is divided into the four parts of symphonic form: The Buddha, The Virgin Island, The Voices of Commerce, The Apparel of a God. The last asserts the permanence of tradition and custom despite the potentially disrupting influence of modern trade. The famous travelling shot of the winging bird startled by the striking of a temple bell is one of the most beautiful in all documentary. In recent years the film has been criticised as superficial, a commercial for commerce, even "pure *National Geographic Magazine.*" Be that as it may, a drab world would become even drabber if all idealisation were to be prohibited by political decree.

TELL ME IF IT HURTS. Script, Direction and Editing: Richard Massingham. Photography: Karl Urbahn. Music: Harry Platts. Players: Russell Waters, Patrick Ross, Freda Silcock, Peter Copley. Production: Richard Massingham. 20 mins.

This is the first production of a personality unique in British cinema. A fully qualified doctor, he gave up medicine to make films, bringing out over the next eighteen years some hundred titles, all shorts, sponsored by the British Council, the Admiralty, the Ministry of Information, the Gas Council and other concerns. He is probably best known for his informational, advisory and admonitory films for the Government during the war—in which, with great humour and charm, he himself played the part of an earnest-minded gentleman doing his best to cope with a plethora of demands and restrictions. His work is noted for its delightful understanding of everyday problems, pains and perplexities. His film made for the Children's Film Foundation, *To The Rescue,* won the 1953 Venice Festival award as the best for children aged between twelve and fifteen. Even in the above first production he shows himself master of current directional fashion. Such was its barbed humour that it was temporarily banned for "ridiculing the dental profession."

## 1935: Facts of Interest

General Film Distributors is set up by C. M. Woolf and J. A. Rank.

Pinewood Studios are opened, with Rank as chairman.

Warner Brothers start production at Teddington.

Alexander Korda becomes producer-owner of United Artists, with Chaplin, Fairbanks, Goldwyn and Mary Pickford.

Twickenham studios are virtually destroyed by fire.

The first Classic Cinema is opened, in Croydon.

The National Film Archive is inaugurated—known in its first years as the National Film Library.

# 1936

*1936: Contrasts from THINGS TO COME. The after-math of the bombing raid. The world of the future.*

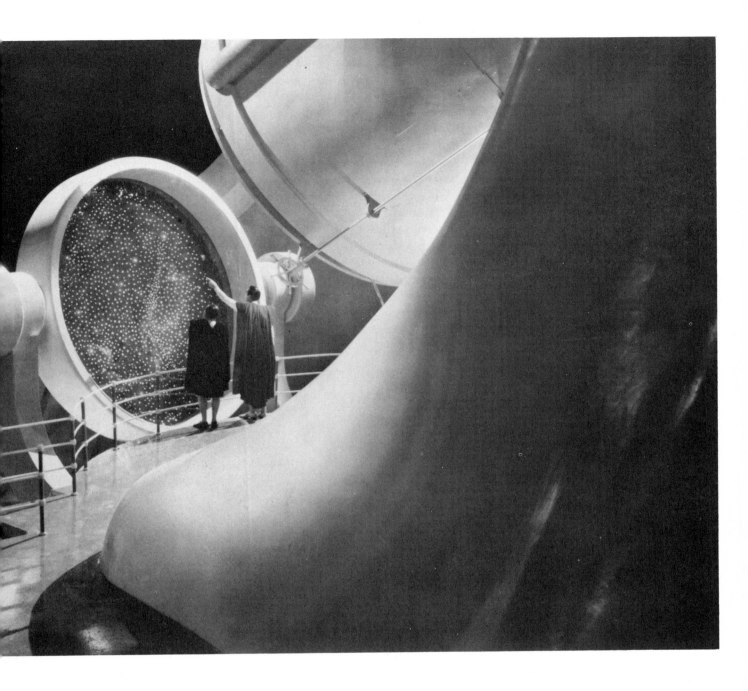

THINGS TO COME. Script: H. G. Wells. Direction: William Cameron Menzies. Photography: Georges Périnal. Music: Sir Arthur Bliss. Art Direction: Vincent Korda. Players: Raymond Massey, Edward Chapman, Ralph Richardson, Margaretta Scott, Ann Todd, Sophie Stewart. Production: London Films. 108 mins.

The most memorable points after thirty years are the menacing approach of the bombers opening the 1940 undeclared war, the magnificent fu-turistic sets (what a nice *clean* world was envisaged—no pollution in sight), and Bliss's stirring music. Its failure is on the human side, where only Raymond Massey is able to inject any reality into the conventionally science-fiction-clothed figures. The worst part of the new world, it seems, will be the speechifying we should have to listen to. For its time the film is a great imaginative feat, in the main successfully realised, and a technical triumph for British studios. The huge vistas of the Space

Gun and other contrivances, the milling crowds and action sequences are hugely impressive, and the chit-chat can always be snoozed through.

REMBRANDT. Script: Carl Zuckmayer. Direction: Alexander Korda. Photography: Georges Périnal. Editing: William Hornbeck. Music: Geoffrey Toye. Art Direction: Vincent Korda. Players: Charles Laughton, Elsa Lanchester, Gertrude Lawrence, John Bryning, Richard Gofe, Meinhard Maur. Production: London Films. 88 mins.

The film treats of the later years of the painter's life, from the death of his wife until his own, his relations with his housekeeper and the little servant girl. They were years of growing poverty and fading reputation, following the outcry from the civic dignitaries when faced with his group portrait of them. The costumes and sets, based on contemporary Dutch paintings, are among the most beautiful to be seen on the screen. Laughton's performance is one of his best. Whether on his own account (he is said to have longed to play the part), or because of strong control from his director, the mannerisms and indulgences which so often mar his work are muted, and the decline of a famous artist into unkempt, shabby old age is uncompromisingly presented. Contemporary criticism found fault with the slow pace of the film, and with the fact that Laughton, fresh from Lincoln at Gettysburg in *Ruggles of Red Gap*, was irrelevantly let loose on the Twenty-third Psalm and Ecclesiastes here. However, though underrated at the time of its appearance, *Rembrandt* has come to be recognized as one of the most successful films yet made about a creative artist.

*1936: Charles Laughton as REMBRANDT.*

**THE GHOST GOES WEST.** Script: R. E. Sherwood. Direction: René Clair. Photography: Harold Rosson. Players: Robert Donat, Eugene Pallette, Jean Parker, Elsa Lanchester, Everly Gregg, Hay Petrie. Production: London Films. 90 mins.

Something of René Clair's miraculously light touch survives transit across the English Channel in this, his only English film, though not perhaps as much as was claimed at the time. It is an amiable satire directed against Scottish clannery and American brashness—telling the story of a millionaire from the States who purchases an old castle, transports it stone by stone, and is delighted to learn that he has also transported its ghost—an unfortunate spirit doomed to haunt it until an insult from a rival clan is avenged. As both ancestor and descendant, Robert Donat gives a masterly comedy performance, revealing himself yet again as one of the most sympathetic and quietly capable of British screen players. Except for an unconvincing period prologue the atmosphere of the old castle is nicely caught, and the photography often beautiful. In particular the supernatural manifestations are well done—as in the shot where the camera slowly approaches a goblet along the deserted dining table and it suddenly and startlingly disintegrates.

**TUDOR ROSE.** Script: Miles Malleson. Direction: Robert Stevenson. Photography: M. Greenbaum. Editing: Terence Fisher. Players: Nova Pilbeam, Sybil Thorndike, Cedric Hardwicke, John Mills, Felix Aylmer. Production: Gainsborough. 78 mins.

Excellent proof that an historical film need not be spectacular to be successful, the tragedy of Lady Jane Grey is told with a quiet restraint and integrity that makes it one of the best, and certainly one of the most moving, of all such reconstructions. The loneliness and pathos of royal pawns, used merely to further the schemes of unscrupulous power-seekers, is all the more affecting for not being dramatically underlined. The film is, in fact, a minor masterpiece, aided by fine performances all around, in particular from the young Nova Pilbeam as the pathetically vulnerable political puppet.

**THE SECRET AGENT.** Script: Charles Bennett, Alma Reville, based on Somerset Maugham's *Ashenden* stories. Direction: Alfred Hitchcock. Pho-

1936: TUDOR ROSE, Nova Pilbeam as the tragic Lady Jane Grey, with Sybil Thorndike.

tography: Bernard Knowles. Editing: Charles Frend. Music: Louis Levy. Art Direction: Otto Werndorff, Albert Jullion. Players: Madeleine Carroll, John Gielgud, Peter Lorre, Roland Young, Percy Marmont, Lilli Palmer, Michael Redgrave. Production: Gaumont British. 83 mins.

A confusion of titles is apt to result from the fact that Hitchcock's following (and better) film is an adaptation of Joseph Conrad's *The Secret Agent*, altered to *Sabotage*. The present film is one of his lesser achievements—partly, according to himself, owing to the anti-hero personality of the protagonist, and the fact that he kills the wrong man. Nevertheless it contains many of the "touches": the single organ note piercing the air and caused by a dead body in a church slumped across the keyboard; the Swiss spy headquarters disguised as a chocolate factory; the death of the man over the cliff; the distorted church bells. The acting is a mixture of styles (from Peter Lorre's grotesquerie to John Gielgud's understatement) which does not really blend. Still, half a Hitchcock is better than none.

**THE GREAT BARRIER.** Script: Michael Barringer, Milton Rosmer, from a story by Alan Sullivan. Direction: Milton Rosmer. Photography: Glen MacWilliams, Sepp Allgeier, Bob Martin. Editing: Charles Frend, B. H. Hipkins. Players: Richard Arlen, Antoinette Cellier, Lilli Palmer, Barry Mackay, Henry Victor, Gilbert Emery. Production: Gaumont British. 81 mins.

A reasonably successful essay in the American grand epic style, concerned with the building of the Canadian Pacific Railway, shot mostly in Canada, with awe-inspiring scenery, and action and spectacle handled with vitality. Of British attempts to emulate Hollywood specialities during the decade, this comes off as one of the best. Faults are the inefficient matching of outdoor magnificence with indoor parsimony, commonplace human situations, and narrative improbabilities. On the whole, however, this is a commendable achievement and Milton Rosmer, well-known actor but comparatively little-known director, shows some of the skill in this larger production which he brought to his fine *Dreyfus* of 1931.

SONG OF FREEDOM. Script: Fenne Sherre, Ingram Diabbes, Claude Wallace, Dorothy Holloway. Direction: J. Elder Wills. Photography: Eric Cross, T. A. Glover, Harry Rose. Editing: Arthur Tavares. Players: Paul Robeson, Elisabeth Welch, George Mozart, Esmé Percy Production: British Lion-Hammer. 80 mins.

The story comes from an African legend which Robeson heard while making *Sanders of the River*. It concerns a young stevedore whose magnificent voice as he sings in an amateur concert causes him to be signed up for a concert tour. He becomes famous but, discovering that he is the descendant of a tribal king and that his people need him, he abandons his career and returns to them. Robeson has stated that for the first time he was given a real part (*Show Boat* was his preceding film), and he rises to the challenge. The songs (which include *Lonely Road* and *Sleepy River*) are among his best, and settings and dances are photographed equally well.

RHODES OF AFRICA. Script: Leslie Arliss, Michael Barringer, from the book by Sarah Gertrude Millin. Direction: Berthold Viertel. Photography: Geoffrey Barkas. Players: Walter Huston, Oscar Homolka, Basil Sydney, Peggy Ashcroft, Frank Cellier, Lewis Casson. Production: Gaumont British. 90 mins.

Though a somewhat whitewashed personal portrait, this film is admirably fair and unbiassed in its presentation of the conflicting interests and activities of Boer and Briton. The account opens with Rhodes mining at Kimberley, hearing that

he has only a few more years to live, and determining that his private vision of South Africa shall become reality before his death. Outstanding is Barkas's photography of African exteriors. Walter Huston labours under the minor disadvantage of being physically unlike Rhodes, and the major one of being a leading film star portraying an historical character: with these reservations he gives a sincere and challenging portrayal. Oscar Homolka is excellent as Kruger.

AS YOU LIKE IT. Script: adaptation from Shakespeare's play suggested by J. M. Barrie, carried out by Carl Meyer, scenario by R. J. Cullen. Direction: Paul Czinner. Photography: Harold Rosson. Music: William Walton. Players: Elisabeth Bergner, Laurence Olivier, Henry Ainley, Leon Quartermaine, Felix Aylmer, Austin Trevor, Richard Ainley. Production: Inter-Allied. 97 mins.

This could have been filmed either in a real forest or in a stylised setting, and either might have come off. As it is, by attempting to make a studio forest look like a real one, it falls with a heavy bump between the two stools. Chunks of Shakespeare have been cut out or moved around to make room for a live lioness and a python. Laurence Olivier, Austin Trevor, and in particular Leon Quartermaine show respect, even some affection, for their author. Elisabeth Bergner (the director's wife) was perhaps cast as Rosalind because it was thought she would look pretty dressed as a boy; it must be admitted she does, rather.

THE MAN WHO COULD WORK MIRACLES. Script: H. G. Wells. Direction: Lothar Mendes. Photography: Bernard Browne, Maurice Forde. Players: Roland Young, Joan Gardner, Ralph Richardson, Ernest Thesiger. Production: London Films. 80 mins.

This light-weight Wellsian morality about a meek little draper's assistant who discovers he can work miracles, placing his services at the disposal of the powers-that-be to make a better world, encountering only opposition, stupidity and greed, and finally wishing his powers away, sinks under the weight of its too-obvious propaganda. Redeeming points are some neat trick work (such as the scene where the draper's shop tidies itself up) and a pleasant performance from Roland Young. It is an unremarkable film as it stands, but with better treatment could have been a fore-runner of the Ealing and the Boulting satires of the Forties and Fifties.

## Short Films and Documentaries

NIGHT MAIL. Direction: Basil Wright, Harry Watt. Photography: F. Jones, H. Fowle. Sound: A. Cavalcanti. Music: Benjamin Britten. Verse: W. H. Auden. Production: John Grierson, for G.P.O. Film Unit. 24 mins.

In content a documentary account of the overnight journey by a mail train from London to Glasgow and the work entailed *en route*, this is in style and approach a visual poem, making use of music and spoken verse to raise a factual documentary to a lyrical evocation. Cutting and pace fit the action to the rhythm of verse or score. Though obviously a method limited in application, it works well in what is in many ways a unique short film.

AND SO TO WORK. Script, Direction, and Editing: Richard Massingham. Photography: Karl Urbahn. Players: Russell Waters, Alan Fosse. Production: Richard Massingham.

Massingham's second film is a purely humorous account of the morning hours in a somewhat shabby boarding-house. It has no ulterior motive, beyond its wry commentary on the way we live now. It was shot, in his spare time, with an old 35mm hand-turned camera, with sound added later.

## 1936: Facts of Interest

The Moyne Committee Report is published.
Michael Balcon leaves Gaumont British and joins M-G-M.
Technicolor opens laboratories in London.
A disastrous fire destroys six studios at Elstree.
The State, Kilburn, London, claimed as the largest cinema in Europe, opens.

# 1937

SABOTAGE (A WOMAN ALONE). Charles Bennett, Alma Reville, from Joseph Conrad's novel *The Secret Agent*. Direction: Alfred Hitchcock. Photography: Bernard Knowles. Editing: Charles Frend. Music: Louis Levy. Art Direction: Otto Werndorff, Albert Jullion. Players: Sylvia Sidney, Oscar Homolka, Desmond Tester, John Loder, Joyce Barbour, Matthew Boulton. Production: Gaumont British. 76 mins.

Despite the fact that Hitchcock himself has expressed considerable reservations about the film, it contains much that is equal to the best work of his British period. Conrad's novel has been moved into a contemporary setting with the foreign agent, Verloc, now the owner of a shabby little East End cinema. The picture house thus replaces the theatre of earlier films and is used to equally good effect, both in suspense and also in ironic comment (for example, when Verloc's wife watches the audience laughing at Disney's *Who Killed Cock Robin?* after receiving the news of her young brother's death and just before she herself kills her husband). The most famous sequence is that in which the young brother is delivering a parcel to Piccadilly Station which, unknown to him, contains a bomb set to explode as part of a campaign to wreck the capital. He dawdles on his way as any twelve-year-old would until finally he climbs on a bus—and the bomb explodes, killing him and all the passengers. It is this scene that Hitchcock later declared to be a mistake, because the killing of the child aroused the audience's resentment, and should have been averted at the last moment. It is, however, arguable that with last minute

escapes from danger appearing in film after film, the reverse process is a salutory shock, besides providing a strong enough motive for Mrs. Verloc to kill her husband without losing sympathy. Seen today the picture remains an outstanding exercise in suspense as well as a study of loneliness—Conrad's own theme. Oddly enough the American title was "A *Woman* Alone."

1937: *Sylvia Sidney and Oscar Homolka before the murder in SABOTAGE.*

VICTORIA THE GREAT. Script: Miles Malleson, Charles de Grandcourt. Direction: Herbert Wilcox. Players: Anna Neagle, Anton Walbrook. Imperator Film Productions. 112 mins.

In considering this film apart from its money-making value (which was great), it must in fairness be borne in mind what it is intended to be—not a reconstruction of a period, nor a serious review of a Queen's life and work. In this respect the title is misleading, for it is not the "Great" Victoria we are here presented with, but the intimate. Though ministers come and go, the centre is her home life and her relationship with dear Albert. Anna Neagle may not be the Victoria of history, but it is an enchanting performance, and—when called for—a strong one also. Anton Walbrook, too, may not be exactly the Albert of dull fact, but nobody could grudge him his Memorial. Craftsmanship as much as flashing genius calls for acknowledgement. A companion picture, *Sixty Glorious Years,* repeated the formula and success of its predecessor in 1938, dealing somewhat more fully with external affairs and ending with Victoria's death.

WINGS OF THE MORNING. Script: Tom Geraghty. Direction: Harold Schuster. Photography: Henry Imus, Jack Cardiff (Technicolor). Editing: James Clark. Players: Annabella, Henry Fonda, John McCormack, Leslie Banks, D. J. Williams, Stewart Rome, Irene Vanbrugh. Production: New World. 86 mins.

With an American director and male star, a French female star and an Irish singer, and a part Irish setting, this unmistakably English film is an exquisite first Technicolor production. The pastel tones and delicate blends and contrasts set a standard which was not reached again until a long time after colour became commonplace. The story —of a Curse, a Horse, and a climactic Derby Race (no prizes for guessing the winner) is a romantic commonplace. Annabella (Anne Carpentier), fresh from her René Clair masterpieces, shows that she is captivatingly transportable, and Henry Fonda charms her charmingly. But what remains in the memory, through all the garish and crude colours that followed after, is the loveliness of that early Technicolor magic.

THE EDGE OF THE WORLD. Script: Michael Powell. Direction: Michael Powell. Photography: Ernest Palmer, Skeets Kelly, Monty Berman. Editing: Derek Twist. Music: Cyril Ray, W. L. Williamson, Women of the Glasgow Orpheus Choir. Players: Niall MacGinnis, Belle Chrystal, John Laurie, Finlay Currie. Production: Rock Studios.

81 mins.

This is the first film to become widely known of one of Britain's most imaginative and exciting directors. It is really a semidocumentary story about the struggle for existence of crofters on a lonely Scottish island. The plot itself is overheated and melodramatic, but already there are signs of Powell's eye for the striking composition—in the seas, crags, rocks, moorlands and grim dwelling-houses finely photographed by his team of three.

THE YOUNG AND INNOCENT (THE GIRL WAS YOUNG). Script: Charles Bennett, Alma Reville, from Josephine Tey's novel *A Shilling for Candles.* Direction: Alfred Hitchcock. Photography: Bernard Knowles. Editing: Charles Frend. Music: Louis Levy. Art Direction: Alfred Junge. Players: Derrick de Marney, Nova Philbeam, Percy Marmont, Arthur Rigby, Mary Clare, John Longden, Basil Radford. Production: Gainsborough. 80 mins.

It is difficult to understand why this should be among the less widely known of Hitchcock's films. It is one of his own favourites and, though of lighter texture than some, is an altogether entertaining and exciting comedy thriller. With the chase as its basic form, it recounts the efforts of a young man, aided later by a girl, to clear himself of the charge of murdering a film star. It shows Hitchcock's semi-humorous handling of the relationship between a man and a woman, and his sense of paradox when terrible consequences may hang on a children's game of blind-man's-buff. It also contains a famous travelling shot, wherein the camera moves from the high roof of a hotel lounge into the large ballroom, past the dancers, up to the bandstand, to finish with an enormous close-up of the drummer's twitching eye—thus providing the audience, but not the characters, with a vital clue.

FIRE OVER ENGLAND. Script: Clemence Dane, Sergei Nolbandov, from A. E. W. Mason's novel. Direction: William K. Howard. Photography: James Wong Howe. Editing: John Denis. Art Direction: Lazare Meerson. Players: Flora Robson, Laurence Olivier, Vivien Leigh, Raymond Massey. Production: Pendennis (Erich Pommer). 91 mins.

A piece of romantic, patriotic swashbuckling about a dashing young naval lieutenant whose

*1937: THE YOUNG AND INNOCENT, the approach
of the camera in the famous travelling shot.*

father is put to death when they are both captured by Spaniards, but who manages to escape and in revenge (plus, of course, Love of the Mother Country) plays a large part in defeating the Armada, a fact Drake must doubtless have appreciated. The film is exciting and colourful on the lines of *Henry VIII* when content to remain a piece of derring-do. At other times is appears too self-conscious a piece of special pleading in a significant period of contemporary dismay. Flora Robson is a dignified but rather lay-figure Elizabeth. Spain, oddly enough, comes off best, the Inquisition scenes being genuinely chilly, and Raymond Massey very sinister as Philip. Laurence Olivier is magnificently acrobatic. He is not called on to be much more.

*1937: OH, MR. PORTER, Will Hay and supporting artist in his most famous film.*

OH, MR. PORTER! Script: Frank Launder, J. O. C. Orton, Val Guest, Marriot Edgar. Direction: Marcel Varnel. Photography: Arthur Crabtree. Editing: R. E. Dearing. Music: Louis Levy. Art Direction: Alex Vetchinsky. Players: Will Hay, Moore Marriott, Graham Moffat, Sebastian Smith, Agnes Lauchlan, Percy Walsh, Dennis Wyndham. Production: Gainsborough. 85 mins.

The best and most popular of the Will Hay comedies, in which he appears as an incompetent railway worker who is made master of a practically derelict station in Ireland, with a couple of scrounging good-for-nothings as staff. Involvements with gun-runners lead to a hectic adventure in a windmill and a frantic chase in a train, with a final explosion. The trio are at their best, and the dialogue and comic invention rarely flag. Gladstone, the game old engine which lays down (or blows up) its life for its country is as fine a character actor as Keaton's *The General*.

STORM IN A TEACUP. Script: James Bridie, from the play by Bruno Frank. Direction: Victor Saville, Ian Dalrymple. Photography: M. Greenbaum. Editing: Hugh Stewart, Cyril Randell. Players: Vivien Leigh, Rex Harrison, Cecil Parker, Sara Allgood, Ursula Jeans. Production: Victor Saville. 87 mins.

Cecil Parker, stalwart character actor in British films for nearly forty years, carries off the honours in this witty and pointed light comedy, although the indomitable Sara Allgood runs him close. A young reporter arrives in a small Scottish town to find it in uproar over an order from the Provost (Parker) that Irish Mrs. Hegarty's pet dog should be destroyed because she cannot pay the licence. He works it up into a national press campaign. Both civic dignity and newspaper stuntings are satirised, if this is not too strong a word for such gentle burlesque. The film progresses from a quiet opening to hectic slapstick and culminates in high comedy courtroom confrontations. All in all, this is a good example of the small-scale production which, while unlikely to feature in any Critics' Ten Best, serves admirably the purpose for which it was made.

ELEPHANT BOY. Script: John Collier, from the stories of Rudyard Kipling. Direction: Robert Flaherty, Zoltan Korda. Photography: Osmond Borrodaile. Editing: Charles Crichton. Players: Sabu, W. E. Holloway, Walter Hudd, Allan Jeayes, Bruce Gordon. Production: London Films. 84 mins.

It is probably unfair to blame Flaherty for the dullness of this film, as he would presumably have preferred to concentrate on the elephants rather than the less interesting boy whose job it is to look after them. As it is, the magnificence of the animals and their scenery only serves to emphasise the pettiness of the human beings and their story. On the whole the animals are the better performers, too.

**Short Films and Documentaries**

RIDERS TO THE SEA. Script: from the play by

J. M. Synge. Direction: Brian Desmond Hurst. Players: Sara Allgood, Ria Mooney, Kevin Guthrie, Denis Johnstone. Production: Flanagan-Hurst. 41 mins.

Though a straight record of the play, the film has some effective cinematic moments—for example the arrival of the black-shrouded mourners down the hill. The heightened prose of Synge's powerful tragedy is beautifully spoken, and the film would be noteworthy if only as a preservation of Sara Allgood's faultlessly moving performance.

### 1937: Facts of Interest

Gaumont British close Shepherd's Bush studios.

Richard Massingham joins the G.P.O. Film Unit. The Odeon, Leicester Square and the Classic, Baker Street, open in London.

*I, Claudius,* the ill-fated film to have starred Charles Laughton, is finally abandoned—after endless production troubles and disagreements between the actor and director von Sternberg—when Merle Oberon, also starring, meets with an accident which would have prevented her from working for some weeks.

Death of Guy Newall.

# 1938

PYGMALION. Script: W. P. Lipscomb, Cecil Lewis, Anthony Asquith, from G. B. Shaw's play. Direction: Anthony Asquith. Photography: Harry Stradling. Editing: David Lean. Music: Arthur Honegger. Art Direction: Laurence Irving. Players: Wendy Hiller, Leslie Howard, Wilfrid Lawson, Marie Lohr, Scott Sunderland, Jean Cadell, David Tree. Production: Gabriel Pascal. 96 mins.

The first important attempt to present Shaw on the screen (there had been two foreign versions of *Pygmalion* and British productions of *Arms and the Man* and *How He Lied to Her Husband*) remains to this day the most successful. Surrounded by his eminent team of collaborators, Asquith created a little masterpiece of Shavian adaptation, preserving all the wit and bite of the text, while bringing to it his own continually developing gift of cinematic humour and irony. An affectionate warmth humanises the Shavian mouthpieces, served by a cast which without exception gives of its distinguished best. The result is an entertainment considerably more exhilarating, amusing and satisfying than the top-heavy, overdressed musical *My Fair Lady*, despite that film's few singable tunes.

THE LADY VANISHES. Script: Sidney Gilliat, Frank Launder, Alma Reville, from Ethel Lina White's novel *The Wheel Spins*. Direction: Alfred Hitchcock. Photography: Jack Cox. Editing: Alfred Roome, R. E. Dearing. Music: Louis Levy. Art Direction: Alex Vetchinsky, Maurice Cater, Albert Jullion. Players: Margaret Lockwood, Michael Redgrave, Paul Lukas, Dame May Whitty, Googie Withers, Cecil Parker, Linden Travers, Basil Radford, Naunton Wayne. Production: Gainsborough. 97 mins.

The last British Hitchcock film, except for the untypical and unmemorable *Jamaica Inn*, this is also the best known. Taking place almost entirely on a train, it deals with the disappearance of an elderly lady on a trans-continental journey, the hunt for her by a young woman and a musician who helps her, and the eventual uncovering of a spy ring. The tone is lighter than some of Hitchcock's earlier work, with more comedy, notably in the extraneous but amusing episodes involving Radford and Wayne as a couple of very English cricket-maniacs. It nevertheless frays the nerves in true Hitchcock fashion, and contains its share of "touches": the sceptical musician finally convinced of the truth of the girl's story by the momentary sticking to the corridor window of a tea-packet label thrown out of the kitchen car. A moment as chilling as any is that in which the girl, thinking she has at last found the old lady sitting in her corner seat, is appalled when under the familiar hat-brim is revealed the cold, challenging face of a young foreign woman. The improbabilities of the plot are accepted as cheerfully by us as by Hitchcock; but the reason for the change of title to its present weak one from the author's far more apt and atmospheric *The Wheel Spins*, remains obscure.

BANK HOLIDAY. Script: Rodney Ackland, Roger Burford. Direction: Carol Reed. Photography: Arthur Crabtree. Editing: R. E. Dearing. Players:

1938: *THE LADY VANISHES, Margaret Lockwood, Michael Redgrave, Kathleen Tremaine (as the Lady's substitute), and Mary Clare.*

John Lodge, Margaret Lockwood, Hugh Williams, René Ray, Merle Tottenham, Linden Travers, Kathleen Harrison, Garry Marsh, Wilfrid Lawson, Felix Aylmer. Production: Gainsborough. 86 mins.

The importance of this modest-budgeted picture of the English at the seaside is that it marks the first appearance of Carol Reed as a director of significance. The slight but moving story of a bereaved young man and the nurse who saves him from suicide is mainly a framework for a kaleidoscopic series of views of differing groups of people on their annual outing. Inevitably the individuals are little more than types—Cockney couple, aspiring beauty queen—but Reed shows his skill in the mingling of broad comedy and near-tragedy, the handling of crowds, and the revelation of character by such small details as he has

time for. Various devices are used for building up a composite picture, linking the seemingly disconnected parties, and the result is a minor but always interesting movie, which today has the added attraction of presenting an unexaggerated record of time past, as well as affording an early glimpse of the development of a major director.

ST. MARTIN'S LANE (SIDEWALKS OF LONDON). Script: Clemence Dane. Direction: Tim Whelan. Photography: Jules Kruger. Editing: Hugh Stewart, Robert Hamer. Music: Arthur Johnston. Art Direction: Tom Morahan. Players: Charles Laughton, Vivien Leigh, Rex Harrison, Tyrone Guthrie. Production: Erich Pommer. 86 mins.

This oddly attractive film met some unde-

*1938: Seaside scene from Carol Reed's BANK HOLI-
DAY.*

servedly harsh criticism on its first appearance and was a commercial failure. Admittedly its story—the clown (in this case a street busker) who helps a girl down on her luck and loses her when she becomes a success—is commonplace and sentimental. But Laughton gives one of his best performances, Vivien Leigh is charming if not wholly convincing, and the less glittering corners of London's theatre-land are affectionately and realistically pictured. Though the plot is hackneyed, the treatment is not.

The very large street set is built in skilful perspective, and the waiting queue outside a theatre door had to be in perspective too—so Central Casting was asked to supply a suitably size-graded group of extras, with heights dwindling from six feet to three feet six inches, to be arranged accordingly.

**A YANK AT OXFORD.** Script: John Monk Saunders, Leon Gordon, Sidney Gilliat, Michael Hogan, Malcolm S. Boylan, Walter Ferris, George Oppenheimer. Direction: Jack Conway. Photography: Harold Rosson. Editing: Margaret Booth. Players: Robert Taylor, Lionel Barrymore, Vivien Leigh, Maureen O'Sullivan, Edmund Gwenn, Griffith Jones, C. V. France, Edward Rigby. Production: M-G-M British (Michael Balcon). 94 mins.

This was the first of the three main works of Anglo-American collaboration during Balcon's apparently none too happy period with M-G-M, the other two being *Good-bye, Mr. Chips* and *The Citadel*. It tells the story of a brash young man from the United States who comes to Oxford University as an undergraduate determined to bring some life to a tottering old institution, finishes up respecting and respected by his English counter-

*1938: Charles Laughton, Tyrone Guthrie, Gus Mc-Naughton and Vivien Leigh as street buskers in ST. MARTIN'S LANE.*

1938: A YANK AT OXFORD. Robert Taylor on the right.

parts, and wins the Boat Race for his team practically single-oared. The American Jack Conway directs with infectious enthusiasm, English and American foibles are amusingly mixed, and the result is a likable if predictable movie, holding the balance fairly between the wisdoms and follies of both sides.

THE CITADEL. Script: Ian Dalrymple, Frank Wead, Elizabeth Hill, Emlyn Williams, from A. J. Cronin's novel. Direction: King Vidor. Photography: Harry Stradling. Editing: Charles Frend. Music: Louis Levy. Players: Robert Donat, Rosalind Russell, Ralph Richardson, Rex Harrison, Emlyn Williams, Penelope Dudley Ward, Mary Clare, Edward Chapman. Production: M-G-M British. 101 mins.

Though the conditions depicted in Cronin's novel are not likely to recur today—and in fact were stated in a libel-watching disclaimer to have ceased to exist at the time of the picture's release—the theme of idealism eroded by success maintains its validity. It seems to be as difficult to make a convincing film about a doctor (television series *ad nauseam* notwithstanding), as about a musician or a painter, but here King Vidor, aided by the superlative integrity of Donat's performance, comes as near it as anyone has yet. The early scenes of struggle are perhaps the most effective but the director, by his handling of a rapid and mounting series of dramatic episodes, holds the attention throughout, making even the slightly contrived and melodramatic turning-point reasonably convincing. The cast is exceptionally strong.

THIS MAN IS NEWS. Script: Roger MacDougall, Allen MacKinnon. Direction: David Macdonald. Photography: Henry Harris. Editing: Reginald

Beck. Players: Barry K. Barnes, Valerie Hobson, Alastair Sim, John Warwick, Philip Leaver, Tom Gill. Production: Pinebrook. 77 mins.

Neither Barry K. Barnes nor David Macdonald is much remembered today, but they came together here to make one of the best comedy thrillers of the period, swift, taut, and vigorous. Barnes plays a newspaper man who tells his editor for a joke that he has witnessed a murder: when the man concerned is actually found dead, the reporter is arrested. The relationship between the newspaper man and his wife recalls the *Thin Man* series, and the general tone of the picture is similar. A sequel, *This Man in Paris,* is almost as good and it seemed that a new school of comedy might have arrived to brighten British screens, but the war was at hand to direct attention to other channels.

SOUTH RIDING. Script: Ian Dalrymple, from Winifred Holtby's novel. Direction: Victor Saville. Photography: Harry Stradling. Editing: Jack Dennis. Players: Edmund Gwenn, Edna Best, Ralph Richardson, Milton Rosmer, Ann Todd, Glynis Johns, John Clements. Production: London Films. 91 mins.

For much of its length this film follows the best-selling novel faithfully, and is a strong drama of rural power politics. Irrelevant today, perhaps, in its political implications, it remains interesting both as a clash of personalities and a picture of a fairly recent past. Victor Saville can be relied on to make the most of the English countryside, and both interiors and exteriors are beautifully photographed. Unfortunately everything slides into a morass of bathos and sentimentality at the end, but for a lot of the way this is one of the better examples of a very British type of film. Ann Todd gives a remarkable performance as the Squire's insane wife.

KEEP FIT. Script: Anthony Kimmins, Austin Melford. Direction: Anthony Kimmins. Photography: John W. Boyle. Editing: Ernest Aldridge. Music and Lyrics: F. E. Cliffe, Harry Gifford. Art Direction: Wilfred Shingleton. Production: Associated Talking Pictures (Basil Dean) 82 mins.

George Formby ranked with Gracie Fields as the top attraction in large areas of England during the Thirties and early Forties and this is a good example of his cheerful, anything-goes style. Mildly satirising the current "Keep Fit" cam-

*1938: KEEP FIT, George Formby in typical pose.*

paigns, and affording Formby the obligatory opportunities to play his ukelele, it is, in the words of a contemporary critic "a riotous comedy, played with all the vitality and swing of a merry-go-round." During his peak period Formby was voted by the American *Motion Picture Herald* as the most popular British star on American screens: in 1944 he was listed as the most popular figure in Russia after Stalin, and was awarded the Order of Merit.

### Short Films and Documentaries

NORTH SEA. Script and Direction: Harry Watt. Photography: H. E. Fowle, Jonah Jones. Editing: R. Q. McNaughton. Art Direction: Edward Carrick. Music: Ernst Meyer. Production: G.P.O. Film Unit (Cavalcanti).

A dramatised documentary of a fishing trawler caught in a storm and isolated from means of summoning assistance: this is one of the most powerful examples of a form which was to reach its full flowering during the coming war.

### 1938: Facts of Interest

The Cinematograph Films Act (1938) is passed, increasing quota figures, banning "blind booking," etc.

Michael Balcon joins the Board of the Ealing group of companies.

Warner Cinema, Leicester Square, opens on the site of Daly's Theatre.

The prestige and number of British films starts to decline again.

130

# 1939

THE STARS LOOK DOWN. Script: J. B. Williams, from A. J. Cronin's novel. Direction: Carol Reed. Photography: Mutz Greenbaum. Editing: Reginald Beck. Art Direction: James Carter. Players: Michael Redgrave, Margaret Lockwood, Emlyn Williams, Nancy Price, Edward Rigby, Cecil Parker, Allan Jeayes. Production: Grafton Films. 105 mins.

Carol Reed's second major film is a grim and realistic portrayal of a coal strike and the conflict over the re-opening of a notoriously unsafe mine, culminating in a disaster when floods inundate the pit. It could be regarded as the first British film to deal really seriously with social problems, and its almost documentary power is weakened only by the caricatured portrait of the mine owner: as so often, a point is overstated and falls back on itself. Apart from this, the bitterness, defiance and grim courage of a mining area during the depression is harrowingly presented, with authentic settings and little concession to the box-office. The disaster itself is vividly done, and the human drama in the larger context lives in the deeply sincere performances of Michael Redgrave and such reliable character actors as Edward Rigby and Cecil Parker.

GOODBYE, MR. CHIPS. Script: R. C. Sherriff, Claudine West, Eric Maschwitz, from James Hilton's novel. Direction: Sam Wood. Photography: F. A. Young. Editing: Charles Frend. Players: Robert Donat, Lyn Harding, Greer Garson, Terry Kilburn, Austin Trevor, Paul van Hernried, Jill Furse. Production: M-G-M British (Victor Saville). 114 mins.

It is difficult to imagine any but the most indiscriminately anti-minded failing to surrender to the charm of this schoolmaster's saga from green young teacher to beloved old fixture. Deplorable as doubtless are its regard for tradition, its respect for institutions, privileges, responsibilities, and virtues unacceptable in these more enlightened and happier days; it nevertheless retains a popularity to the present time that would seem to suggest a lasting quality which extends beyond the mere story interest. The atmosphere and activities of small public school life through the changing years are beautifully caught by the American director and, except for a patently phoney and overlong sequence in the Tyrol, not a false note is struck. Donat's endearing performance is justly famed, and Greer Garson, with the blight of Mrs. Miniver not yet on her, is wholly enchanting in the small role of the girl he marries and loses so soon. There are few more sensitively handled moments in any film than those in which the news of her death is brought to him as he sits at his desk in school, and they are representative of the whole tone of this kindly, gentle, totally unsentimental film. The "musical" re-make, which updated and transmogrified the story, added some unmemorable songs and is—except perhaps for Peter O'Toole's performance—best forgotten.

ON THE NIGHT OF THE FIRE. Script: Brian Desmond Hurst, Patrick Kirwan, Terence Young. Direction: Brian Desmond Hurst. Photography: Günther Krampf. Editing: Terence Young. Music: Miklos Rozsa. Art Direction: John Bryan. Players: Ralph Richardson, Diana Wynyard. Production:

*1939: Michael Redgrave in THE STARS LOOK DOWN.*

*1939: Old and new, Robert Donat and young friend in GOOD-BYE, MR. CHIPS.*

Josef Somlo. 93 mins.

This film seems to have been submerged in the world events that followed on its release so swiftly, which is regrettable, for it is a brilliant study of character under stress, built on an exciting story of theft and murder, and written, acted and directed with imaginative skill. Ralph Richardson excels as the small-time barber who steals a sum of money, is blackmailed and driven to murder, and Diana Wynyard is hardly less effective in an untypical part as his extravagant wife. The grim story is told with uncompromising realism, but illuminated and warmed by the devotion of the couple to each other. The emphasis is on the psychological rather than the physical events, and the result is original and unfailingly gripping. It is the apparently total disappearance of movies such as this, by no means world-shattering but by any standards worthy of preservation, that make the life of the cinema enthusiast one of quiet desperation.

*1939: ON THE NIGHT OF THE FIRE, Romney Brent and Ralph Richardson.*

THE LION HAS WINGS. Direction: Michael Powell, Brian Desmond Hurst, Adrian Brunel. Players: Merle Oberon, Ralph Richardson, June Duprez, Flora Robson, Robert Douglas. Narrator: Lowell Thomas. Production: Alexander Korda. 70 mins.

The purpose of this fictionalised documentary film was to "inspire quiet confidence in the hearts of those who saw it"—and like most highly publicised propaganda efforts it fell fairly flat on its face, despite a number of well constructed episodes and the sponsorship of the Ministry of Information. It opens with Britain happily at peace: enter shadows of Nazi Germany, marching feet, ranting Hitler, outbreak of war, Chamberlain on radio, Kiel raid: climax—a long demonstration of Britain's unassailable air defences. In the months to come this film, had anyone the temerity to show it, may have had a somewhat sawdusty taste in the mouths of the underground shelterers.

NURSE EDITH CAVELL. Script: Michael Hogan. Direction: Herbert Wilcox. Photography: F. A. Young, Joseph H. August. Art Direction: L. P. Williams. Players: Anna Neagle, Edna May Oliver, George Sanders, Zasu Pitts. Production: Herbert Wilcox. 98 mins.

Dealing with a famous—or infamous—incident in the first war against Germany, this appeared just after the start of the second, which may have coloured some critical reactions to it. In actual fact it is notable for its lack of antagonism, treating the Germans as in the grip of an evil power too strong for resistance (a popular viewpoint), and for the general restraint of Wilcox's direction. Anna Neagle's Cavell stands up well against Sybil Thorndike's, and won her an Oscar nomination.

THE WARE CASE. Script: Roland Pertwee, Robert Stevenson, from the play by George Pleydell. Direction: Robert Stevenson. Photography: Ronald Neame. Editing: Charles Saunders. Art Direction: O. F. Werndorff. Players: Clive Brook, Jane Baxter, Barry K. Barnes. Production: Capad (Michael Balcon). 78 mins.

Noteworthy as Balcon's second independent Ealing production (the first, *The Gaunt Stranger*, is of less interest), *The Ware Case* is a competent, inexpensive version of a well-known stage play. Though in no way typical of Ealing films as they are generally recognised, it can be appreciated for a good dramatic story, effective courtroom scenes, and sound performances from Barry K. Barnes and Clive Brook in particular.

### Short Films and Documentaries

THE FIRST DAYS. Script: Robert Sinclair. Editing: R. Q. McNaughton. Production: G.P.O. Film Unit (Cavalcanti). 23 mins.

An interesting and often entertaining record of the first days of Britain at war: the atmosphere of cheerful calm, friendly fortitude and quiet determination is inevitably emphasised against the equally existent misery and gloom, but is not unduly played up.

### 1939: Facts of Interest

J. A. Rank becomes a member of the Odeon board and the circuit takes over Paramount Theatres.

Filippo Del Giudice forms Two Cities Films.

All cinemas are closed at the outbreak of war on September 3. On the fifth, the Pier Cinema, Aberystwyth, Wales, shows its defiant independence by reopening "on the discretion of the Chief Constable of Cardiganshire," and remains staunchly functioning. After a week or so, cinemas in "neutral" and "reception" areas are permitted to open until 10:00 p.m. This is extended throughout the country within three weeks, but with restricted hours. Many cinema buildings are requisitioned for war purposes. Food is stored at Pinewood studios, and parts of Denham. Elstree is taken over, Associated British moving to Welwyn.

# 1940

GASLIGHT. Script: A. R. Rawlinson, Bridget Boland, from Patrick Hamilton's play. Direction: Thorold Dickinson. Photography: Bernard Knowles. Editing: Sydney Cole. Music: Richard Addinsell. Art Direction: Duncan Sutherland. Players: Anton Walbrook, Diana Wynyard, Cathleen Nesbitt, Robert Newton, Frank Pettingell. Production: British National. 88 mins.

With war and the menace of bombs and destruction shadowing everybody's mind, the best British film of the year was a Victorian thriller. The film has been the victim of a notorious piece of commercial vandalism, bought up and suppressed (legally) by a company intending to produce another version. There could be a temptation to build up the reputation of Dickinson's version from sheer indignation at its treatment, but in fact, as those fortunate enough to have seen it on its original release will fondly remember, it is an excellent piece of period *Grand Guignol* in its own right. The opening sequence, showing a man's hands strangling an elderly woman, is brilliantly shot in eerie silence, setting the tone for the claustrophobic horror to follow. Diana Wynyard gives one of her best performances as the increasingly terrified wife, with Anton Walbrook a splendidly smooth villain. Victorian London is brought vividly to life, though the music hall sequence, admirable in itself, intrudes on the suspense which the rest so relentlessly sustains. The fine thriller is in every way superior to the travesty that replaced it.

THE PROUD VALLEY. Script: Herbert Marshall, Fredda Brilliant, Louis Golding. Direction: Pen Tennyson. Players: Edward Chapman, Paul Robeson, Clifford Evans, Simon Lack, Jack Jones. Production: Capad (Michael Balcon). 77 mins.

Another realistic documentary-style coal mining drama, with the inevitable explosion and pit collapse. The main difference between this and *The Stars Look Down* is in Pen Tennyson's lyrical approach to the grey realities of life in the little Welsh village, and in the presence of Paul Robeson as a Negro stoker who arrives in search of work and eventually sacrifices his life to save his companions. Played with great sincerity from a mixed professional and non-professional cast, the film has a nobility of purpose which raises it above a certain technical immaturity, and makes Tennyson's death before his promise could be fully realised the more regrettable. It was only three days in production when war was declared, and the last reel was apparently altered to incorporate a new ending suitable for the changed circumstances; this may account for a lessening of grip in the final moments.

PASTOR HALL. Script: Ernst Toller, Leslie Arliss, Anna Reiner, Haworth Bromley. Direction: Roy Boulting. Photography: Mutz Greenbaum. Music: Charles Brill. Players: Wilfrid Lawson, Nova Pilbeam, Seymour Hicks, Marius Goring, Brian Worth, Percy Walsh. Production: Charter Films. 98 mins.

Inspired by the story of Pastor Niemöeller, the film is memorable, when one considers the time of its production, for the way in which it transcends

*1940: GASLIGHT, Anton Walbrook and Diana Wynyard in Thorold Dickinson's excellent—and suppressed—thriller.*

even the gross infamy of its particular events, and becomes a tribute to personal courage in any place, at any time, against any tyranny. This is partly due to the superb performance of Wilfrid Lawson—an actor who when given the chance (which was not always) could hold his audience in a vice—and also very much to the restraint and dignity of Boulting's direction. The final moments as Hall walks down the aisle of his church to the waiting Storm Troopers is as moving as anything on the screen. The film's comparative neglect can be put down only to its emergence at a time when denunciation of National Socialism was deemed no longer necessary as steps were being taken to bring about its downfall, but its universal relevance removes it from the limitations of time.

**TWENTY-ONE DAYS.** Script: Graham Greene, Basil Dean, from John Galsworthy's play *The First and the Last*. Direction: Basil Dean. Photography: Jan Stallich. Editing: Charles Crichton. Music: Louis Levy. Art Direction: Vincent Korda. Players: Vivien Leigh, Laurence Olivier, Leslie Banks, Francis L. Sullivan. Robert Newton, Esmé Percy, David Horne. Production: Alexander Korda. 75 mins.

Though completed in 1939, *Twenty-One Days* was not shown publicly until twelve months later, possibly to take advantage of Vivien Leigh's success in *Gone With The Wind*. The not unfamiliar situation of an innocent man accused of murder and the real killer's dilemma is presented here with the accent on the moral and internal struggle

136

*1940: Paul Robeson as a miner in THE PROUD VAL-
LEY.*

*1940: Marius Goring, Bernard Miles and Wilfrid Law-
on in PASTOR HALL.*

rather than the external action. Even so, Basil Dean works up some very strong suspense, particularly in small ominous touches reminiscent of Hitchcock. There is a tense courtroom scene and a neat anti-climactic finish. The film was Olivier's prelude to Hollywood stardom in *Wuthering Heights* and *Rebecca,* as it was Vivien Leigh's in *Gone with the Wind.*

### Short Films and Documentaries

LONDON CAN TAKE IT. Direction: Humphrey Jennings, Harry Watt. Narration: Quentin Reynolds. Production: Crown Film Unit. 10 mins.

A brief account of the first night of the London Blitz, in the form of a despatch from an American correspondent, skilfully put together and integrated with the spoken word, preparing the way for the great war documentaries to follow. The film was enthusiastically received in the United States.

### 1940: Facts of Interest

George Pearson joins the Colonial Film Unit.

*1940: Stand-by in LONDON CAN TAKE IT, Humphrey Jennings's documentary of the blitz.*

The Prince of Wales Theatre, Piccadilly, turns to films for the screening of Chaplin's *The Great Dictator.*

Death of John Maxwell.

# 1941

49TH PARALLEL (THE INVADERS). Script: Emeric Pressburger. Direction: Michael Powell. Photography: F. A. Young. Editing: David Lean. Music: Ralph Vaughan Williams. Art Direction: David Rawnsley. Players: Leslie Howard, Eric Portman, Raymond Massey, Anton Walbrook, Laurence Olivier. Production: Ortus Films (Michael Powell). 123 mins.

War films, especially those made during actual hostilities, must suffer from the fact that the "enemy"—whichever side he may be—must be in the wrong, must be at least a fairly dark shade of grey, and must in the end be done down. Both suspense and characterisation are inevitably limited, and contrivance is the order of the day. Allowing for these circumscriptions, this is a very good adventure story, episodically following the adventures of a bunch of fanatical Nazis landed by submarine in Canada. The film, produced on the grand scale, was backed by the Ministry of Information, and its obvious purpose is propaganda coated with entertainment. The coating is the best part, and the most interesting character is the chief Nazi, played by Eric Portman.

THE THIEF OF BAGHDAD. Script: Lajos Biro, Miles Malleson. Direction: Ludwig Berger, Tim Whelan, Michael Powell. Photography: Georges Périnal, Osmond Borrodaile (Technicolor). Editing: William Hornbeck, Charles Crichton. Music: Miklos Rozsa. Art Direction: Vincent Korda. Players: Conrad Veidt, Sabu, John Justin, June Duprez, Miles Malleson. Production: Alexander Korda. 106 mins.

*The Thief of Baghdad* had a very protracted genesis, which resulted in its appearing much later than had been planned. Though no more than a pantomime-style fantasy, it is produced on a most spectacular scale, and its ravishing use of colour forecasts the Powell eye for visual effect to be seen later when he and Emeric Pressburger form their famous partnership. The trick photography is among the best yet seen. The story— beautiful daughter of Sultan, nasty Grand Vizier, wicked magicians, djinns in jars— is told with sufficient wit and panache to entrance old as much as young. At the time it was a more than welcome splash of colour in a dingy world: revived in after years, it affords pleasure beyond that of mere enjoyment recalled.

THE PRIME MINISTER. Script: Michael Hogan, Brock Williams. Direction: Thorold Dickinson. Players: John Gielgud, Owen Nares, Fay Compton, Stephen Murray, Frederick Leister, Lyn Harding. Production: Warners. 109 mins.

Thorold Dickinson follows up a Victorian thriller with Victorian politics in this well-made, if somewhat conventionally worthy study of some forty years of Disraeli's working life during which the British Empire was consolidated: it needed less time to disintegrate. His career is followed from that of popular young novelist to statesman returning, aging and lonely, from the Congress of Berlin, bearing Peace with Honour. The patriotic motives are a little obtrusive but not belaboured— indeed, the fact that at the end we admire Disraeli for having *saved* the country from war

1941: THE THIEF OF BAGHDAD, "the Powell eye
for visual effect."

might be taken as an ironic reflection on the contemporary situation. The highlights are the scenes in the House of Commons, but all the period detail is reproduced with the care to be expected from the maker of *Gaslight*. Gielgud's subtle Disraeli is matched by the forthright Gladstone of Stephen Murray.

**MAJOR BARBARA.** Script: G. B. Shaw, Harold French, from Shaw's play. Direction: Gabriel Pascal. Photography: Ronald Neame. Editing: Charles Frend. Music: William Walton. Art Direction: Vincent Korda, John Bryan. Players: Wendy Hiller, Rex Harrison, Robert Morley, Emlyn Williams, Sybil Thorndike, Deborah Kerr. Production: Gabriel Pascal. 121 mins.

A more or less straightforward transference of the play, affording Wendy Hiller to follow up her Eliza with another impressive Shavian portrayal. Apart from this, the film's main claim on our gratitude is that the length of time it took to make at Ealing helped Michael Balcon in persuading the Ministry of Supply not to requisition the studio.

**KIPPS.** Script: Sidney Gilliat, from the novel by H. G. Wells. Direction: Carol Reed. Photography: Arthur Crabtree. Editing: Alfred Roome. Music: Louis Levy. Art Direction: Alex Vetchinsky. Players: Michael Redgrave, Diana Wynyard, Phyllis Calvert, Max Adrian, Edward Rigby, Helen Haye. Production: Twentieth-Century Productions. 112 mins.

Carol Reed was now approaching the threshold of his greatest work, and this second version of Wells's little-draper romance shows in particular his skill with actors: Michael Redgrave's performance is wholly charming. Lightweight Reed, but on its own level delightfully done.

*Michael Redgrave as KIPPS, Arthur Riscoe on the right.*

DANGEROUS MOONLIGHT. Script: Terence Young. Direction: Desmond Brian Hurst. Music: Richard Addinsell. Players: Anton Walbrook, Sally Gray, Derrick de Marney, J. H. Roberts, Cecil Parker, John Laurie. Production: R.K.O. Radio British. 98 mins.

Far more dangerous than the moonlight in this wartime romantic rigmarole is the Warsaw Concerto—not so much on its own account, but because it sowed the seeds of similar compositions which were to form the rhapsodic climaxes of peacetime romantic rigmaroles.

## Short Films and Documentaries

TARGET FOR TONIGHT. Script and direction: Harry Watt. Photography: Jonah Jones, Edward Catford. Editing: Stewart McAllister. Music: Leighton Lucas. Art Direction: Edward Carrick. Production: Crown Film Unit (Ian Dalrymple). 50 mins.

The first major wartime documentary follows the progress of a single bomber on a raid over Germany, the damage it suffers, the wounding of one of the crew, its return. Reality is dramatised, but the very fact that it seems dated today—in its determined understatement and reticence—is an indication of its contemporary truthfulness. Its influence on the British documentary of the near future was immense.

LISTEN TO BRITAIN. Script, direction, editing: Humphrey Jennings, Stewart McAllister. Production: Crown Film Unit (Ian Dalrymple). 20 mins.

In a brilliant one-third of an hour Jennings and McAllister collect together the music of the Forces Orchestras and Dame Myra Hess at the piano, the songs of dance-halls and canteens, the noise of tanks, planes, marching feet, the clash and clang of ordnance and other factories—and weave them together in a sound-and-vision picture of wartime Britain.

## 1941: Facts of Interest

J. A. Rank is chairman of Odeon (306 cinemas) and Gaumont British (251 cinemas).

The British Film Producers' Association is formed.

It is estimated that 170 cinemas are closed by enemy action.

Death of Oscar Deutsch.

# 1942

IN WHICH WE SERVE. Script: Noël Coward. Direction: Noël Coward, David Lean. Photography: Ronald Neame. Music: Noël Coward. Art Direction: David Rawnsley. Players: Noël Coward, John Mills, Bernard Miles, Celia Johnson, Michael Wilding, Richard Attenborough, Kay Walsh, James Donald, Leslie Dwyer, Joyce Carey. Production: Two Cities. 114 mins.

Inspired by the sinking of H.M.S. Kelly off Crete, the story of a destroyer is followed from her first building until her last battle, with flashbacks linking the lives of the crew with their home ties. Most of the film is itself a long flashback as the Captain and members of the crew cling to a raft in the oil covered water. It is an astonishing all-round *début* for Noël Coward, and though undoubtedly part of its enormous success was due to the exact timing of its release, it remains, with Carol Reed's *The Way Ahead,* among the most enduring and convincing films of the war—in neither case was any close personal contact with the enemy involved. The shifts between past and present are unfussily achieved, and the on-shore sequences, air-raid, music hall, domestic scenes are as true in their setting as those on board.

NEXT OF KIN. Script: Thorold Dickinson, Basil Bartlett, Angus MacPhail, John Dighton. Direction: Thorold Dickinson. Editing: Ray Pitt. Photography: Ernest Palmer. Music: Sir William Walton. Art Direction: Tom Morahan. Players: Mervyn Johns, Nova Pilbeam, Stephen Murray, Reginald Tate, Jack Hawkins, Mary Clare. Production: Ealing—for the War Office (Michael Balcon) 101 mins.

Originally intended for screening to H. M. Forces only as a cautionary tale against careless talk, *Next of Kin* later proved one of the most successful wartime films among the general public. One test of a film made for a limited contemporary purpose is how it holds the attention when its primary *raison d'être* no longer exists, and *Next of Kin* passes this with almost contemptuous ease, despite some very obvious studio settings. It is, in fact, a first-class suspense-and-spy story, cunningly put together and entirely uncompromising in its grim climax. Mervyn Johns gives a superb performance as the agent who, by collecting information on a coming commando raid, enables the enemy to exact a heavy penalty when it takes place: the quiet ending after scenes of death and destruction, with the unnoticeable little man setting out to profit by more "careless talk," is chillingly effective.

ONE OF OUR AIRCRAFT IS MISSING. Script: Michael Powell, Emeric Pressburger. Direction: Michael Powell. Photography: Ronald Neame. Editing: David Lean. Art Direction: David Rawnsley. Players: Godfrey Tearle, Eric Portman, Hugh Williams, Bernard Miles, Hugh Burden, Emrys Jones, Pamela Brown, Googie Withers. Production: British National (Michael Powell). 106 mins.

A more or less straightforward adventure story, beginning in documentary fashion with the briefing and execution of a bombing raid (the briefing being done by Powell himself), and continuing

*1942: NEXT OF KIN, the Commandos' raid.*

with the baling out of a crew and their escape from occupied Holland. The most impressive sequences are the raid itself and the plane crash (the latter opening the film and repeated later in context). The remainder, though quite exciting on a thriller level, is not so convincing, perhaps because of well-known stars like Pamela Brown, Googie Withers, Alec Clunes (as a church organist) and Peter Ustinov (parson) appearing in Holland to help the boys on their way. As a first attempt to portray life in occupied countries, however, the film has interest.

*1942: Eric Portman, Hugh Burden and Googie Withers in ONE OF OUR AIRCRAFT IS MISSING.*

THE FOREMAN WENT TO FRANCE. Script: Angus MacPhail, John Dighton, Leslie Arliss. Direction: Charles Frend. Photography: Wilkie Cooper. Editing: Robert Hamer. Music: Sir William Walton. Art Direction: Tom Morahan. Players: Tommy Trinder, Clifford Evans, Constance Cummings, Gordon Jackson. Production: Ealing (Cavalcanti). 87 mins.

Founded on the true incident of a works foreman who crossed the English Channel to retrieve some vital equipment after the collapse of France, this is a notable second film by a young director (his first was *The Big Blockade*) hitherto known as a skilled editor. France, being out of bounds as a location, was cleverly re-created in Cornwall. Much good work lay ahead of Frend—*San Demetrio London, Joanna Godden, Scott of the Antarctic, The Cruel Sea*—but this early feature, aided by an excellent script, will stand well in comparison with the future.

THE FIRST OF THE FEW (SPITFIRE). Script: Anatole de Grunwald, Miles Malleson. Direction: Leslie Howard. Photography: Georges Périnal. Editing: Douglas Myers. Music: Sir William Walton. Art Direction: Paul Sheriff. Players: Leslie Howard, David Niven, Rosamund John, Roland Culver. Production: British Aviation Pictures. 118 mins.

This was Leslie Howard's last appearance as an actor before his tragic death. (He was to co-produce *The Gentle Sex* and *The Lamp Still Burns,* in 1943). It tells simply and unostentatiously the life and work of R. J. Mitchell, inventor of the Spitfire plane. In a sense it has little to do with war, it could be the story of any man's struggle to realise his dream. Howard's performance is wholly sympathetic throughout and his quiet death scene doubly poignant when viewed with the knowledge of what was so soon to follow. Walton's music includes the famous Spitfire Fugue, which is excitingly integrated with the action.

WENT THE DAY WELL? Script: John Dighton, Diana Morgan, Angus MacPhail, from a story by Graham Greene. Direction: Alberto Cavalcanti. Photography: Wilkie Cooper. Editor: Sidney Cole. Music: Sir William Walton. Art Director: Tom Morahan. Players: Leslie Banks, Basil Sydney, Frank Lawton, Elizabeth Allan, Valerie Taylor, John Slater. Production: Ealing (Michael Balcon). 92 mins.

Less often figured in accounts of British wartime production, this underrated film views with a coldly appraising eye what might have happened in a remote village if the Germans had landed. A company of "Royal Engineers" surprises the villagers, but is welcomed and billeted. Once they have been revealed as the enemy, the captive community, despite all the official advice and warnings they have received, are helpless. Attempt after attempt to raise an alarm fails. Eventually relief arrives, but not until some unpleasant lessons have been learnt. The gradual arousal of suspicion by trivial incidents works up to a pitch of real suspense, and the feeling of helplessness is disturbingly possible. Only the characters are dull stereotypes, though well played. This was Cavalcanti's first full-length British feature.

*1942: "British" troops invade an English country church in WENT THE DAY WELL.*

*1942: COASTAL COMMAND, a Crown Film Unit documentary.*

## Short Films and Documentaries

COASTAL COMMAND. Script and direction: J. B. Holmes. Photography: Jonah Jones, F. Gamage. Music: Ralph Vaughan Williams. Art Direction: Edward Carrick. Production: Crown Film Unit (Ian Dalrymple).

Dealing with the co-operation between the Navy and aircraft based on shore, in ensuring the safe conduct of convoys, this may be regarded as a companion piece to *Target for Tonight*: made with standard efficiency and noteworthy for the score by Vaughan Williams.

## 1942: Facts of Interest

The number of British films over one hour in length falls to a low of forty-six, but the general standard of production is good.

Death of C. M. Woolf.

# 1943

NINE MEN. Script: Harry Watt. Direction: Harry Watt. Photography: Roy Kellino. Editing: Sidney Cole. Music: John Greenwood. Art Direction: Duncan Sutherland. Players: Jack Lambert, Gordon Jackson, Grant Sutherland, Richard Wilkinson. Production: Ealing. 67 mins.

Harry Watt's first feature film after a distinguished career in short documentaries is a modest-budget production set in North Africa (and filmed on a small stretch of sand in Wales), telling of a group of men caught in the desert and holding out in a derelict tomb until they are relieved. This stalwart situation of tough fiction is given immediacy by Watt's skill and experience in the realistic field, and also by the inspired casting of Jack Lambert (a Scot as stalwart as the situation, and at the time second-in-command of a battalion of the Royal Scots) as the sergeant who takes over when his officer is killed. The film was attacked later because of its attitude towards the Italian enemy, one of whom is shot while trying to escape: no outcry was made at the time.

MILLIONS LIKE US. Script: Frank Launder, Sidney Gilliat. Direction: Frank Launder, Sidney Gilliat. Photography: Jack Cox, Roy Fogwell. Editing: R. E. Dearing. Art Direction: John Bryan. Players: Eric Portman, Lilli Palmer, Patricia Roc, Gordon Jackson, Anne Crawford, Joy Shelton. Production: Gainsborough. 103 mins.

Launder and Gilliat come together for the first time as joint feature directors in this treatment of a less often recorded aspect of war activity—the munitions factory. A likeable, lively and realistic film, it combines the all-in-it-together situation indicated by the title with shrewd comments on the breaking up of class barriers by the war, and the difficulties that might have to be faced in the brave new world to come, from the feminine point of view. The factory sequences are treated in documentary fashion, but the human stories play a larger part in this account of civilians on the home front. The production was a good augury for the partnership to follow. Eric Portman stands out as a forthright Yorkshire foreman, and all the girls are good.

SAN DEMETRIO, LONDON. Script: Robert Hamer, Charles Frend. Direction: Charles Frend. Photography: Ernest Palmer. Editing: Eily Boland. Music: John Greenwood. Art Direction: Duncan Sutherland. Players: Walter Fitzgerald, Robert Beatty, Mervyn Johns, Ralph Michael, Gordon Jackson, Frederick Piper. Production: Ealing (Michael Balcon). 105 mins.

The oil tanker San Demetrio was set on fire and practically cut in two by enemy shells—then patched up and brought home by its crew after they had been drifting in one of its boats for three days. The Ministry of Information issued a special account of the exploit, and Balcon decided it was a subject worthy of film treatment. The result is not a documentary, nor even a semi-documentary, any more than a film of the Battle of Trafalgar would be. It is a reconstruction of history with a number of professional actors and studio sets. The fact that the history is recent only means that accuracy is probably (though not necessarily) easier

*: Desert warfare in Harry Watt's NINE MEN.*

*1943: MILLIONS LIKE US, the distaff side in the munitions factories, with Patricia Roc and Megs Jenkins.*

to achieve. Judged as fact-based fiction, it is a tightly directed picture with all the qualities of the British war-time renaissance, and does for the Merchant Navy what earlier productions had done for the Royal Navy and the R.A.F. The Army's turn was yet to come.

**THE LIFE AND DEATH OF COLONEL BLIMP.** Script: Michael Powell, Emeric Pressburger. Photography: Georges Périnal. Editing: John Seabourne. Music: Allan Gray. Players: Anton Walbrook, Deborah Kerr, Roger Livesey. Production: Archers (Powell and Pressburger). 163 mins.

Based on the cartoon character of David Low, the film traces the life and career from the Boer War to the Second World War and the Home Guard, of a bumbling, blustering military type. As played by Livesey (the original choice had been Laurence Olivier), he emerges a good deal softened from Low's bullying, boasting and viciously stupid martinet: what results is not a bitter satire but an amiable, enjoyable comedy-drama, shot in good colour and with good performances—particularly by Deborah Kerr as three women of different generations in the soldier's life. Eye and mind are constantly delighted by the directors' *penchant* for the imaginative composition—but it is interesting to speculate how much influence the period of its creation had in altering its tone.

**THE DEMI-PARADISE.** Script: Anatole de Grunwald. Direction: Anthony Asquith. Photography: Bernard Knowles. Editing: Reginald Beck. Music: Nicholas Brodsky. Art Direction: Paul Sheriff. Players: Laurence Olivier, Penelope Dudley Ward, Marjorie Fielding, Margaret Rutherford, Felix Aylmer, Michael Shepley. Production: Two Cities. 115 mins.

A light-weight film which affords Asquith a welcome chance to exercise his gift for gently satirical comedy. Only marginally connected with the war, and evidently intended as a friendly gesture towards the Soviet Union, its main attraction is the performance of Olivier as the Russian engineer who arrives in England to oversee the production of a propellor of his own invention. The other characters are little more than embodiments of "amusing" or "lovable" English characteristics, put there for him to react to, but the whole thing is so unpretentious and good-houmoured that, taken as it is offered, there is much to enjoy.

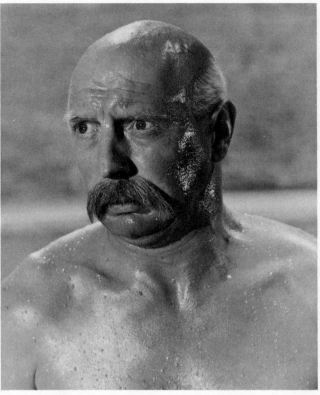

*1943: A striking photograph of Roger Livesey in the title role of THE LIFE AND DEATH OF COLONEL BLIMP.*

**THE MAN IN GREY.** Script: Leslie Arliss, Margaret Kennedy, from Eleanor Smith's novel. Direction: Leslie Arliss. Photography: Arthur Crabtree. Editing: R. E. Dearing. Music: Cedric Mallabey. Art Direction: Walter Murton. Players: Margaret Lockwood, James Mason, Phyllis Calvert, Stewart Granger. Production: Gainsborough. 116 mins.

Making a boldly incongruous entry into the world of global conflict, James Mason's Regency buck made himself heard above all the din of bombs and shells. The immense popularity of this elaborate period melodrama, with its emphasis on sex and violence in pretty costumes, set in motion a wave of similar pictures, brought increased prominence to its stars, made a great deal of money, and thus had an importance far beyond its intrinsic worth—which (apart from full-blooded acting and technical elegance) is not very much. The personalities of Mason and Margaret Lockwood acquired a sort of aura of Regency raffishness which was to take some time to fade into the light of common day. The film is linked to the present by a fairly irrelevant prologue and epilogue featuring a Jamaican pilot and a WREN.

## Short Films and Documentaries

FIRES WERE STARTED. Script and Direction: Humphrey Jennings. Photography: C. M. Pennington-Richards. Editing: Stewart McAllister. Music: William Alwyn. Art Direction: Edward Carrick. Players: George Gravitt, Philip W. Dickson, Fred Griffiths. Production: Crown Film Unit (Ian Dalrymple). 63 mins.

A reconstruction of a single night's activity by an Auxiliary Fire Service sub-station in the 1940 blitz, raised above the level of flat commentary or tribute by the poetic quality of its presentation, and the humanity and warmth with which it de-

picts a diverse group of men brought together by a common purpose and a common courage. Despite reminders that the sub-station is linked to a whole network, the one element lacking (admittedly consistent with its immediate intention, and perhaps physically inevitable) is a sense of the sheer vastness of the battle to be fought—of night after night of holocaustic fury when whole streets went up in flame. In this instance, despite its many qualities, the part somehow fails to convey the full meaning of the whole.

DESERT VICTORY. Direction: Roy Boulting. Photography: Army Film Photographic Unit. Editing: Roy Boulting, Richard Best, Frank Clarke. Music: William Alwyn. Commentary: J. L. Hodson. Production: Army Film Production Unit,

*1943: WORLD OF PLENTY, Paul Rotha's courageously forward-looking documentary on the conquest of hunger.*

151

R.A.F. Film Production Unit (David McDonald). 60 mins.

The skill in editing a mass of material, and the intelligent integration of explanatory maps and diagrams make this hour-long account of the Egyptian-Libyan campaign from El Alamein to Tripoli a model documentary of its kind. Several of the unnamed cameramen were killed or taken prisoner as they worked.

WORLD OF PLENTY. Script, direction, production: Paul Rotha.

A documentary that, after looking back at the world food situation before the war and examining the position during it, looks forward courageously beyond it to the possibility of nationally and internationally controlled distribution. It breaks new ground by anticipating television techniques in the presentation of discussion for and against the various proposals.

## 1943: Facts of Interest

Odeon forms a Children's Cinema Club.

Alexander Korda takes charge of M-G-M British production.

Death of R. W. Paul. Leslie Howard is killed in a plane destroyed by enemy action.

# 1944

HENRY V. Script: Alan Dent, Laurence Olivier, from Shakespeare's play. Direction: Laurence Olivier. Photography: Robert Krasker, Jack Hildyard (Technicolor). Editing: Reginald Beck. Music: Sir William Walton. Art Direction: Paul Sheriff. Players: Laurence Olivier, Renee Asherson, Leslie Banks, Esmond Knight, Robert Newton, Felix Aylmer, Harcourt Williams. Production: Two Cities (Laurence Olivier).

Olivier's *Henry V* burst like a rising sun on the cinema screen at the end of 1944: seldom can a film's timing have been more apt. The word of the day was "breakthrough"—for the war, for the Britain of the future—and for Shakespeare on the screen. The opening sequences in the Globe Theatre, the illuminated-missal settings into which they merged, the spectacular pageantry of the battle, the return through picturebook to Globe, the treatment of the soliloquys, the respect without inflated reverence for great verse, the humanity of Olivier's Henry, the bright but not gaudy colour—all was magnificent. Since then, inevitably, have come reservations. The three conventions do not wholly integrate, the sheer scope and invention of the visual aspects work to the detriment of the verbal, and so on. Justified though some such criticisms may be, the film remains a landmark both in the presentation of Shakespeare and in the history of British cinema. The film's opening, with its panorama of Elizabethan London, the Globe pennant flying, the players bustling into their costumes, the audience gathering, is so full of fascinating detail that one longs for more of it. The battle charge of Agincourt, to Walton's most stir-ring music, and culminating in the whirring flight of a thousand arrows, is unlikely ever to be surpassed.

THE WAY AHEAD. Script: Eric Ambler, Peter Ustinov. Direction: Carol Reed. Photography: Guy Green. Editing: Fergus McDonell. Music: William Alwyn. Art Direction: David Rawnsley. Players: David Niven, William Hartnell, Raymond Huntley, Leslie Dwyer, Hugh Burden, John Laurie, James Donald, Peter Ustinov, Jimmy Hanley, Stanley Holloway, Renee Asherson. Production: Two Cities. 115 mins.

The production that was to speak for the Army as *In Which We Serve* had for the Navy, and arguably the best war film of them all. With a brilliant script to work from, Reed tells with the utmost sympathy, humour, fidelity and compassion the story of a diverse group of men called up just after Dunkirk, made to undergo a long period of training, and finally shipped off to take part in the North African invasion. A conventional enough formula, but so handled that even the contrivance of gathering together "one of each type" does not destroy reality. The progress from simulated to actual danger, from the controllable to the uncontrollable event, moves with superbly conveyed inevitability until the first grinding menace of the approaching enemy tanks is heard. The direction is backed with a number of flawless performances —William Hartnell, Raymond Huntley and David Niven perhaps outstanding, but all of an excellence that defies comparison. The final scene, with each individual—moulded into a fighting group, per-

*Contrasting styles in HENRY V. (a) The Globe Theatre. (b) At Agincourt.*

*(a)*

*(b)*

haps, but remaining in the last resort desperately vulnerable and alone—trudging through the enveloping smoke-screen towards the unseen, uncertain future, is as moving today as when the film first appeared.

*1944: The recruits meet the sergeant. Raymond Huntley, William Hartnell, John Laurie, Stanley Holloway and Jimmy Hanley in Carol Reed's THE WAY AHEAD.*

**ON APPROVAL.** Script: from the play by Frederick Lonsdale. Direction: Clive Brook. Photography: C. Friese-Greene. Editing: Fergus McDonell. Music: William Alwyn. Art Direction: Tom Morahan. Players: Clive Brook, Beatrice Lillie, Googie Withers, Roland Culver. Production: Clive Brook. 80 mins.

Clive Brook's one film as director is a surprising oddity. Transferring a Twenties comedy into an Edwardian setting, he has treated it in a half-parodying style, dressed up its rather wilting wit with such cinematic devices as a commentator (interrupted at times by the characters themselves) and a fantastic dream sequence, and finished up with a mixture of period piece and surrealism which is unexpectedly satisfying. The production encountered criticism from one quarter for being too "frothy and irresponsible" for such grave and glum times.

**TAWNY PIPIT.** Script: Bernard Miles, Charles Saunders. Direction: Bernard Miles, Charles Saunders. Photography: Eric Cross. Editing: Douglas Myers. Music: Noël Mewton-Wood. Art Direction: Alex Vetchinsky. Players: Bernard Miles, Niall McGinnis, Rosamund John, Lucie Mannheim, Christopher Steele, John Schofield. Production: Two Cities (F. Del Giudice). 81 mins.

Miles makes an auspicious *début* as director in this unassuming little tilt at rural life and overbearing officialdom. Telling of the discovery of a rare pair of wild birds nesting near a Cotswold village, and of the inhabitants' determination to see they are left undisturbed by army exercises, agricultural planners, or just plain egg-stealers, the story is rather too self-consciously quaint, but this is largely offset by its humour, and by much beautiful photography of country scenes: and the points made, however gently, are valid ones.

**A CANTERBURY TALE.** Script and direction: Michael Powell, Emeric Pressburger. Photography: Erwin Hillier. Art Direction: Alfred Junge. Players: Eric Portman, Sheila Sim, John Sweet, Dennis Price. Production: Independent Producers. 125 mins.

One of Powell and Pressburger's strangest films, arousing almost as much controversy as *Peeping Tom*, which Powell made on his own in 1959. It combines two stories: one concerning the tracking-down of a neurotic organist who spends his evenings smearing glue on the hair of the village girls, the other the journey to Canterbury Cathedral of four people in search of penance or blessing. The symbolic contrast between good and evil is obvious, but the interweaving of the two is complex and the result is a bit of a puzzle—beautifully photographed by Erwin Hillier. The glue-smearing organist caused some critical offence, though placed among the cinematic perversion and sadism of today his aberration is mild. Michael Powell has described the film as a crusade against materialism.

**WATERLOO ROAD.** Script: Frank Launder, Sidney Gilliat, Val Valentine. Direction: Sidney Gilliat. Photography: Arthur Crabtree. Editing: Alfred Roome. Music: Louis Levy, Bob Busby. Art Direction: Alex Vetchinsky. Players: John Mills, Stewart Granger, Alastair Sim, Joy Shelton, Beatrice Varley, George Carney, Alison Leggatt. Production: Gainsborough. 77 mins.

A wartime melodrama about a young soldier who takes leave of absence to sort out his private life and rescue his wife from the clutches of a black-

*1944: The villagers meet to protect the TAWNY PIPIT.*

*1944: Eric Portman and Sheila Sim in a CANTER-BURY TALE.*

market profiteer, this is notable for its realistic scenes of London slum life, and for its furious fight between Mills and Granger, one of the most savage ever screened. The picture foreshadows the tough "spiv" and petty crime stories to follow immediately after the war.

## Short Films and Documentaries

WESTERN APPROACHES. Script: Pat Jackson, Gerry Bryant. Direction: Pat Jackson. Photography: Jack Cardiff (Technicolor). Art Direction: Edward Carrick. Music: Clifton Parker. Production: Crown Film Unit (Ian Dalrymple).

Among the best of the war documentaries, this is a reconstruction of an encounter which took place during the struggle against the U-Boat menace to British shipping in the Atlantic: photographed by Jack Cardiff, soon to become one of Britain's finest cameramen.

## 1944: Facts of Interest

The Rank Organisation forms a Children's Entertainment Division under Mary Field, and produces its first picture, *Tom's Ride*.

A Committee is appointed to examine the monopoly position existing in the film industry.

British cinemas in the South-east suffer further damage from flying-bombs.

Death of Percy Smith.

# 1945

BRIEF ENCOUNTER. Script: Noël Coward, David Lean, Anthony Havelock-Allan, from the one-act play by Noël Coward. Direction: David Lean. Photography: Robert Krasker. Editing: Jack Harris. Music: Rachmaninov's Piano Concerto Number Two, played by Eileen Joyce. Art Direction: L. P. Williams. Players: Celia Johnson, Trevor Howard, Cyril Raymond, Stanley Holloway, Joyce Carey. Production: Cineguild. 86 mins.

Probably no other major film has suffered such a reversal of opinion as this. A writer has recently described a London audience as "convulsed with loathing" of it. At the time of its first appearance it was hailed as one of the truest and most moving experiences to be gained from any film; one in which "the subject of love has seldom been so sensitively handled outside the French cinema." The slight story, no more than an episode, of two people—both with ties—who meet, fall in love, and realise they must part, is well-known. The small railway junction is the symbol of their loneliness, their meeting and their parting: the atmosphere of dingy postwar austerity is woven into their own story. This is told and played with sincerity, compassion, and considerable subtlety (e.g. the close-up of Cyril Raymond's face after the last flashback). The sentiments and standards may be out of keeping with the tougher, more enlightened, sharper-visioned, protest-conscious, brave new world of today: but the inability to appreciate problems other than those that seem important to oneself may—if these are presented with sincerity —be a sign of immaturity or emotional sterility. It is just possible that a "convulsion of loathing" may reflect to some extent on the audience, as well as on the film.

1945: Celia Johnson at home with her crossword-addict husband, Cyril Raymond, as the memories of her BRIEF ENCOUNTER pass through her mind.

THE WAY TO THE STARS (JOHNNY IN THE CLOUDS). Script: Terence Rattigan, Anatole de Grunwald. Poems: John Pudney. Direction: Anthony Asquith. Photography: Derek Williams. Editing: Fergus McDonell. Music: Nicholas Brodsky. Art Direction: Carmen Dillon. Players: Michael Redgrave, John Mills, Rosamund John, Douglass Montgomery, Renee Asherson, Stanley Holloway, Trevor Howard, Felix Aylmer, Jean Simmons, Bonar Colleano. Production: Two Cities. 109 mins.

Though in its setting a war film, *The Way to the*

*Stars* concentrates much more on the personal problems of the characters than on the wider issues, and the time of its appearance, after the war in Europe was over, helps to wrap it in a nostalgic atmosphere which—owing to the skill of Asquith's direction—strengthens rather than weakens its impact. Set in 1942, it opens with shots of a deserted and dead airfield, then describes the men connected with it who lived, loved, flew, and died. The "variegated group" formula is kept from cliché by the way in which the director is able to arouse a feeling of indignation at *all* the waste of young lives. But this is no mournful moan of despair: the keynote of the film is John Pudney's poem *Johnny Head-in-Air,* with its last line—increasingly significant as the war drew to an end and awoke memories of the aftermath of other wars—"See that his children are fed."

DEAD OF NIGHT. Script: John V. Baines, Angus MacPhail, T. E. B. Clarke, from stories by J. V. Baines, E. F. Benson, H. G. Wells. Direction: Cavalcanti, Basil Dearden, Robert Hamer, Charles Crichton. Photography: Jack Parker, H. Julius. Editing: Charles Hassey. Music: Georges Auric. Art Direction: Michael Relph. Players: Mervyn Johns, Roland Culver, Michael Redgrave, Googie Withers, Frederick Valk, Sally Ann Howes, Miles Malleson, Basil Radford, Naunton Wayne. Production: Ealing (Michael Balcon). 104 mins.

Britain's first entry into the sphere of the macabre is still one of the most striking of all supernatural films. Consisting of five episodes strung along a linking story, it is memorable for the steady progression—both from episode to episode and in the linking story—from the light of day to the darkness of night, and far beyond. The one comedy interlude, with Radford and Wayne, though amusing enough in itself, is out of key with the rest, and seems too consciously brought in because of the conventional need for "comic relief." Apart from this, the tension is steadily increased until the horrifying climax. The final episode, directed by Cavalcanti and superbly played by Michael Redgrave as the ventriloquist who is mastered by his doll, is rightly regarded as the high spot—but the sense of nightmare in the first brief history of the hearse-driver (by Basil Dearden who also directs the linking story) is unnervingly created. The construction of the story is extremely in-

genious. At first glance the shape of the whole film, episodes and linking story, appears to be circular. The entire thing turns out to be a dream. The dreamer awakes, sweating but relieved—answers a call on the telephone, and sets off on the same course we have already seen in the nightmare. But—by a brilliant stroke contained in one momentary shot, we are informed that *this* time it is no mere dream, there will be no merciful awakening. This time—the horror is real.

*1945: Michael Redgrave, superb as the haunted ventriloquist in DEAD OF NIGHT.*

I KNOW WHERE I'M GOING. Script: Michael Powell, Emeric Pressburger. Direction: Michael Powell, Emeric Pressburger. Photography: Erwin Hillier. Editing: John Seabourne. Music: Allan Gray. Art Direction: Alfred Junge. Players: Wendy Hiller, Roger Livesey, Pamela Brown, Sybil Thorndike. Production: Archers. 91 mins.

Against the lovely scenery of the Western Isles, presented with all the flair to be expected from the firm of Powell and Pressburger, is set the seemingly commonplace story of a self-assured young woman who finds her plans to marry for money thwarted by her love for a laird without any. No prizes for a correct solution, but the story is commonplace only in its outline, and the picture is as stimulating as a breath of fresh air in a cinema. Without being a widely popular success (though it has done well in New York), it has always remained a favourite with a discriminating few.

BLITHE SPIRIT. Script: from the play by Noël Coward. Direction: David Lean. Photography: Ronald Neame (Technicolor). Editing: Jack Harris. Art Direction: C. P. Norman. Players: Rex Harrison, Constance Cummings, Kay Hammond, Margaret Rutherford. Production: Two Cities. 96 mins.

A more or less straight adaptation of the play. Lean has wisely let Coward's dialogue speak for itself; apart from one or two witty touches, scenes outside the room add little to the original, and the ghostly effects are strangely less effective than in the theatre. It came at a time when the country was weary for a bit of colour and light, and was enormously popular.

THE SEVENTH VEIL. Script: Muriel and Sydney Box. Direction: R. Compton Bennett. Photography: Reginald Wyer. Editing: Gordon Hale. Music: Ben Frankel. Pianist for Ann Todd: Eileen Joyce. Art Direction: Jim Carter. Players: Ann Todd, James Mason, Herbert Lom, Albert Lieven, Hugh MacDermott. Production: Sydney Box-Ortus. 84 mins.

The outstanding box-office success of this Svengali melodrama, with its supercharged romantic story and glossy "artistic" background, has resulted in its virtues (and there are some) being decried in the more fastidious fastnesses of film criticism. There is, firstly, the fact that the music which is so important a part of it is treated with a certain respect (in contrast to poor old Tchaikovsky's pieces in Ken Russell's hyper-pretentious *Music Lovers*); secondly there is Ann Todd's virtuoso performance; thirdly there is the sheer craftsmanship with which it is put together, staged and photographed; lastly, there is James Mason doing his own thing as only he can. If novelettes are to be filmed, this is the way to film them.

I LIVE IN GROSVENOR SQUARE (A YANK IN LONDON). Script: Maurice Cowan, Nicholas Phipps, W. D. Bayles. Direction: Herbert Wilcox.

1945: A traumatic moment in the young pianist's life, Ann Todd in THE SEVENTH VEIL.

Photography: Otto Heller. Editing: Vera Campbell. Art Direction: William C. Andrews. Players: Anna Neagle, Rex Harrison, Dean Jagger, Robert Morley. Production: Associated British Pictures. 114 mins.

This is the first of a vastly remunerative series of romantic comedy-dramas, generally with a West End of London setting and later Michael Wilding, expert, predictable, full of well-dressed, good-looking people. In essence they are musicless musical comedies. They may not be worth much in terms of art, but they cannot be ignored in terms of cinema history. Wilcox explained their success by saying that the public were sick of "gloomy horrors and wanted films about nice people." Judging by the receipts, he could have been right.

CAESAR AND CLEOPATRA. Script: Marjorie Deans, from G. B. Shaw's play. Direction: Gabriel Pascal. Photography: F. Young, Robert Krasker, Jack Hildyard, Jack Cardiff. Editing: F. Wilson. Music: Georges Auric. Art Direction: John Bryan. Players: Claude Rains, Vivien Leigh, Stewart Granger, Flora Robson, Francis L. Sullivan, Basil Sydney, Cecil Parker, Raymond Lovell. Production: Gabriel Pascal.

This wildly extravagant production was intended to prove to the world that Britain could make a spectacular as good as anyone, and at the same time provide mental stimulation as well as emotional. Unhappily, despite desperately good acting, it provided neither. With picture postcard

*1945: I LIVE IN GROSVENOR SQUARE, Robert Morley, Anna Neagle and Rex Harrison.*

settings and pasteboard characters posturing in front of them, what was meant to be a monster film turned out merely a monstrous bore.

### Short Films and Documentaries

THE TRUE GLORY. Script: Eric Maschwitz, Arthur Macrae, Jenny Nicholson, Gerald Kersh, Guy Trosper. Direction: Carol Reed, Garson Kanin. Photography: Army Film Unit, American Army Pictorial Service. Editing: Robert Verrell. Music: William Alwyn. Production: U.S. Office of War Information, The Ministry of Information. 84 mins.

This full-scale account of the Normandy invasion from its inception until the meeting at the River Elbe is in reality a masterpiece of compilation, taken from the records of fourteen hundred cameramen, and accompanied by an unusually impressive commentary spoken by men of the invading armies. A prodigiously complex undertaking has been reduced to clarity and human perspective without losing the sense of its vast scope.

### 1945: Facts of Interest

David Hand arrives from America to form a cartoon film unit under Rank—the *Musical Paintbox* series, etc., but the project is not successful.

Some 330 cinemas are estimated to have been destroyed by enemy action during the war. One of the worst incidents of the Blitz, the destruction of the Café de Paris in Coventry Street, was caused by a bomb which went through the ceiling and floor of the Rialto Cinema above it. Death of Sinclair Hill.

# 1946

A MATTER OF LIFE AND DEATH (STAIRWAY TO HEAVEN). Script: Michael Powell, Emeric Pressburger. Direction: Michael Powell, Emeric Pressburger. Photography: Jack Cardiff. Editing: Reginald Mills. Music: Allan Gray. Art Direction: Alfred Junge. Players: David Niven, Kim Hunter, Marius Goring, Roger Livesey, Abraham Sofaer, Raymond Massey. Production: Archers. 104 mins.

A wounded airman undergoing a brain operation has hallucinations that he is being tried for his life by a supernatural court, his defence being undertaken by various historical characters. This extraordinary film, described as a stratospheric joke, is made with a flamboyance and technical bravura outstanding for its period. Much of the action takes place on an enormous staircase—as impressive a set piece as the War Room in *Doctor Strangelove* (or a Busby Berkeley dance sequence!). Monochrome and colour are blended in a manner commonplace today, but unusual then. Miraculously, the characters are not wholly swamped by their settings. The film has been interpreted as a plea for better understanding between Britain and America—among other things—but it is not for its Matter that the production can still amaze, but for its sheer exuberance of imagination. Accusations of bad taste (and there were some) are irrelevant in such an exhilarating and beautiful display of cinematic fireworks.

GREAT EXPECTATIONS. Script: David Lean, Ronald Neame, from Dickens's novel. Direction: David Lean. Photography: Guy Green. Editing: Jack Harris. Music: Walter Goehr. Art Direction: Wilfred Shingleton. Players: John Mills, Alec Guinness, Valerie Hobson, Bernard Miles, Francis L. Sullivan, Finlay Currie, Anthony Wager, Jean Simmons, Martita Hunt. Production: Cineguild. 118 mins.

The nearest rival to this supreme Dickens film is the director's own *Oliver Twist* (1948). By drastic and intelligent pruning of the novel, Lean proves once for all that the essence of a sprawling masterpiece can be distilled for the screen, and proves himself, had he made no other film, a major director. The photography, from mistiness to razor-sharp etching, catches every mood exactly, and cutting is inspired to the single frame. The shock of the convict's first appearance has not been surpassed to this day, even when we know it is coming. Lean is equally successful with his cast, and if Guinness is picked out for his endearingly timorous and gentle Herbert Pocket, it is only to welcome the first appearance on the screen of one of its finest actors. To say that the early part of the film comes off best is only to compare two standards of excellence. The one fatal flaw is that of the book itself—the happy ending, forced on Dickens, that belies all that has gone before. If only the film had had the final courage to do for Dickens what he was prevented from doing for himself, and incorporate his original intention!

THE OVERLANDERS. Script and Direction: Harry Watt. Photography: Osmond Borrodaile. Editing: E. M. Inman Hunter, Leslie Norman. Music: John Ireland. Players: Chips Rafferty,

*1946: Roger Livesey in one of the remarkable settings
created for A MATTER OF LIFE AND DEATH.*

Daphne Campbell, John N. Hayward, Jeanne Blue. Production: Ealing (Michael Balcon). 91 mins.

Bringing the Australian land for the first time vividly to the screen, this tells the story of a two thousand mile trek across desert country, undertaken to save cattle from a scorched-earth policy adopted in the fear of possible Japanese invasion in 1942. Personal dramas take second place to the documentary recording of the journey itself, and Watt's treatment raises the subject to epic level while expressing the courage and determination of a small community—a notable accomplishment in strange surroundings and unfamiliar circumstances.

MEN OF TWO WORLDS. Script: Thorold Dickinson, Herbert W. Victor, Joyce Cary. Direction: Thorold Dickinson. Photography: Desmond Dickinson. Editing: Alan Jaggs. Music: Sir Arthur Bliss. Art Direction: Tom Morahan. Players: Eric Portman, Phyllis Calvert, Robert Adams, Orlando Martins, David Horne, Cathleen Nesbitt. Production: Two Cities. 109 mins.

A sincere attempt to present the contemporary problems of a Negro standing as it were between two cultures, and his struggles to fulfil himself, this story of a well-known musician who returns to his native Africa took three years to make, and shows evidence of the care taken to attain both

*1946: GREAT EXPECTATIONS, John Mills as Pip and Finlay Currie as Magwitch in David Lean's inspired version.*

*1946: Trek across the Australian desert from Harry Watt's epic of THE OVERLANDERS.*

factual accuracy and the general "feel" of a strange country. Praised as a serious contribution to racial understanding, its good intentions are obvious even if in execution it falls short of its director's best. It was made with the help of the Tanganyikan government.

**THEIRS IS THE GLORY.** Direction: Brian Desmond Hurst. Commentators: Alan Wood, Stanley Maxted. Production: Castleton Knight. 82 mins.

As a reconstruction of past events, not a document of actual facts, this account of the ill-starred 1944 Arnhem landing inevitably loses something in immediacy. It derives authenticity, however, from the very recent memories of its participants, and, aided by the commentaries of the war correspondents, is probably as close a re-living of the tension, drama and despair of those few days as it would be possible to achieve.

## 1946: Facts of Interest

J. A. Rank launches *This Modern Age*, a film review intended as a British equivalent to the American *March of Time*. The first issue is *Homes for All*, and subsequent subjects included *The Police, Development Areas, Home and Beauty, Antarctic Whale Hunters, Palestine, Women in Our Time, Gambling, The Coal Crisis*. The series was to run until 1949.

The British Film Academy is formed.

John Davis becomes Managing Director of the Rank Organisation.

# 1947

ODD MAN OUT. Script: F. L. Green, R. C. Sherriff, from Graham Greene's novel. Direction: Carol Reed. Photography: Robert Krasker. Editing: Fergus McDonell. Music: William Alwyn. Art Direction: Ralph Brinton. Players: James Mason, Kathleen Ryan, Robert Beatty, Robert Newton, W. G. Fay, Fay Compton, F. J. McCormick. Production: Two Cities. 115 mins.

On the basis of a straightforward thriller, Carol Reed has constructed what many consider still to be one of his most significant films, following the course of a political leader in Belfast from his injury during an attempt to raise funds for his organisation by robbery to his death within reach of safety. The film is extremely close-knit, occurring within about eight hours and in a circumscribed space within sight of the street clock which serves both as symbol and as physical hub of the action. Mason gives an outstanding performance in what is really a passive role: the mainspring of the episodic events is not the hunted man but the reactions of those with whom he comes in contact. The story is thus less a tragedy than a deeply penetrating study of human behaviour. It is not —above all—a picture of undeserved human suffering. The man knew what he was doing, he knew the risks he was deliberately taking in breaking the law and thieving. The measure of Reed's powerful handling of the theme is the deep involvement with the man's fate which, in spite of everything, he arouses in the watcher.

BLACK NARCISSUS. Script: Michael Powell, Emeric Pressburger, from the novel by Rumer Godden. Direction: Michael Powell, Emeric Pressburger. Photography: Jack Cardiff. Editing: Reginald Mills. Music: Brian Easdale. Art Direction: Alfred Junge. Players: Deborah Kerr, Sabu, David Farrar, Flora Robson, Jean Simmons, Esmond Knight, Kathleen Byron. Production: Archers. 100 mins.

This story of five Anglo-Catholic nuns who open a school and hospital in a remote spot in the Himalayas is a study of frustrated women in rather superficially religious settings. At first the mission appears to be a success, then one of the sisters begins to plant flowers instead of vegetables, another treats a village child who dies, thereby incurring the enmity of the local people, a third becomes insane, runs away, and finally loses her life, a young native pupil also deserts. The film is ravishingly beautiful, in colour unsurpassed for its time: shots such as the start of the rains, with great drops splashing on the enormous green leaves, are unforgettable. It has been accused of lapses of taste, but in actual fact the treatment of a fundamentally serious theme, brought out in terms of human conflict and set against awe-inspiring mountain backgrounds, never lapses into mere melodrama. It is throughout vividly imaginative, dramatic and often very moving.

HUE AND CRY. Script: T. E. B. Clarke. Direction: Charles Crichton. Photography: Douglas Slocombe. Editing: Charles Hasse. Music: Georges Auric. Art Direction: Norman Arnold. Players: Harry Fowler, Frederick Piper, Vida Hope, Jack Warner, Alastair Sim, Valerie White, Jack Lam-

*1947: ODD MAN OUT, James Mason and Fay Compton in one of Carol Reed's "most significant films."*

*1947: A beautiful still from BLACK NARCISSUS.*

bert. Production: Ealing (Michael Balcon). 82 mins.

The first "real Ealing" comedy is a simple tale of a group of children who use the bombed buildings of London's City as their playground: through the astute reasoning of a fifteen-year-old boy, they realise that a popular children's paper is being used as a code by a gang of fur thieves. The story of their capture of the criminals is photographed with a fine sense of setting, e.g. St. Paul's Cathedral looming above its shattered surroundings, and the high spirits and soaring imaginations of the young cast exhilaratingly fill the screen. A spirit of hope is engendered in the sight of a new vitality among the reminders of recent destruction and tragedy. Later Ealing comedies were to have more bite and satire, more finesse and polish, but none exceeds the sheer gaiety of this opening fanfare.

**IT ALWAYS RAINS ON SUNDAYS.** Script: Angus MacPhail, Robert Hamer, Henry Cornelius, from a novel by Arthur La Bern. Direction: Robert Hamer. Photography: Douglas Slocombe. Editing: Michael Turner. Music: Georges Auric. Art Direction: Duncan Sutherland. Players: John McCallum, Googie Withers, Edward Chapman, Susan Shaw, Patricia Plunkett, Sidney Tafler, Jack Warner. Production: Ealing. 92 mins.

Though overshadowed by its descendants, this was notable at the time as a forerunner of the new drab-realistic school. Following the fortunes of an escaped convict until his recapture, it seeks to present life in East London (Bethnal Green) in a totally unromanticised light. The result is a sad film, as grey as the wet English Sunday that opens it, but one which is important in its intentions and influence, if not altogether in its own results. It also has the courage (which Galsworthy in his twice-filmed play *Escape,* for instance, lacked) of making the escaped man thoroughly undesirable. The final scenes among the railway sidings are excellently done, and Slocombe's photography exactly captures the prevailing melancholy mood.

**FRIEDA.** Script: Angus MacPhail, Ronald Millar, from the latter's play. Direction: Basil Dearden. Photography: Gordon Dines. Editing: Leslie Norman. Music: John Greenwood. Art Direction: Jim Morahan. Players: Mai Zetterling, David Farrar, Glynis Johns, Flora Robson, Albert Lieven, Barry Jones. Production: Ealing. 98 mins.

Though somewhat contrived, particularly in its melodramatic ending, *Frieda* presents a contemporary problem (the acceptance of a German girl in an English family) with sympathy and insight. Its theme extends beyond the confines of its own time and circumstances to the general and ever-present question of the treatment of outsiders, whether ex-enemy or just plain alien. The production marks the British film *début* of the Swedish actress Mai Zetterling, quietly and wholly convincing as the German girl.

**MINE OWN EXECUTIONER.** Script: from the novel by Nigel Balchin. Direction: Anthony Kimmins. Photography: Wilkie Cooper. Editing: Richard Best. Music: Benjamin Frankel. Art Direction: William C. Andrews. Players: Burgess Meredith, Dulcie Gray, Michael Shepley, Christine Norden, Kieron Moore, Barbara White. Production: London Films. 108 mins.

An interesting attempt to deal with psychiatry and psychiatric treatment as a subject in itself, and not merely as a convenient explanation of behaviour in a thriller or a drama, *Mine Own Executioner* concentrates on the practitioner, a layman reluctant to take on a case that he feels is beyond his powers, and who becomes disastrously involved in his patients' circumstances. The intelligent, if rather literary, script makes the whole thing uncomfortably credible, and mounts with growing tension to its climax. The sequence on the fire-escape ladder should drive anyone afraid of heights either out of the theatre or deep into his seat.

**NICHOLAS NICKLEBY.** Script: John Dighton, from Charles Dickens's novel. Direction: Cavalcanti. Photography: Gordon Dines. Editing: Leslie Norman. Music: Lord Berners. Art Direction: Michael Relph. Players: Derek Bond, Cedric Hardwicke, Mary Merrall, Sally Ann Howes, Jill Balcon, Bernard Miles, Athene Seyler, Sybil Thorndike, Emrys Jones, Alfred Drayton. Production: Ealing. 125 mins.

Coming when it did, this inevitably suffered from comparisons with David Lean's two Dickens masterpieces. Nevertheless, it has definite merits of its own, mainly in the performances (Sybil Thorndike and Alfred Drayton as the Squeerses, Cedric Hardwicke's stiffly villainous Ralph, Jill Balcon, in her film *début,* as Madeline Bray), and

*1947: Mai Zetterling in FRIEDA, her first English-speaking film, with David Manners.*

1947: BRIGHTON ROCK, a young Richard Attenborough brilliant as the vicious Pinkie, with William Hartnell.

in some of the always photogenic Dickensian settings. Its main fault is too much concentration on the melodramatic main plot and too little on the wonderful peripheral characters such as the Mantalinis.

BRIGHTON ROCK. Script: Graham Greene, Terence Rattigan, from the novel by Graham Greene. Direction: John Boulting. Photography: Harry Waxman. Editing: Peter Graham Scott. Music: Hans May. Art Direction: John Howell. Players: Richard Attenborough, Hermione Baddeley, Carol Marsh, William Hartnell, Wylie Watson, Harcourt Williams, Nigel Stock. Production: Boulting Brothers. 92 mins.

The film misses the subtle overtones and nuances of character in Greene's between-the-wars book, concentrating more on the sensational externals, and the activities of the ruthless racing gang. It does, however, capture the mood of nihilist despair and hopeless fear of those dark days. Richard Attenborough, at the beginning of an illustrious and adventurous career, transports from the stage his razor-sharp portrait of the vicious, sadistic, mean and cowardly seventeen-year-old, Pinkie.

THE WOMAN IN THE HALL. Script: Ian Dalrymple, G. B. Stern, Jack Lee, from G. B. Stern's novel. Direction: Jack Lee. Photography: C. M. Pennington-Richards, H. E. Fowle. Editing: John Krish. Music: Temple Abady. Art Direction: Peter Proud. Players: Ursula Jeans, Jean Simmons, Cecil Parker, Jill Raymond, Joan Miller, Edward Underdown. Production: Wessex. 93 mins.

This most unusual film, about a widow who decides to become a professional beggar to bring up her two daughters, claiming distant relationship with various well-off families and living a parasitical existence of their grudging charity, is original both in subject and treatment. Some of the later complications become theatrical, but the character of the Woman, and the outcome of her activities, remain admirably consistent, and are explored in some depth. The result, excellently played by Ursula Jeans, with Jill Raymond and Jean Simmons as the daughters, is a very interesting curiosity.

THE UPTURNED GLASS. Script: J. P. Monaghan, Pamela Kellino. Direction: Lawrence Huntington. Photography: Reginald Wyer. Editing: Alan Osbiston. Music: Bernard Stevens. Art Direction: Andrew Mazzei. Players: James Mason, Rosamund John, Pamela Kellino, Ann Stephens, Morland Graham, Henry Oscar. Production: Sydney Box. 86 mins.

The particular interest of this murder drama about a paranoid surgeon who kills a woman whom he thinks was responsible for the death of his girl and is apprehended because he delays disposing of the body to save a child's life, is in the fragmented time method by which the story is told. As Mason, in an excellent performance, tells his students about the supposedly hypothetical crime, both flashback and flash-forward are used in a manner now reduced to a *cliché* but a decided rarity at the time.

THE BROTHERS. Script: Muriel and Sydney Box, from L. A. G. Strong's novel. Direction: David Macdonald. Photography: Stephen Dade. Music: Cedric Thorpe Davie. Art Direction: George Provis. Players: Patricia Roc, Will Fyffe, Duncan Macrae, Finlay Currie, Maxwell Reed. Production: Sydney Box. 98 mins.

Grim cold comfort here, in 1900 Skye, where the arrival of an orphan girl brings to a head the rivalry between two fishing families (what would happen to fishing films if fishing families loved one another?), and among brothers even in the same family. Relentlessly realistic, unhappy ending and all, the film is impressive both in its scenic photography and in its reconstruction of details of island life at the turn of the century. Moral for young girls: if you join a fishing community, don't untie your pigtails.

## 1947: Facts of Interest

The Dalton Duty is imposed on imported films, an unfortunate step leading to ill-will with America and an embargo on exports to Britain.

The Circuits Management Association is formed, comprising the Odeon and Gaumont British circuits.

Shepperton Studios are acquired by Alexander Korda.

Death of G. B. Samuelson.

# 1948

HAMLET. Script: Alan Dent, from Shakespeare's play. Direction: Laurence Olivier. Photography: Desmond Dickinson. Editing: Helga Cranston. Music: Sir William Walton. Art Direction: Roger Furse, Carmen Dillon. Players: Laurence Olivier, Eileen Herlie, Basil Sydney, Norman Wooland, Felix Aylmer, Terence Morgan, Jean Simmons, Peter Cushing, Stanley Holloway, John Laurie, Anthony Quayle, Harcourt Williams. Production: Two Cities. 155 mins.

Olivier explains his use of black-and-white rather than colour by saying that he sees *Hamlet* as engraving rather than a painting. This is a cool, not to say a cold *Hamlet*, both as regards the play and the Prince—interesting rather than moving. It is, too, a *Hamlet* in which the Castle predominates, dwarfing, with obvious intent, the small figures who act out their human tragedy within it. The constant movement of the camera along those enormous passages and up those massive steps has been wrongly criticised as finicky: rather, they make of the camera itself a watchful inhabitant of the Castle, an intimate courtier as one writer has put it, almost seeming at times to eavesdrop on the events. Cuts in the text are, of course, inevitable, and generally acceptable: one may see Rosencrantz and Guildenstern go with mild regret, but the final entry of Fortinbras is a real loss, depriving us of the important life-goes-on finish so vital to the tragedies. Ophelia's death and the sea-battle are visualised: well enough, but perhaps some of the lost text could have been substituted. Gertrude is made to drink from the cup knowing that it is poisoned: the point is subtly made, justified or not. The final comment on Olivier's *Hamlet*, however, must be that it is a noble one—in conception and in execution. This all-important quality overrides any minor criticisms.

OLIVER TWIST. Script: David Lean, Stanley Haynes, from Charles Dickens's novel. Direction: David Lean. Photography: Guy Green. Editing: Jack Harris. Music: Arnold Bax. Art Direction: John Bryan. Players: Alec Guinness, John Howard Davies, Robert Newton, Henry Stephenson, Mary Clare, Francis L. Sullivan, Anthony Newley, Maurice Denham, Diana Dors, Peter Bull, Gibb McLaughlin. Production: Cineguild (Ronald Neame). 116 mins.

Comparisons between this and the same director's *Great Expectations* may be invidious but are inevitable. *Great Expectations* probably has the edge, if only because of the unaccountable omission of Fagin's last hours in *Oliver Twist*. On the other hand, nothing in either is more impressive than the opening of the second film, as the girl with the baby in her arms struggles across the lowering landscape to the grim stone building. Superb, too, are the scenes in the workhouse and in Fagin's boy-thieves' kitchen. The murder of Nancy, shown only by the bull-terrier's frantic scrabbling at the door, is one of the most terrifying examples of horror induced by indirect means, in all cinema. Guinness's Fagin, wheedling, imperious, fawning, sinister, impish, genial, oily, waspish by turn, is justly renowned, which makes all the more regrettable the shortening of the role. Altogether both of these films can only cause regret that Lean has not since made any other Dickens film: what of *Dombey and Son*, or even *The*

1948: Laurence Olivier's HAMLET, "an engraving
rather than a painting."

1948: *Robert Newton as Sikes and Alec Guinness as Fagin in David Lean's OLIVER TWIST.*

*Old Curiosity Shop?*

THE FALLEN IDOL. Script: Graham Greene, from his own story *The Basement Room.* Direction: Carol Reed. Photography: Georges Périnal. Editing: Oswald Hafenrichter. Music: William Alwyn. Art Direction: Vincent Korda, James Sawyer. Players: Ralph Richardson, Michèle Morgan, Bobby Henrey, Sonia Dresdel, Bernard Lee, Karel Stepanek. Production: London Films. 94 mins.

The first film with Carol Reed and Graham Greene together as director and writer. The idol is a butler (one of Ralph Richardson's finest performances), the idolator a small boy. Drawn into the butler's tangled personal life during a weekend when his parental guardianship is absent, the boy suffers disillusionment, then staunchly tries to defend his friend, who he mistakenly thinks has committed murder. Ironically, in his innocence he hides the very information which will prove the butler's innocence. As a suspense story this is on the highest level, but this is the least of its intentions. It is as a study of a child's awakening to human fallibility that the film must be considered. On the whole it succeeds, though there is a certain distance between our viewpoint and the boy's that is not altogether bridged. Perhaps only in the wonderful sequence of his flight through the wet, night-lit streets do we fully share his experiences rather than witness them, perhaps simply because the boy is so brilliantly directed that we subconsciously cannot but be aware of the skill of Reed's guiding hand. Even so, the film is always enthralling and often moving. When, in the closing moments, the boy runs into the arms of his returning family, we doubt whether he will ever again put in them or anyone, the trust he would have had three days before.

THE RED SHOES. Script: Michael Powell, Em-

1948: The butler and his idolator, Ralph Richardson
and Bobby Henry in THE FALLEN IDOL.

eric Pressburger, from a story by Hans Andersen.
Direction: Michael Powell, Emeric Pressburger.
Photography: Jack Cardiff (Technicolor). Editing:
Reginald Mills. Music: Brian Easdale. Art Direc-
tion: Hein Heckroth, Arthur Lawson. Players:
Anton Walbrook, Moira Shearer, Leonid Massine,
Robert Helpmann, Marius Goring, Albert Basser-
mann, Ludmilla Tcherina, Esmond Knight. Pro-
duction: Archers. 136 mins.

This is the most famous Powell-Pressburger film,
and almost as important in its influence on American acceptance as was *Henry V* fifteen years before. Presenting the world of ballet; dancers,
music, composers, impresarios; with enormous panache and flamboyance which fills the screen with
colour and movement, more from its incidentals
than its comparatively commonplace story. The
long, subjective ballet sequence is a *tour-de-force*
in which camera, director, choreographer, de-
signer and dancers combine to marvellous effect.
Moira Shearer, already famed as a dancer, makes
an enchanting *début*, with a strong cast going all
out in support. Powell and Pressburger are once
again refreshingly contemptuous of accusations of
vulgarity and lack of taste (e.g. in the final train
disaster): their films of this disillusioned, austerity-
stricken period stand out like bright splashes of
colour in the memory. A stringent test of a film
such as this is whether, when seen without its
colour on the small television screen, it can still
grip the attention. It can.

SCOTT OF THE ANTARCTIC. Script: Walter
Meade, Ivor Montagu. Direction: Charles Frend.

*1948: THE RED SHOES, Moira Shearer and news-paper partner.*

Photography: Jack Cardiff, Osmond Borrodaile, Geoffrey Unsworth (Technicolor). Editing: Peter Tanner. Music: Ralph Vaughan Williams. Art Direction: Arne Akermark. Players: John Mills, Derek Bond, Harold Warrender, James Robertson Justice, Reginald Beckwith, Diana Churchill. Production: Ealing. 111 mins.

A reconstruction of the tragic expedition, undertaken with immense care for detail, for which Ponting's film of many years earlier was found of considerable use. The breathtaking scenery and wild animal sequences almost overwhelm the human story, but the whole is treated in the epic manner, and it says much for the portrayals by Mills and the rest of the cast that involvement in their predicament becomes complete. So much of the viewer's reaction to the famous adventure is preconditioned by knowledge of its end that it is difficult to assess how much of this involvement is due to the film itself, but the dignity and integrity of the production are never in doubt, yet never self-consciously evident.

SARABAND FOR DEAD LOVERS (SARABAND). Script: John Dighton, Alexander Mackendrick. Direction: Basil Dearden. Photography: Douglas Slocombe (Technicolor). Editing: Michael Truman. Music: Alan Rawsthorne. Art Direction: Jim Morahan, William Kellner. Players: Stewart Granger, Joan Greenwood, Françoise Rosay, Flora Robson, Peter Bull. Production: Ealing. 96 mins.

The period reconstruction is stunning and seemingly accurate; the subject is interesting—the little-

known love of the wife of George Louis of Hanover (later King George I of England) for Count Konigsmark, and its tragic outcome. Directed with a fine swirling action, in beautiful sets, with two outstanding character performances from Flora Robson and Peter Bull, this is a most superior example of romanticised history. Ventures off the trodden beat such as this bring credit to British cinema.

QUARTET. Script: R. C. Sheriff, from Somerset Maugham's short stories. Direction: Ralph Smart, Harold French, Arthur Crabtree, Ken Annakin. Photography: Ray Elton, Reg Wyer. Editing: A. Charles Knott. Music: John Greenwood. Art Direction: Cedric Dawe. Players: Dirk Bogarde, Cecil Parker, Mervyn Johns, Basil Radford, Naunton Wayne, Françoise Rosay, Susan Shaw, Mai Zetterling. Production: Sydney Box, for Gainsborough. 120 mins.

Linked only by their author, the four stories are simply and efficiently treated by their four direc-

*1948: One of the magnificent period settings in SARABAND FOR DEAD LOVERS, Stewart Granger behind the pillar.*

tors, bringing out the well-known Somerset Maugham cynicism with brevity and wit. The experiment is a success in itself, and was followed in 1950 by the equally successful *Trio*. This type of compilation film could have opened a way for the filming of short stories, much preferable to that of stretching them to feature length. Unhappily the idea did not catch on, and has rarely been realised since.

### Short Films and Documentaries

THE CUMBERLAND STORY. Direction: Humphrey Jennings. Photography: Chick Fowle. Music: Arthur Benjamin. Player: James Nimmo. Production: Crown Film Unit. 39 mins.

Through the description of a mining engineer's experiences in refurbishing a run-down coal mine, Jennings paints a compelling picture of Cumberland country, with its sharp juxtaposition of natural beauty and man-made grime. Though not of the standard of some of his earlier work, the film contains many examples of his creative editing and his skill in raising the material from prosaic information to poetic interpretation.

### 1948: Facts of Interest

A.B.C. Elstree studios are opened.

Hammer Films Company is formed, with studios at Bray.

The Radcliffe Report is issued, suggesting fundamental changes in the objectives of the British Film Institute.

# 1949

**THE THIRD MAN.** Script: Graham Greene. Direction: Carol Reed. Photography: Robert Krasker. Editing: Oswald Hafenrichter. Music: Anton Karas. Art Direction: Vincent Korda. Players: Joseph Cotten, Orson Welles, Trevor Howard, Valli, Bernard Lee, Wilfred Hyde-White. Production: London Films. 93 mins.

Rarely can the atmosphere of postwar existence in a defeated city have been captured with such devastating accuracy than in this masterpiece of a film. The weary, cold resignation of the aftermath permeates every scene and every character, embodied in the gradual disillusionment of Holly Martins in his search for Harry Lime. Unforgettable scenes and shots abound: the first glimpse of Lime in the doorway with the kitten at his feet; the footsteps ending in the empty, echoing Square; the anti-climactic ride of Martins in the taxi; the famous duologue on the fairground wheel; the small boy's accusation of Martins and the ensuing chase; the high-angle shot of the three tiny figures on the bridge; Lime's last gesture of assent as he clings to the grating; the long, last shot of the girl's walk towards the waiting Martins—the list could be extended indefinitely in a film where every shot counts, but it is the overall picture that haunts the mind: a city, a world, a concept of life itself in defeat. Even the zither music, cheapened by overexposure and by attachment to a dismal television series, renews its magical aptness when seen again accompanying the film for which is was composed. The story of blackmarketeering, corruption, shabby compromises, bitterness and death, relentlessly holding though it is, seems itself a background to the battered city, with its bare, gimcrack offices erected in the midst of ruined Baroque palaces. With every viewing the power and stature of this great moving picture increases— one of the peaks of British, or any other country's, achievement.

**PASSPORT TO PIMLICO.** Script: T. E. B. Clarke. Direction: Henry Cornelius. Photography: Lionel Banes. Editing: Michael Truman. Music: Georges Auric. Art Direction: Roy Oxley. Players: Stanley Holloway, Raymond Huntley, Margaret Rutherford, Hermione Baddeley, Barbara Murray, Paul Dupuis, John Slater. Production: Ealing. 84 mins.

*Passport to Pimlico* may have lost some of its immediate edge nowadays with the removal of the restrictions it satirises, but its comic spirit, and indeed the relevance of its anti-bureaucratic standpoint, are as sharp as ever. The discovery that a small piece of Pimlico in South West London does not belong to Britain, but was decreed Burgundian for ever in a Fifteenth century charter, is the single joke (taken from an actual event in connection with the Dutch Royal family's exile during the war) from which comic invention spreads like the branches of a tree, beautifully combining the absurd with the eminently possible. For a country still under bondage to anachronistic wartime restraints, the whole affair afforded a joyous vicarious release. Script and direction combine in a vitality which never languishes, and though the characters may seem very much the conventional English comedy types, it is not they that matter so much as the situations in which they find themselves,

1949: THE THIRD MAN, *the climactic sequence in the sewers.*

1949: Barbara Murray, Stanley Holloway, Betty Warren and Paul Dupuis in Ealing's PASSPORT TO PIMLICO.

and the skill with which they deal with them.

THE QUEEN OF SPADES. Script: Rodney Ackland, Arthur Boys, from Pushkin's story. Direction: Thorold Dickinson. Photography: Otto Heller. Editing: Hazel Wilkinson. Music: Georges Auric. Art Direction: Oliver Messel, William Kellner. Players: Edith Evans, Anton Walbrook, Ronald Howard, Yvonne Mitchell, Mary Jerrold. Production: World Screen Plays. 90 mins.

After a slow start, this macabre story of an old Russian countess who is supposed to have sold her soul to the devil in return for the secret of winning at cards, mounts through four great climaxes to a height of tension and terror. The fantastically elaborate settings and *décor* might well have swamped the characters, but Edith Evans's toweringly sinister performance beats everything in sight, stand-

180

ing out still as one of the supreme examples of the grand manner on the screen. Dickinson's creation of a Russia of the imagination, of Pushkin's imagination, is a remarkable achievement, as is his whole handling of the nightmarish story, particularly when it is realised that he was called in only when all the preliminary work on the script had been completed. Cunning use of sound adds to the suspense, and only the very difficult final climax, when the old lady's killer thinks he sees her grinning at him from the Queen of Spades playing card, fails to come off.

KIND HEARTS AND CORONETS. Script: John Dighton, Robert Hamer. Direction: Robert Hamer. Photography: Douglas Slocombe. Editing: Peter

*1949: "A toweringly sinister performance." Edith Evans in THE QUEEN OF SPADES.*

*1949: KIND HEARTS AND CORONETS, Ealing's most stylish comedy, with Dennis Price and Joan Greenwood.*

Tanner. Music: Mozart's *Don Giovanni*. Art Direction: William Kellner. Players: Alec Guinness, Dennis Price, Joan Greenwood, Valerie Hobson, Audrey Fildes, Miles Malleson. Production: Ealing. 106 mins.

The most stylish of the Ealing comedies, this relates, with a diverting sense of black comedy at this time rare in the cinema, how an unscrupulous Italian Count plots the elimination of eight members of a noble family standing between him and the title, in revenge for their refusal to allow his mother to be buried in the ancestral vault. The various deaths are ingeniously varied and the whole thing carried off with the utmost sparkle and polish. Dennis Price seizes a chance he has only too infrequently had to show his skill at light comedy as a likeable scoundrel, and Alec Guinness as all eight victims presents a set of perfect cameos, if inevitably in somewhat small scale. Joan Greenwood is at her most captivating. It is to Hamer's credit that, except for a very few dullish patches, he preserves through a comic style so brittle, so easily fractured.

## THE SMALL BACK ROOM (HOUR OF GLORY).

Script: Michael Powell, Emeric Pressburger, from Nigel Balchin's novel. Direction: Michael Powell, Emeric Pressburger. Photography: Christopher Challis. Editing: Reginald Mills. Music: Brian Easdale. Art Direction: Hein Heckroth, John Hoesli. Players: David Farrar, Kathleen Byron, Jack Hawkins, Cyril Cusack. Production: Archers. 106 mins.

In a lower-toned key than usual, Powell and Pressburger return to the recent war in this study of frustration and animosities among the backroom boys—scientists thinking up bigger and better means of destruction, or prevention, of course, provided it is for their own side. It is an enclosed film, dealing with the clash of human personalities: efficiently done, not noticeably the work of its makers except for one surrealistic sequence ("bad taste," of course, from some critical quarters) depicting an alcoholic nightmare. The climax of the film is a triumph of suspense, as the hero dismantles an unexploded bomb on a deserted beach. Brilliantly angled shots add to the skin-crawling tension: the bomb hugely menacing in the foreground, the tiny figures watching in the distance as slowly—slowly—the metal grinding against itself, he disconnects the lethal parts.

## WHISKY GALORE (TIGHT LITTLE ISLAND).

Script: Compton Mackenzie, Angus MacPhail, from Compton Mackenzie's novel. Direction: Alexander Mackendrick. Photography: Gerald Gibbs. Editing: Joseph Sterling. Music: Ernest Irving. Art Direction: Jim Morahan. Players: Basil Radford, Joan Greenwood, James Robertson Justice, Gordon Jackson, Duncan Macrae, Jean Cadell. Production: Ealing. 82 mins.

It is the dreariest year (1943) of a dreary war, and the dreariest spot in the United Kingdom is the island of Toddy (or Todday—in reality Barra) in the Outer Hebrides, deprived as it is of the water of life, whisky. So when a ship with fifty thousand cases is wrecked off its coast the world—despite the efforts of the authorities to prevent looting—is transformed. With Ealing in a bumper year proving once again how much can be ground from a single joke, Mackendrick has drawn from an amusing novel a hilarious film, beautifully played by English character reliables. Fantasy is allowed to prevail over fact (the story is reputedly based on a true occurrence), to everyone's satisfaction.

## THE HISTORY OF MR. POLLY.

Script: Anthony Pelissier, from H. G. Wells's novel. Direction: Anthony Pelissier. Photography: Desmond Dickinson. Editing: John Seabourne. Music: William Alwyn. Art Direction: Duncan Sutherland. Players: John Mills, Sally Ann Howes, Finlay Currie, Betty Ann Davies, Edward Chapman, Megs Jenkins, Diana Churchill. Production: Two Cities. 94 mins.

In his first feature, Anthony Pelissier shows a nice sense of period, both characters and setting and is aided by some extremely attractive photography. Though rather disjointed, an episodic rather than continuous History, and missing the social implications of Wells's book, this saga of the small-time draper who burns his shop to start a new life offers many incidental delights—not least in the performance of John Mills, who also makes his *début* as producer.

### 1949: Facts of Interest

Islington studios are closed.

Rank sells Shepherd's Bush studios to television.

The National Film Finance Corporation is set up.

Cinema attendance show a drop to 27 million (from 31 million in 1946).

*1949: "A triumph of suspense." Dismantling the new-type bomb in THE SMALL BACK ROOM.*

# 1950

SEVEN DAYS TO NOON. Script: Frank Harvey, Roy Boulting, from a story by Paul Dehn, James Bernard. Direction: John Boulting. Photography: Gilbert Taylor. Editing: Roy Boulting. Music: John Addison. Art Direction: John Elphick. Players: Barry Jones, Olive Sloane, Andre Morell, Sheila Manahan, Joan Hickson, Ronald Adam. Production: Boulting Brothers, for London Films. 94 mins.

The strength in this suspense thriller about a deranged scientist who steals an atomic bomb and threatens to destroy London unless such weapons of destruction cease to be made, is in its frightening reality. The scenes of mounting anxiety, the mass evacuation in every conceivable means of transport, the shots of a deserted, doom-awaiting capital, are only too appallingly "possible"—the impression of actuality strengthened by the avoidance of star names in the cast, the cool, matter-of-fact narrative, and the unobtrusive direction. The darkly pessimistic message—that the only man sane enough to stand against the insane course that supposedly sane mankind is taking is, by official standards, insane himself—is given an added grimness by the fact that the authorities who "save" London (i.e. civilisation) are still, at the end, continuing policies which may eventually destroy it. Audience sympathy is most cunningly manipulated and confused. Barry Jones as the scientist is horribly reasonable and logical, and at the same time conveys a sense of tragic loneliness —a loneliness echoed in Olive Sloane's beautifully conceived portrait of the warm-hearted, music hall comic actress who befriends him. After this film

the Boulting Brothers enter a retreat, to emerge once more (in 1956) with the first of a series of films in which they comment on the contemporary scene in a more light-hearted and satirical fashion —but in the meantime they have given the anxious-minded filmgoer plenty to worry about.

1950: SEVEN DAYS TO NOON, Barry Jones as the "deranged scientist," with Olive Sloane.

CHANCE OF A LIFETIME. Script: Walter Greenwood, Bernard Miles. Direction: Bernard Miles. Photography: Eric Cross. Editing: Alan Osbiston. Art Direction: Donald Russell. Players: Basil Radford, Bernard Miles, Niall MacGinnis, Geoffrey Keen, Kenneth More, Josephine Wilson. Production: Bernard Miles. 89 mins.

In its day a pioneer attempt to tackle the thorny question of labour relationships in a realistic and unbiassed manner, *Chance of a Lifetime* would appear to have as much, if not more, relevance at the present time, with its story of workers who—at the challenging invitation of the boss—take over the running of a factory. For a time they succeed, then run into difficulties, finally the boss returns, and there is an increase of mutual respect all around. The inexpensively made, studio-free production was a refreshing novelty when it first appeared: its gritty, grey, shabby factory setting and untheatrical playing give it a semi-documentary appearance of truth. It does not cloud the issues, even if the end result is more satisfactory than appears to be possible in real life. The film deserved greater public response and a wider showing than it achieved at the time of its release.

*1950: Julian Mitchell and Bernard Miles in CHANCE OF A LIFETIME.*

THE BLUE LAMP. Script: T. E. B. Clarke. Direction: Basil Dearden. Photography: Gordon Dines. Editing: Peter Tanner. Music: Ernest Irving. Art Direction: Jim Morahan. Players: Jack Warner, Dirk Bogarde, Peggy Evans, Jimmy Hanley, Robert Fleming. Production: Ealing. 84 mins.

Jack Warner's kindly copper suffered a Lazarus-like miracle after his brief death-concluded role in *The Blue Lamp,* and has been restored to apparently everlasting life in a television series. This inevitably colours views of the film from today's standpoint, but even at the time it was assailed (by a minority only, for it was hugely successful) as a false and cosy picture of police life and activities. It is, even so, an honest attempt to treat the conventional cops-and-robbers story in a realistic, near documentary way, and in its portrayal of routine, its carefully selected locations, in fact in most of its externals it very nearly succeeds. Unfortunately the casting of popular figures such as Warner and Jimmy Hanley at once predisposes the viewer to see a custom-honoured type of film, and it is the lesser-known crooks (notably Dirk Bogarde) who come most naturally to life. However, it contains several sequences of merit (the shooting down of P. C. Dixon is a genuine shock), and demonstrably succeeded as entertainment: it had a most salutory effect on British box-office receipts at a time when this was badly needed.

THE WOODEN HORSE. Script: Eric Williams, from his novel. Direction: Jack Lee. Photography: C. M. Pennington-Richards. Editing: John Seabourne, Peter Seabourne. Music: Clifton Parker. Art Direction: William Kellner. Players: Leo Genn, David Tomlinson, Anthony Steele, Bryan Forbes, Jacques Brunius. Production: Wessex. 101 mins.

The first part of this famous prisoner-of-war escape film, showing the digging of the tunnel under the vaulting-horse, is by far the most interesting—the subsequent wanderings around the countryside being conventional and surprisingly slow. Though based on a true story, the characterisation is thin, the real atmosphere of a prison camp hardly noticeable, and the whole brave venture treated in the manner of a boy's action story.

THE MUDLARK. Script: Nunnally Johnson. Direction: Jean Negulesco. Photography: Georges Périnal. Editing: Thelma Myers. Music: William Alwyn. Art Direction: C. P. Norman. Players: Irene Dunne, Alec Guinness, Andrew Ray, Finlay Currie, Beatrice Campbell, Anthony Steele. Production: Twentieth-Century Fox. 98 mins.

A minor pleasure is this story, based on a determinedly lasting legend, of a mudlark (small boys who scraped a living from the shores of the River Thames before it was embanked) who broke into Buckingham Palace to catch a glimpse of Queen Victoria whom he worshipped unseen, and was partially responsible for bringing her from her post-Albert Memorial seclusion. The latter part of the tale may be taken as apocryphal. The film, beautifully photographed, treats this little whimsy with just the right amount of seriousness-without-solemnity, pathos-without-sentimentality, humour-

*1950: THE BLUE LAMP, Jack Warner as P. C. Dixon, the character he later restored to apparently everlasting life in the TV series DIXON OF DOCK GREEN.*

without-facetiousness. A subplot about two lovers can be (in fact, had better be) forgotten. Alec Guinness obviously enjoys himself as Disraeli, and his long speech in Parliament, striking a more serious note, is a splendid interpolation. Andrew Ray is charming and unself-conscious as the mudlark. Irene Dunne has an earnest and rather endearing shot at Queen Victoria—not piercing that formidable personality, but perhaps inflicting a slight graze.

**LAST HOLIDAY.** Script: J. B. Priestley. Direction: Henry Cass. Photography: Ray Elton. Editing: Monica Kimick. Music: Francis Chagrin. Art Direction: Duncan Sutherland. Players: Alec Guinness, Beatrice Campbell, Kay Walsh, Coco Aslan, Bernard Lee, Wilfred Hyde-White. Production: A.B.P.C. 88 mins.

This modest film is sufficiently interesting and original to make it a matter for regret that Priestley's direct work for the screen has been so limited. A mild little man learns from his doctor that he has only a month to live and decides to spend everything on a lavish last fling in a high-class seaside hotel. Here, owing to a strike by the staff, he finds himself for the first time in his life a success. The potential sentimentality of the subject is skilfully avoided both in Priestley's literate script and in Guinness's subtle and wholly unself-pitying performance. The ending is a grim double-twist, and it is this refusal to compromise with a forced happy ending, perhaps, which was mainly responsible for the film's very moderate success.

**STAGE FRIGHT.** Script: Whitfield Cook, from Selwyn Jepson's novel, *Man Running.* Direction: Alfred Hitchcock. Photography: Wilkie Cooper. Editing: Edward Jarvis. Music: Leighton Lucas. Art Direction: Terence Verity. Players: Marlene Dietrich, Jane Wyman, Michael Wilding, Richard Todd, Alastair Sim, Sybil Thorndike, Kay Walsh. Production: A.B.P.C. 111 mins.

Hopes that a return to England might have led to a happy marriage between the best of Hitchcock's very distinguishable American and British work are not, alas, realised, despite the film's close connection with one of his favourite and generally most effective milieux, the theatre. The reason may lie in the script, which is confused and overlong, the characters (Hitchcock himself puts the

failure down to the weakness of the villain), or a mixed Anglo-American cast of which no-one is very good except perhaps Richard Todd and, though miscast, Alastair Sim. Much of the best Hitchcock was yet to come, but his one return home (up to 1971) was, in spite of two or three vintage sequences, a sad disappointment.

**STATE SECRET.** Script: Sidney Gilliat. Direction: Sidney Gilliat. Photography: Robert Krasker. Editing: Thelma Myers. Music: William Alwyn. Art Direction: Wilfred Shingleton. Vosnian Language: Georgina Shield. Players: Douglas Fairbanks, Jr., Glynis Johns, Jack Hawkins, Walter Rilla, Herbert Lom. Production: British Lion (Launder and Gilliat). 104 mins.

The 1950 Launder and Gilliat is a very well-made escape thriller describing the plight of an American surgeon who is called on to operate on the chief of a mythical police state, fails to save his patient's life, and realises he will also lose his own unless he escapes quickly. Fine all-round performances, and fast action leading to a magnificent mountain climb, make this a superior thriller in the Hitchcock style, particularly in the gradually dawning suspicion that something is rotten in the state of Vosnia. A special credit is deservedly given to the inventor of a complete foreign language in comparison with which Sanskrit sounds simple.

*1950: Douglas Fairbanks Jr. and Glynis Johns escape over the mountains in STATE SECRET. Hans Moser as the guide.*

## 1950: Facts of Interest

The British Film Production Fund is set up, financed by Eady money—named after the Second Secretary of the Treasury, Sir Wilfred Eady. A sum is deducted from box-office receipts and shared out between British films according to the relative amount of their earnings. The fund is voluntary, but becomes statutory in 1957.

The British Board of Film Censors introduces the "X" Certificate.

The number of British cinemas is estimated at 4,584.

Death of Humphrey Jennings.

# 1951

THE LAVENDER HILL MOB. Script: T. E. B. Clarke. Direction: Charles Crichton. Photography: Douglas Slocombe. Editing: Seth Holt. Music: Georges Auric. Art Direction: William Kellner. Players: Alec Guinness, Stanley Holloway, Sidney James, Alfie Bass, Marjorie Fielding, Edie Martin, John Gregson. Production: Ealing. 78 mins.

This year saw two of Michael Balcon's crowning achievements at Ealing, both featuring brilliant performances from Guinness, both directed with verve, wit and polish, and both from scripts which combine ingeniously twisting stories with shrewd tilts at social, commercial and political anomalies. In *The Lavender Hill Mob*, the slighter but more hilarious of the two, Guinness appears as an unnoticeable, respectable little employee whose job it is to supervise the transfer of gold bullion to the bank, and who, when temptation offers, works out an ingenious scheme for helping himself, melting down the metal with the aid of a maker of souvenir models, and shipping the result abroad in the shape of little Eiffel Towers. The ensuing chaos, involving among other things a chase after six tourist schoolgirls who have unwittingly bought the precious models, is itself a model of what an action sequence should be, mounting to heights of fantastic absurdity. The scenes in which the two resourceful amateur crooks mix up police messages and cause official cars to finish up in inextricable confusion are among the funniest of any comedy at any time.

THE MAN IN THE WHITE SUIT. Script: Roger Macdougall, John Dighton, Alexander Mackendrick. Direction: Alexander Mackendrick. Photography: Douglas Slocombe. Editing: Bernard Gribble. Music: Benjamin Frankel. Art Direction: Jim Morahan. Players: Alec Guinness, Joan Greenwood, Cecil Parker, Ernest Thesiger, Michael Gough. Production: Ealing. 85 mins.

A low-grade employee at a textile mill invents a fabric that will last for ever and repel all dirt: the confusion into which big business is thrown by this, the intrigues, chicanery and plotting by both workers and bosses when they realise how it will affect their own fortunes, are presented with considerable satiric force and the implications are quite seriously discussed. The last word comes from a humble washerwoman who asks what will become of her livelihood when nothing gets dirty any more. Less frenetically farcical than its predecessor, the film is a more solid achievement. The closing sequence, as Guinness suffers terrible humiliation when it is discovered his invention is a failure and his white suit falls off his body, is nearer tragedy than comedy—but the final moment reveals his undefeated determination to discover the error and start anew. The building where he works takes on the look of a sandbagged wartime dugout as his constant explosions shatter the windows and walls: and his bubbling, plopping, grunting chemical apparatus is a completely eloquent character in itself.

THE BROWNING VERSION. Script: Terence Rattigan, from his play. Direction: Anthony Asquith. Photography: Desmond Dickinson. Editing: John D. Guthridge. Art Direction: Carmen Dillon.

*1951: Alec Guinness and Stanley Holloway in THE LAVENDER HILL MOB.*

*1951: Alec Guinness in THE MAN IN THE WHITE SUIT.*

Players: Michael Redgrave, Jean Kent, Nigel Patrick, Wilfred Hyde White, Brian Smith, Ronald Howard.

The stage production of Rattigan's play about the closing moments in the career of an unsuccessful, humiliated and unhappily married classics master made an unforgettable impression, and the moment when the cold protective shell he had built around him was cracked by a kindly gesture from one of his pupils was almost unbearably moving. The film, with Michael Redgrave equally magnificent in the part played in the theatre by Eric Portman, follows the original closely and with as strong an effect—until the wholly disastrous ending, an ending which contradicts all that has gone before and leaves one wondering what all the fuss has been about. If this is a pusillanimous pandering to public taste, then it is as unnecessary as it is insulting. Beside this betrayal of trust (unhappily far from a solitary example) between film-maker and filmgoer, the miscasting of Jean Kent is of minor importance.

TALES OF HOFFMANN. Script: Michael Powell, Emeric Pressburger. English Libretto: Dennis Arundel, from the French text of Jules Barbier. Direction: Michael Powell, Emeric Pressburger. Photography: Christopher Challis (Technicolor). Editing: Reginald Mills. Music: Jacques Offenbach. Conductor: Sir Thomas Beecham. Art Direction: Arthur Lawson, Hein Heckroth. Players: Robert Rounseville, Robert Helpmann, Moira Shearer, Frederick Ashton, Leonide Massine, Ludmilla Tcherina. Singers: Bruce Dargavel, Monica Sinclair, Dorothy Bond, Graham Clifford, Murray Dickie. Production: London Films (Pow-

1951: Michael Redgrave as the humiliated classics master in THE BROWNING VERSION, with Jean Kent and Nigel Patrick.

ell and Pressburger). 127 mins.

On the whole, this filming of Offenbach's fantasy opera has been achieved with astonishing success. The fact that the style of the Prologue and the three Tales differs is clearly dictated by the original work. In the film each act has its special appeal: the dancing doll of Act One to the eye; the story of the Venetian courtesan in Act Two, to eye and ear; the tragedy of the singer and her grief-stricken widowed father in Act Three, where the camera is less adventurous and the setting less fantastic, mainly to the ear, as the music takes first place. Some of the synchronised voices of the singers do not match too well with their visible counterparts—notably Robert Helpmann—but in the main the device is acceptable. The whole is a fine display of colour, music, movement, fantasy, bravura camerawork—most successful, perhaps, in its earlier part, but enjoyable throughout.

AN OUTCAST OF THE ISLANDS. Script: W. E. C. Fairchild, from Joseph Conrad's novel. Direction: Carol Reed. Photography: John Wilcox. Editing: Bert Bates. Music: Brian Easdale. Art Di-

*1951: TALES OF HOFFMANN, Ludmilla Tcherina and Robert Helpmann in the second act of the beautiful Powell and Pressburger opera-film.*

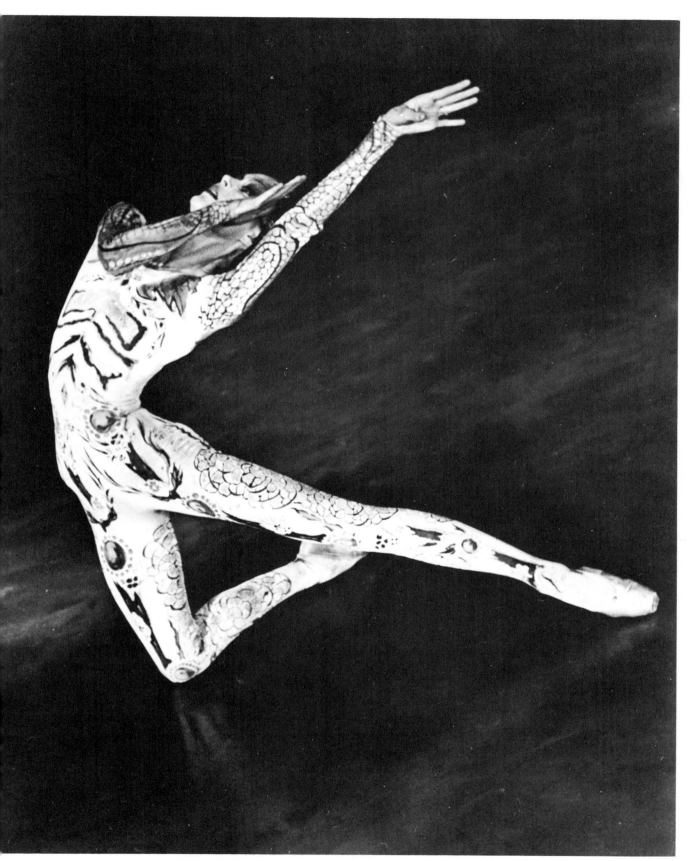

*1951: Moira Shearer in the Prologue to TALES OF
HOFFMANN.*

*1951: Robert Donat as William Friese-Greene in the Festival of Britain film THE MAGIC BOX, with Basil Sydney and Cecil Trouncer.*

rection: Vincent Korda. Players: Trevor Howard, Ralph Richardson, Robert Morley, Kerima, Wendy Hiller, George Coulouris, Frederick Valk. Production: London Films. 102 mins.

Conrad's strange, dark-shadowed studies of the shifting complexities of human nature are notoriously difficult to transpose to stage or screen. Here Reed probably comes as near as possible to visualising one of the earlier novels, aided by Trevor Howard's powerful, wide ranging performance as the self-destroying Willens. The atmosphere and the appearance of the Conrad locale has been well caught by Vincent Korda, aided in his turn by John Wilcox's sensitive lighting and

camera work. A strangely assorted cast is integrated with surprising success, except perhaps for Ralph Richardson as the man who befriends the outcast—a strange, eccentric performance interesting in itself but out of key with the rest. Reed secures an appearance of smouldering passion from Kerima as the dumb brunette.

THE MAGIC BOX. Script: Eric Ambler. Direction: John Boulting. Photography: Jack Cardiff (Technicolor). Editing: Richard Best. Music: William Alwyn. Art Direction: John Bryan. Bryan. Players: Robert Donat, Maria Schell, Margaret Johnston, Richard Attenborough, Robert Beatty, Renee Asherson, John Howard Davies, Stanley Holloway, Marjorie Fielding, Glynis Johns, Miles Malleson, Michael Redgrave, Eric Portman, Kay Walsh, Frederick Valk, Laurence Olivier. Production: Festival Film Productions (Ronald Neame). 118 mins.

Made as the industry's contribution to the Festival of Britain, and at the same time a homage to William Friese-Greene, the film is not so over-weighted with its own worthy intentions as might have been feared. Without material of high drama to build on, director and writer have been content to create a number of episodes in the cinema pioneer's private and personal life, often amusing, sometimes moving and only occasionally dull. Robert Donat is quietly charming, and Laurence Olivier stands out in his two-minute scene as a stolidly sceptical policeman.

## Short Films and Documentaries

WATERS OF TIME. Script, direction and editing: Basil Wright, Bill Launder. Photography: Reginald Hughes. Music: Alan Rawsthorne. Words: Paul Dehn. Speakers: James McKechnie, Paul Dehn, Felix Felton, John Slater. Production: Basil Wright, for Festival of Britain. 35 mins.

The first of the special Festival documentaries, made for the Telekinema, this deals with the numerous activities of the Pool of London. Poetic commentary (or heightened prose) and music are fitted to the photography in a manner reminiscent of prewar work in the field. The treatment is by now familiar, but the film is assembled with a

*Music-hall comedian Arthur Lucan made one film a year almost continuously between 1936 and 1952 with enormous success throughout the provinces, playing an old Irish washerwoman, with his wife, Kitty McShane, who generally appeared as his daughter. OLD MOTHER RILEY'S JUNGLE TREASURE, shown above, appeared in 1951.*

technical perfection that makes it worthy of its occasion.

## 1951: Facts of Interest

Denham studios are closed.

The Telekinema, later to become the first home of the National Film Theatre, opens at the Festival of Britain.

The Children's Film Foundation is formed.

A Documentary Film Festival is held at Edinburgh.

# 1952

THE SOUND BARRIER (BREAKING THE SOUND BARRIER). Script: Terence Rattigan. Direction: David Lean. Photography: Jack Hildyard. Editing: Geoffrey Foot. Music: Malcolm Arnold. Art Direction: Joseph Bato, John Hawksworth. Players: Ralph Richardson, Ann Todd, Nigel Patrick, John Justin, Dinah Sheridan, Denholm Elliott. Production: London Films. 118 mins.

By far the most successful parts of the film are the flying sequences, which are superb. With great skill Lean avoids the danger of monotony inherent in the fact that a pilot at the controls is one of the most limited objects it is possible to photograph (see the endlessly repetitive strained faces—goggled or not according to period—in one air-combat after another), and succeeds in involving the viewer in some of the stress and excitement of flying. The human story, concerned with a test pilot married to the daughter of a man ruthlessly determined to prove his scientific theories, is less interesting; and important questions such as the responsibilities of such inventors to the society on whom they inflict the results of their work, are too summarily dismissed. Now that supersonic bangs seem likely to add to the miseries of life for ever, the pilot's eventual success tastes more sour than sweet. However, taken as a picture of human endeavour somewhat superficially regarded, it will pass.

THE AFRICAN QUEEN. Script: James Agee, John Huston, from C. S. Forester's novel. Direction: John Huston. Photography: Jack Cardiff (Technicolor). Editing: Ralph Kemplen. Music: Allan Gray. Art Direction: Wilfred Shingleton. Players: Katharine Hepburn, Humphrey Bogart, Robert Morley, Peter Bull. Production: Sam Spiegel. 103 mins.

This famous British film (American director, American producer, American scriptwriters, American stars—beautifully photographed by English cameraman Jack Cardiff) is to all intents and purposes a twosome for Katharine Hepburn as a straitlaced but indomitable mission sister, and Humphrey Bogart as a tough sea-captain, as they journey on a dirty little trading boat escaping from German East Africa in the First World War. Despite many diverting scenes, and a few horrible ones (e.g. leech-sticking), monotony is only avoided in the end by the excellence of the two protagonists, bouncing performances off each other's personalities like a first-class ball game. The ending, with shipwrecks, a last-minute marriage, and an even laster-minute providential escape, is amusing but out of key. The couple should have died in the reality of their real stranded vessel rather than become involved in the artificiality of the gunboat activities.

THE SECRET PEOPLE. Script: Thorold Dickinson, Wolfgang Wilhelm, with acknowledgement to Joyce Cary. Direction: Thorold Dickinson. Photography: Gordon Dines. Editing: Peter Tanner. Music: Roberto Gerhardt. Art Direction: William Kellner. Players: Valentina Cortesa, Serge Reggiani, Charles Goldner, Audrey Hepburn, Angela Foulds, Irene Worth, Athene Seyler. Production: Ealing. 96 mins.

The theme of *The Secret People* is the attitude of the individual conscience to violence, and whether it is ever excusable to combat violence with more violence. Set in the Thirties, it deals with the plight of two sisters sent away from an unspecified European dictatorship for their own safety, following their father's death for political activities. Hating violence, the elder is drawn unwillingly into a plot to assassinate the dictator: the plan misfires, an innocent man is killed, she goes to the police and finally is herself killed. A bald outline necessarily omits many subtleties and ramifications in a strong plot. It is a remarkable film, full of original cinematic touches, and, in the framework of an exciting political thriller, dealing with one of the most fundamental problems of all times.

*1952: Valentina Cortesa in THE SECRET PEOPLE.*

MANDY (THE CRASH OF SILENCE). Script: Nigel Balchin, Jack Whittingham, from the novel *The Day Is Ours,* by Hilda Lewis. Direction: Alexander Mackendrick. Photography: Douglas Slocombe. Editing: Seth Holt. Music: William Alwyn. Art Direction: Jim Morahan. Players: Phyllis Calvert, Jack Hawkins, Terence Morgan, Godfrey Tearle, Mandy Miller, Marjorie Fielding. Production: Ealing. 93 mins.

The problem of the deaf child is treated with compassion and integrity: one of the great qualities of the film is the way in which Mackendrick has skirted the pitfalls of easy sentiment in the effect of the situation on the little girl's parents. His spare, cool direction allows the story to speak for itself, refraining from underlying the inherent pathos. Most ingenious use is made of the opportunities offered by the particular subject in the soundtrack. From little Mandy Miller Mackendrick coaxes an almost miraculous performance. Scenes such as her experiments with the balloon are deeply moving, and indeed the whole effect of the film is to widen the understanding of more fortunate families of the problems facing those afflicted. Much of the film was shot in an actual residential school for the deaf.

THE YELLOW BALLOON. Script: Anne Burnaby, J. Lee Thompson. Direction: J. Lee Thompson. Photography: Gilbert Taylor. Editing: Richard Best. Music: Philip Green. Art Direction: Robert Jones. Players: Andrew Ray, Kathleen Ryan, Kenneth More, William Sylvester, Bernard Lee. Production: A.B.P.C. 80 mins.

An excellent suspense story, made on a modest budget, tells of a small boy who, playfully snatching away a balloon he covets from a friend, gets himself involved in robbery and murder. Natural surroundings, realistic characters and backgrounds, and a skilful use of lighting and camera angles succeed in making the danger and drama frighteningly convincing, no small credit being due to Lee Thompson's skill with Andrew Ray, a skill he later repeats in a not dissimilar but subtler situation with the young Hayley Mills (see 1959).

BRANDY FOR THE PARSON. Script: John Dighton, Walter Meade, from a story by Geoffrey Household. Direction: John Eldridge. Photography: Martin Curtis. Editing: John Trumper. Music: John Addison. Art Direction: Ray Simm. Players: James Donald, Kenneth More, Jean Lodge, Frederick Piper, Charles Hawtrey. Production: Group 3 (John Grierson). 79 mins.

The Group 3 company was set up in 1951 to make second feature films. Their first production, *Judgement Deferred,* was unremarkable, but *Brandy for the Parson,* their second, is an amusing smuggling tale, rather similar in both style and content to the Ealing comedies, though on a smaller scale. Much use is made of countryside locations, and the whole thing has a disarming air of shared enjoyment.

THE CARD (THE PROMOTER). Script: Eric

*1952: MANDY, teaching the deaf to "hear" by means of a balloon. Mandy Miller as the little girl.*

*1952: Andrew Ray fleeing from his pursuer in THE YELLOW BALLOON.*

Ambler, from Arnold Bennett's novel. Direction: Ronald Neame. Photography: Oswald Morris. Editing: Clive Donner. Music: William Alwyn. Art Direction: T. Hopwell Ash. Players: Alec Guinness, Glynis Johns, Valerie Hobson, Petula Clark, Edward Chapman. Production: British Film Makers. 91 mins.

This version of Arnold Bennett's perky comedy about a Midlands washerwoman's son who starts his career with a smart bit of forgery and ends by becoming a town's youngest Mayor is really a series of loosely connected episodes set not too securely in the vividly created Five Towns country of the original. It is really a one-man picture, fortunately in the hands of Alec Guinness, who creates a believable character, more likeable if less bumptious than in the book and sufficiently colourful to keep the viewer amusedly interested in his lighthearted career.

### 1952: Facts of Interest

The Crown Film Unit is closed down.

The Telekinema becomes the National Film Theatre.

Death of Henry Edwards.

# 1953

GENEVIEVE. Script: William Rose. Direction: Henry Cornelius. Photography: Christopher Challis (Technicolor). Editing: Clive Donner. Music: Larry Adler. Art Direction: Michael Stringer. Players: John Gregson, Dinah Sheridan, Kenneth More, Kay Kendall, Geoffrey Keen. Production: Sirius. 86 mins.

One of the most commercially successful of all British comedies, and revived with monotonous regularity for years. On a straightforward story line of a vintage car rally between London and Brighton, scriptwriter and director have built a witty, energetic and often pungent little film about the effects of such an event on the relationship of the young couple involved and on their two friends who are also involved in the run. The pace is unflagging both on the road and during the midway Brighton interlude, rising to a climax when the two couples, mutually irritated by personal and mechanical rivalries, race each other back to London. Comparison with Ealing is inevitable, particularly as both writer and director had worked there, but the general tone is a little more acid than the blander Ealing product of previous years—indicating a trend of the times. The film is blessed with four superlative comedy performances but the real star is Genevieve herself, and enjoyable though the film is, its extraordinary and lasting success is at least partly due to the pathological British infatuation with anything on wheels.

THE CRUEL SEA. Script: Eric Ambler, from the novel by Nicholas Monsarrat. Direction: Charles

1953: *Three of the stars of GENEVIEVE, Kenneth More, Kay Kendall, and vintage car.*

Frend. Photography: Gordon Dines. Editing: Peter Tanner. Music: Alan Rawsthorne. Art Direction: Jim Morahan. Players: Jack Hawkins, Donald Sinden, John Stratton, Denham Elliott, Stanley Baker, Virginia McKenna, Moira Lister. Production: Ealing. 126 mins.

Monsarrat's long novel about the experiences of a number of naval officers during the Battle of the Atlantic, their lives on board and ashore, has inevitably suffered from the compression of its four hundred pages into a couple of hours screen time. As usual, action sequences far outclass human entanglements at home. The horrors of shipwreck by torpedo are depicted with terrifying realism: both the spirit and the material aspects of the period are reconstructed by a director notable for his wartime productions, with sufficient accuracy to give the impression that the film could have been a contemporary production. And at least there is no attempt to present war as really rather an exciting adventure, if a bit grim at times.

THE MAN BETWEEN. Script: Harry Kurnitz, from a story by Walter Ebert. Direction: Carol Reed. Photography: Desmond Dickinson. Editing: A. S. Bates. Music: John Addison. Art Direction: Andre Andrejew. Players: James Mason, Claire Bloom, Hildegarde Neff, Geoffrey Toone. Production: London Films. 101 mins.

With its story of black-marketeering and blackmail, kidnapping and killing in a war-scarred city, this film seems deliberately to invite comparisons with the same director's *The Third Man*. In neither story, characterisation. nor atmosphere, however, is it comparable with that earlier masterpiece. The story is much more conventional and melodramatic, Mason's character—most sensitively played though it is—has not the strangely epic quality of Harry Lime; the haunting sense of a cold, efficient, immeasurably deep world-weariness which so unforgettably permeates *The Third Man*, is missing. All the same, there are lesser compensations. The grey, grim despair of a Berlin which has not yet begun to rise from its ruins is well caught, and on a purely thriller level the film is gripping. Had it not appeared under the vast shadow of its predecessor, it would have served well enough.

*953: Hildegarde Neff and James Mason in THE MAN BETWEEN.*

THE KIDNAPPERS. Script: Neil Paterson. Direction: Philip Leacock. Photography: Eric Cross. Editing: John Trumper. Music: Bruce Montgomery. Art Direction: Edward Carrick. Players: Duncan Macrae, Jean Anderson, Adrienne Corri, Jon Whiteley, Vincent Winter. Production: Sergei Nolbandov, Leslie Parkyn. 95 mins.

Aided by coach Margaret Thomson, Leacock draws from Jon Whiteley and Vincent Winter two entirely captivating performances as a couple of small boys who, refused permission to have a dog, delightedly adopt a baby they find in the woods, and feed it on goat's milk. Grave consequences follow, and though all ends well this is no children's fantasy. Set in a grim Nova Scotia community during the early 1900s, the enclosed little neighbourhood ruled over by a dour patriarch consumed with hatred for the Boers who killed his son and who are represented among the local population, is drawn with uncompromising realism, even if his change of heart at the end is a little glib. Though no such comparable masterpiece, something of the atmosphere of René Clément's *Jeux Interdits* is discernible in the secret games of children isolated in a grey, sullen and uninterested adult community.

THE TITFIELD THUNDERBOLT. Script: T. E. B. Clark. Direction: Charles Crichton. Photography: Douglas Slocombe (Technicolor). Editing: Seth Holt. Music: Georges Auric. Art Direction: C. P. Norman. Players: Stanley Holloway, George Relph, Naunton Wayne, John Gregson, Godfrey Tearle, Gabrielle Brune, Hugh Griffith, Jack MacGowran. Production: Ealing. 84 mins.

A minor Ealing, perhaps even a little tired towards the evening of their long comedy day, but a very pleasant sunset for all that. The plot follows the familiar formula of ingenious comic situations branching from a central joke—in this case the determination of a group of people to run independently an unprofitable line of railway track. Gentle fun is poked at "foolish but lovable" English customs and manners but no real barbs are permitted to be thrown. It is all very nice and nostalgic to look at, and the Thunderbolt herself ties with Genevieve the old car for a high place in the acting honours for the year.

THE BEGGAR'S OPERA. Script: Dennis Cannan,

*1953: THE KIDNAPPERS, Vincent Winter and Jon Whiteley, with their "adopted" baby.*

Christopher Fry, from the original text by John Gay. Direction: Peter Brook. Photography: Guy Green (Technicolor). Editing: Reginald Beck. Musical additions and arrangements: Sir Arthur Bliss. Art Direction: William C. Andrews. Players: Laurence Olivier, Dorothy Tutin, Stanley Holloway, Daphne Anderson, Mary Clare, George Devine. Singers: Adele Leigh, Joan Cross, Bruce Boyce, Edith Coates. Production: Herbert Wilcox, Laurence Olivier. 94 mins.

The first film production of Peter Brook, noted stage director, seems in retrospect to be more of an exercise than a completed work. The lack of unity exemplified in the mixture of singing actors and synchronised singers is apparent in other aspects also, even to the colour values. One is left with an odd wish to shake the parts together in a vast bowl and hope they will coagulate into something more of a whole. It was an ambitious first venture to translate Gay's stylised semi-opera to the screen, and it would be interesting to see how the director would tackle it today.

**Short Films and Documentaries**

SUNDAY BY THE SEA. Script, direction: Anthony

202

Simmons. Photography: Walter Lassally. Editing: Lusia Krakowska. Piano: Betty Lawrence. Singers: Joan Sterndale-Bennett, John Hewes. Production: Leon Clore. 13 mins.

On a pre-recorded series of popular songs and ballads Anthony Simmons has constructed a kaleidoscopic picture of seaside visitors enjoying themselves at Southend. With a keen sense of the oddities and charm of human beings in moments of unguarded relaxation he combines a sense of pictorial values which Walter Lassally preserves in his beautiful, gentle-toned photography. Some of the incidents have been re-created for the camera, but the director has coaxed his amateurs to do what comes naturally, and the result looks wholly spontaneous—viewed with an affectionate and discerning eye. Here is Free Cinema before the term was coined.

THE BLAKES SLEPT HERE. Script: Jacques Brunius, Roy Plomley. Direction: Jacques Brunius, Richard Massingham. Photography: Robert Navarro (Technicolor). Editing: Bill Megarry. Music: Eric Spear. Art Direction: Bernard Sarron. Players: David King-Wood, Dorothy Gordon, Peter Coke, Ursula Howells, Rachel Gurney, Mary Kerridge, Bill Shine, David Marham, Erica (Kika) Markham, Petra Markham. Production: Richard Massingham, Jacques Brunius, for the Gas Council. 38 mins.

Richard Massingham's last film (he died before it was completed) is in some ways his most elab-

*1953: Richard Massingham's last film, THE BLAKES SLEPT HERE; Petra Markham and admirer.*

orate, with a very large professional cast and a time span of four generations, recounting the history of a house belonging to a typical middle-class family. Much use is made of small objects—doorbells, ornaments, furnishings, radios, telephones—to indicate the passing of time, in addition to old newsreels and photographs. The development of gas for light and heating is, of course, recorded, but not emphasised.

THE OWL AND THE PUSSYCAT. Direction: John Halas (Technicolor). Music: Matyas Seiber. Singer: Maurice Bevan. Production: Halas and Batchelor. 6 mins.

Claimed to be the first three-dimensional cartoon of fiction, this tells Lear's story of the journey to the Bong Tree land with grace and charm, and with a respect for their author's creations that might serve as a model for other animators.

## 1953: Facts of Interest

CinemaScope is first publicly shown in Britain at the Odeon Theatre, Leicester Square (*The Robe*).

The television threat to cinema audiences is accelerated by the great success of the Queen's Coronation coverage.

Death of Cecil Hepworth and Richard Massingham.

# 1954

ANIMAL FARM. Script: John Halas, Joy Batchelor, from the book by George Orwell. Direction: John Halas, Joy Batchelor. Animation Director: John Reed. Photography: S. G. Griffiths, J. Gurr, W. Traylor, R. Turk (Technicolor). Music: Matyas Seiber. Layout: Geoffrey Martin. Voices of all the animals: Maurice Denham. Narrator: Gordon Heath. Production: Halas and Batchelor. 97 mins.

The most interesting feature of a rather uninteresting year is this first British full-length animated film, which is also the first to present a story of over an hour in length with a serious theme rather than a fairy-tale. It contains 750 scenes and some 300,000 drawings and is for its time a major achievement in its field. Some blunting of the Orwellian barbs were probably inevitable, but much sharp comment remains, though the softened ending is a sad let-down, the author's whole point being that pigs and men were in the long run indistinguishable. It is difficult to see how a film of such integrity with regard to its source could have so compromised itself in its final moments. This, however, is its only major flaw. The draughtsmanship is at worst acceptable and at best inspired. The characterisations, aided by Maurice Denham's vocal *tour-de-force*, re-create the originals with commendable accuracy—most commendable in avoiding the ghastly cuteness and comicalities which would certainly have emanated from other stables. If Shaw is supposed to have written *Saint Joan* to have saved her from Drinkwater, we can only be thankful that Halas and Batchelor made *Animal Farm* and saved it from . . .

THE DIVIDED HEART. Script: Jack Whittingham, Richard Hughes. Direction: Charles Crichton. Photography: Otto Heller. Editing: Peter Bezencenet. Music: Georges Auric. Art Direction: Edward Carrick. Players: Yvonne Mitchell, Cornell Borchers, Armin Dahlen, Alexander Knox, Geoffrey Keen. Production: Ealing. 89 mins.

1954: Yvonne Mitchell gives a moving performance in
THE DIVIDED HEART.

A couple have brought up a young child whom they believe to be a war orphan. When he is ten years old, and looked on as one of the family, the International Refugee Organisation informs them that the real mother has been discovered to be alive and wishes to have him back. This account of an actual case in war-shattered Europe is treated with great sincerity and restraint by director and cast—all the more moving because it is entirely without emotional storms. Flashbacks, now so often used for mere self-indulgent effect, come naturally in a situation where memories are of such importance. The treatment of the Court and other officials—deliberately one-dimensional against the complex human beings with whom they have to deal, is particularly interesting.

**KNAVE OF HEARTS (LOVERS, HAPPY LOVERS).** Script: Hugh Mills, Réne Clément, Raymond Queneau. Direction: Réne Clément. Photography: Oswald Morris. Editing: Vera Campbell. Music: Roman Vlad. Art Direction: Ralph Brinton. Players: Gérard Philipe, Natasha Parry, Percy Marmont, Valerie Hobson, Joan Greenwood. Production: Transcontinental Films. 103 mins.

André Ripois, a sort of second-class Don Juan, is unable to form a lasting attachment: even when, at the end of the film, after a faked attempt at suicide which nearly turns out to be the real thing, he finishes up in a bath chair, held securely on one hand by his English wife, and on the other by her best friend whom he has tried to seduce—even then, he cannot control his roving eye. This is sophisticated black comedy, essentially heartless and cynical, directed with the requisite distance from his characters by René Clément, and played with cool elegance by the principals. An unusual film, perhaps out of its time for it did not do too well at the box-office of the period.

**THE MAGGIE (HIGH AND DRY).** Script: William Rose. Direction: Alexander Mackendrick. Photography: Gordon Dines. Editing: Peter Tanner. Music: John Addison. Art Direction: Jim Morahan. Players: Paul Douglas, Alex Mackenzie, James Copeland, Dorothy Alison, Geoffrey Keen, Mark Dignam. Production: Ealing. 92 mins.

Mackendrick followed his moving study of a deaf child's struggle to communicate, with a return to the Ealing comedy setting of his *Whisky*

*1954: The ironic ending to KNAVE OF HEARTS, Natasha Parry, Valerie Hobson and a captive Gérard Philipe.*

*Galore.* The Maggie is a small ship working among the islands which, like the Titfield Thunderbolt, has outlived its usefulness and is in danger of retirement. Through guile and cunning, her captain induces an American business man to fall in love with Maggie, to the extent even of losing his own cargo and paying for the continuance of the boat's working life. With a cast of mainly unknown Scottish players as the sailors Mackendrick exhibits an entertaining gallery of regional traits, neatly contrasted with the American of Paul Douglas.

**THE COLDITZ STORY.** Script: Guy Hamilton, Ivan Foxwell, from the book by P. R. Reid. Direction: Guy Hamilton. Photography: Gordon Dines. Editing: Peter Mayhew. Music: Francis Chagrin. Art Direction: Alex Vetchinsky. Players: Eric Portman, John Mills, Christopher Rhodes, Bryan Forbes, Lionel Jeffries, Frederick Valk, Ian Carmichael, Anton Diffring. Production: Ivan Foxwell. 97 mins.

An ambitiously mounted prisoners-of-war escape story, based on fact, and working up a considerable suspense. The whole set-up is treated as a boy's adventure story, and, except in a purely superficial way, nothing seems to have bothered the men less than months of confinement with daily uncertainty at the whim of an enemy, and with no knowledge how long their predicament would last. On its level the film is a well-made action yarn, and it is perhaps unfair to judge it by standards to which it is not intended to conform: but—based on fact—the viewer fortunate enough never to have undergone such an ordeal cannot but wonder . . .

FATHER BROWN (THE DETECTIVE). Script: Thelma Schnee, Robert Hamer, based on G. K. Chesterton's stories. Direction: Robert Hamer. Photography: Harry Waxman. Editing: Gordon Hales. Music: Georges Auric. Art Direction: John Hawksworth. Players: Alec Guinness, Joan Greenwood, Peter Finch, Ernest Thesiger, Cecil Parker, Bernard Lee. Production: Facet Films. 91 mins.

Though physically the exact opposite of Chesterton's runcible priest-detective, Guinness is so captivating in the part that this matters little. The emphasis is on detection rather than deduction from character as in the stories, but this does not seem to matter either, with Peter Finch, Joan Greenwood at their best, Hamer directing with unobtrusive style, and Cecil Parker leading a strong supporting cast. The religious element is played down to a degree, but Father Brown does have a few sharp points to make from the pulpit.

THE BELLES OF ST. TRINIAN'S. The daunting task of transferring Ronald Searle's horrific schoolgirls from cartoon to screen is triumphantly accomplished by Frank Launder and Sidney Gilliat. Three St. Trinian sequels appeared: BLUE MURDER, PURE HELL and TRAIN ROBBERY.

## Short Films and Documentaries

THURSDAY'S CHILDREN. Script, Direction: Lindsay Anderson, Guy Brenton. Photography: Walter Lassally. Music: Geoffrey Wright. Commentary spoken by: Richard Burton. Production: Morse Films and World Wide. 22 mins.

*Mandy* treated as a fictional story a particular case of a deaf child. *Thursday's Children* looks at an actual school where the training of such children is undertaken, from the understanding and recognition of words in themselves to the use of them as a means of communication. It is a simple, unaffected but affectionate record of children and teachers, apparently entirely unconscious of the camera, working together—often by instinct as much as deliberate instruction—to this end.

BOW BELLS. Script, Direction: Anthony Simmons. Photography: Walter Lassally. Editing: Lusia Krakowska. Piano: Betty Lawrence. Singers: Joan Sterndale-Bennett, John Hewes. Production: Leon Clore. 14 mins.

With the same team and the same basis of construction (popular songs) as in *Sunday by the Sea*, Simmons describes a day in the East End of London (with a brief journey to the West for contrast) at work and play, from the fish market to the chair in the sun by the front door, and to the traffic in the river. It forms a worthy companion piece to its predecessor as a record of life—brief and oddly touching—as it is lived in a small corner of time and space.

### 1954: Facts of Interest

Signs begin to grow—following the success of *The African Queen*—of American investment in British production.

British Lion announces huge losses.

Cinerama opens at the London Casino (originally the Prince Edward Theatre).

# 1955

RICHARD III. Script: Alan Dent, from Shakespeare's play. Direction: Laurence Olivier. Photography: Otto Heller (Technicolor). Editing: Helga Cranston. Music: Sir William Walton. Art Direction: Roger Furse. Players: Laurence Olivier, John Gielgud, Ralph Richardson, Cedric Hardwicke, Claire Bloom, Mary Kerridge, Pamela Brown, Alec Clunes, Stanley Baker. Production: London Films. 161 mins.

This is the most straightforward of the Olivier Shakespeares, if we except the recorded theatre of *Othello,* and generally held to be the most satisfactory. It opens with the crowning of Edward IV from the end of Henry VI Part III. Textual changes and transpositions have in the main been made with discretion, and for reasons of clarity deemed necessary for the swifter action of the film and the wider audience it was hoped to capture. The whole production is stimulatingly fullblooded, vivid and colourful. Olivier's magnificently evil (and totally libellous, but this is his author's fault) portrait of Richard gains rather than loses by the close eye of the camera. Only the battle disappoints—a skimpy scuffle, despite the King's splendidly acrobatic death.

THE LADYKILLERS. Script: William Rose. Direction: Alexander Mackendrick. Photography: Otto Keller (Technicolor). Editing: Jack Harris. Music: Tristram Cary. Art Direction: Jim Morahan. Players: Alec Guinness, Cecil Parker, Peter Sellers, Herbert Lom, Danny Green, Katie Johnson. Production: Ealing. 97 mins.

The last of the "Ealing comedies" is quite a grim affair at times, with Alec Guinness's Professor a truly sinister leader of a gang of thieves. The arrival of his horrific group at an old house near King's Cross where the Professor has taken lodgings with a respectable elderly landlady, ostensibly to play chamber music, in reality to plan an ingenious robbery, leads to some superbly bizarre confrontations. The gang are magnificently exaggerated types, and their interminglings with the landlady's genteel friends are among the highspots of all the Ealing series. The setting of the oddly baleful old house isolated amid the grimy railway surroundings is eerily atmospheric, and the film is also notable for its weirdly effective lighting—for instance the appearance of the policeman at the front door. Peter Sellers makes a comparatively brief and muted appearance in his only Ealing comedy, at the start of his career, and Katie Johnson, at the close of hers (for she died in 1957 after only one more film) achieved and deserved stardom after many years in supporting roles, as the vague, refined but by no means characterless landlady.

THE DAM BUSTERS. Script: R. C. Sherriff, based on accounts by Paul Buckhill and Guy Gibson. Direction: Michael Anderson. Photography: Erwin Hillier, Gilbert Taylor. Editing: Richard Best. Music: Leighton Lucas, Eric Coates. Art Direction: Robert Jones. Special effects: George Blackwell. Players: Richard Todd, Michael Redgrave, Basil Sydney, Derek Farr, Patrick Barr, Raymond Huntley. Production: A.B.P.C. 125 mins.

This great box-office success re-opened a door

# RICHARD III

*1955: Laurence Olivier's "magnificently evil" RICHARD III.*

*1955: Gang and landlady; Alec Guinness, Katie Johnson, Peter Sellers and Danny Green in THE LADY-KILLERS.*

which had never been very tightly closed, to a succession of Second World War films, of which it still ranks one of the best. The technical preparations for the raid on the Ruhr dams are factual enough to be interesting, and sufficiently dramatised to be exciting. For the raid itself a model of about twenty feet across was erected in a studio set of lake and countryside one hundred feet square: at the appropriate moment the water was disturbed by submerged air-jets and an actual full-scale explosion superimposed. The result, except for one or two approach shots, is reasonably convincing, at least on a first viewing. Commendably, the film—devoid of heroics—sets the loss of life against the success of the mission in the final summing up—of British life, that is. What happened to any farms and homesteads in the path of the loosened floodwaters is not so closely considered.

*1955: THE DAM BUSTERS, the huge model set created for the raid sequence.*

211

THE PRISONER. Script: Bridget Boland, from her own play. Direction: Peter Glenville. Photography: Reginald Wyer. Editing: Freddie Wilson. Music: Benjamin Frankel. Art Direction: John Hawkesworth. Players: Alec Guinness, Jack Hawkins, Wilfred Lawson, Kenneth Griffith, Raymond Huntley, Jeannette Sterke, Ronald Lewis. Production: Facet Films. 94 mins.

Though often supposed to have been based on the character and ordeal of Cardinal Mindzenty, Bridget Boland's play was in fact written before the trial and its aftermath were known. The subtle interplay between the priest and his interrogator forms the core of the film, as of the play, and the opening out of the action to follow an irrelevant love affair and include scenes of the city beyond the building weakens the essential claustrophobic atmosphere of imprisonment and examination. Apart from this the grip is unrelenting, totally compelling in the shifting play of character and argument, and superbly played by Guinness in his original stage role, and Jack Hawkins as the Interrogator. The measure of Peter Glenville's success in direction is the power of these two great performances.

THE QUATERMASS EXPERIMENT (THE CREEPING UNKNOWN). Script: Richard Landau, based on the television play by Nigel Kneale. Direction: Val Guest. Photography: Jimmy Harvey. Editing: James Needs. Art Direction: J. Elder Wills. Players: Brian Donlevy, Jack Warner, Margia Dean, Richard Wordsworth. Production: Hammer. 82 mins.

Preceding by two years the Hammer upsurge set off by *The Curse of Frankenstein* (and culminating in the company's receiving the Queen's Award to Industry), this is a modestly made essay in horror derived from an exceedingly successful television serial. The sole survivor of a space rocket team begins, soon after his return in a state of shock, to turn into a nasty kind of fungus-like vegetable. His wife is understandably put out at this transformation, and he leaves her to wander around London feeding on human and animal blood, ending up—a mere slimy mess—in, of all places, Westminster Abbey. Unperturbed, Professor Quatermass, who began it all, starts work on another rocket (and another mess, no doubt). A brisk, matter-of-fact approach, smart direction and ex-

cellent effects suspend disbelief for as long as is necessary, and there is even a touch of pity as well as horror for the veg-man. Quatermass will be in trouble again in 1967, this time with the discovery of evil personifications buried deep below the London Underground system.

RAISING A RIOT. Script: Ian Dalrymple, Hugh Percival, James Matthews, from a novel by Alfred Toombs. Direction: Wendy Toye. Photography: Christopher Challis (Technicolor). Editing: Albert Rule. Music: Bruce Montgomery. Art Direction: Joseph Bato. Players: Kenneth More, Shelagh Fraser, Mandy Miller, Gary Billings. Production: Wessex. 91 mins.

Kenneth More continues to build on his reputation as one of the British cinema's most engaging personalities, as he tries to cope single-handed with three energetic children by running his house with Naval discipline. A light comedy in the *Genevieve* tradition (though without the earlier film's bite), this is an example of the small-scale, fill-up production which not infrequently affords more pleasure by its general expertise and cinematic sense than many a more pretentious effort.

### Short Films and Documentaries

THE BESPOKE OVERCOAT. Script: Wolf Mankowitz. Direction: Jack Clayton. Photography: Wolfgang Suschitzky. Editing: Stanley Hawkes. Music: Georges Auric. Art Direction: Anthony Masters. Players: Alfie Bass, David Kossoff, Alan Tilvern, Alf Dean. Production: Remus (Jack Clayton). 33 mins.

This short, about a little Jewish clerk's yearning for a warm sheepskin coat, marks Jack Clayton's *début* as director after wide experience as assistant and in production. In it he shows already the sensitivity and feeling for the medium which are to give quality to his regrettably infrequent films in the years to come.

### 1955: Facts of Interest

A new British Lion Company is formed, acquiring by an issue of shares the net assets of the old.

The number of cinemas in Britain is approximately 4,500.

# 1956

MOBY DICK. Script: Ray Bradbury, John Huston, from Herman Melville's novel. Direction: John Huston. Photography: Oswald Morris, Freddie Francis (Technicolor). Editing: Russell Lloyd. Music: Philip Stainton. Players: Gregory Peck, Richard Basehart, Orson Welles, Leo Genn, Harry Andrews, Bernard Miles, Mervyn Johns. Production: Moulin Pictures (John Huston). 115 mins.

The "layers of meaning" which enwrap the symbolism of Melville's great book are probably impossible to represent in visual terms, and Huston's film treats the story as a straightforward adventure, with little suggestion of the mysterious and awesome terror of the original. Moby Dick is a dangerous whale rather than an ominous portent; Ahab is a man with an anti-whale fixation rather than a being racked and rent with emotions he himself cannot consciously comprehend. If no more is looked for, this is a notable achievement. The action sequences are thrilling, the color startlingly beautiful. For the latter Huston and Oswald Morris worked out a special desaturation process, overlaying the three colour negatives with a grey fourth to give the appearance of an old aquatint. For all its ultimate failings, this is the most interesting picture of the year—an honourable failure. And there are Orson Welles's tremendous few minutes as Father Mapple.

REACH FOR THE SKY. Script: Lewis Gilbert, based on Paul Brickhill's biography. Direction: Paul Brickhill. Photography: Jack Asher. Editing: John Shirley. Music: John Addison. Art Direction: Bernard Robinson. Players: Kenneth More, Muriel Pavlov, Lyndon Brook, Alexander Knox, Lee Patterson. Production: Pinnacle Productions. 135 mins.

The fact that the subject (Douglas Bader) of a true story of personal courage and mental resilience is a still living legend, and is portrayed by a popular actor, inevitably results in a feeling of restraint, of a sense of "not being able to tell all" that places a sort of glass wall between the viewer and the events viewed. Paradoxically, it is possible to get closer to a figure in a remoter past, about whom in all probability less can be discovered. The sincere intentions and general integrity of the film is clear, but it is impossible not to wonder, while watching it, what Douglas Bader is thinking of Kenneth More's portrayal of him—actor and sub-

1956: REACH FOR THE SKY, Kenneth More as Douglas Bader.

ject thus remain separated. More plays with charm, humour, and a conscientious lack of sycophancy towards the original, and the film, as film-making, is as competent as the majority of war-based epics. But always there is the feeling —justified or not—of hands being tied.

THE BATTLE OF THE RIVER PLATE (PURSUIT OF THE GRAF SPEE). Script, Direction: Michael Powell, Emeric Pressburger. Photography: Christopher Challis (Technicolor). Editing: Reginald Mills. Music: Brian Easdale. Art Direction: Arthur Lawson, Hein Heckroth. Players: John Gregson, Peter Finch, Ian Hunter, Jack Gwillim, Bernard Lee. Production: Arcturus (Powell and Pressburger). 119 mins.

A straightforward reconstruction, in documen-tary style, of the naval battle which resulted in the sinking of the Graf Spee, told with the emphasis—both of importance and sympathy—fairly evenly divided. The outstanding performance is that of Peter Finch as Captain Langsdorff. All concerned, in fact, seem to have behaved in gentlemanly fash-ion when not actually trying to kill one another. The film is, let us say, solidly made, and gives an impression of scrupulous accuracy, but it is doubt-ful if, without knowing the makers, any filmgoer would recognise the work of Powell and Press-burger, whose flamboyantly exhilarating imagi-nations are here firmly—perhaps too firmly—under control.

YIELD TO THE NIGHT (BLONDE SINNER). Script: John Cresswell, Joan Henry, from the lat-

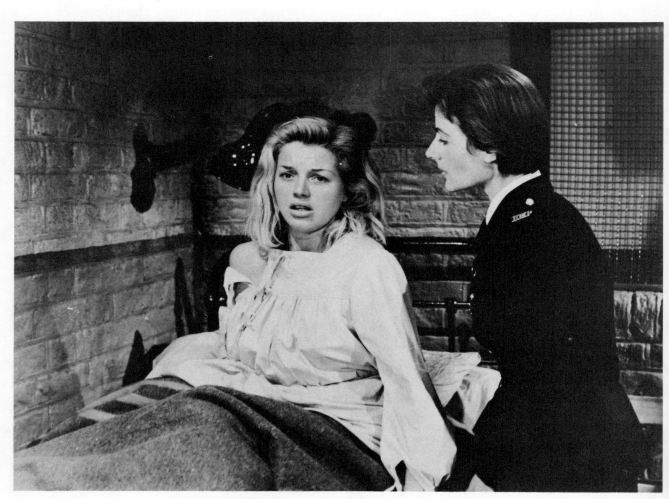

*1956: Diana Dors in an unusual role in YIELD TO THE NIGHT, with Yvonne Mitchell.*

ter's novel. Direction: J. Lee Thompson. Photography: Gilbert Taylor. Editing: Richard Best. Music: Ray Martin. Art Direction: Robert Jones. Players: Yvonne Mitchell, Diana Dors, Michael Craig, Marie Ney, Geoffrey Keen, Liam Redmond, Olga Lindo. Production: Associated British. 99 mins.

This is a serious attempt to study the mind of a murderess. Diana Dors plays (remarkably well) Mary Hilton, an unhappily married woman who falls in love with a night club pianist. She leaves her husband, he his girl friend. Later, still infatuated with his girl friend and now turned down by her, he kills himself. Mary, broken and desperate, kills the girl. From this deliberately commonplace story, told from the condemned cell in flashbacks, director and writer investigate the mental make-up of the woman which led her to do what she did. Soberly directed and played, no concessions made, the film is interesting and often moving, even if—as a case against capital punishment —its circumstances are too special for its arguments to be conclusive.

**THE GREEN MAN.** Script: Sidney Gilliat, Frank Launder, from their play, *Meet a Body*. Direction: Robert Day. Photography: Gerald Gibbs. Editing: Bernard Gribble. Music: Cedric Thorpe Davie. Art Direction: Wilfred Shingleton. Players: Alastair Sim, George Cole, Jill Adams, Terry-Thomas, Colin Gordon, Dora Bryan, Raymond Huntley. Production: Grenadier Films (Launder and Gilliat). 80 mins.

In a year devoid of peaks, this minor but enjoyable comedy-thriller may be noted, with Alastair Sim at his best as a professional assassin on the job, Raymond Huntley at his best as the potential and pompous victim, and a story which, despite a few dull patches and elderly jokes, is brightened by quick and competent direction. The chaos brought to a small and respectable South Coast hotel is the highlight and might have been made more of, but at least the film has the sense to know it shouldn't go on too long.

**THE LONG ARM.** Script: Janet Green, Robert Barr. Direction: Charles Frend. Photography: Gordon Dines. Editing: Gordon Stone. Music: Gerbrand Schurmann. Players: Jack Hawkins, John Stratton, Dorothy Alison, Michael Brooke, Geof-

*1956: Alastair Sim, versatile character actor for over thirty years of British cinema, especially in parts that combine the eccentric and the sinister, as he appears in THE GREEN MAN.*

frey Keen. Production: Ealing. 96 mins.

This crime thriller has the melancholy distinction of being the last film to come from Ealing studios before they were sold to television. As the final curtain to a long and famous run one could have wished, perhaps, for something more striking. However, it is a neat enough mystery, with a good *dénouement* at the Royal Festival Hall. As an example of well-made, unpretentious entertainment, it will suffice as a modest farewell to one of the most successful and affectionately remembered episodes of the British cinema story.

### Short Films and Documentaries

**TOGETHER.** Script: Denis Horne. Direction: Lorenza Mazzetti. Photography: Hamid Harari, Geoffrey Simpson, Walter Lassally, John Fletcher. Editing: Lindsay Anderson. Music: Daniele Paris. Players: Michael Andrews, Eduardo Paolozzi, Valy,

Denis Richardson, Cecilia May. Production: British Film Institute Production Committee. 52 mins.

A study of two deaf-and-dumb dock workers who live together in a single room in a shabby East London house. The ending is tragic—when one of the men is killed by a member of a group of children who have been mocking them—and the film as a whole draws a grey, desolate picture of the essential loneliness of life. Compassion and insight lift it far above the merely depressing, so that for a brief hour we share, rather than merely pity, the enclosed lives of the afflicted.

THE HISTORY OF THE CINEMA. Script: John Halas, Nicholas Spargo. Direction: John Halas. Photography: Bill Traylor, Roy Turk (Eastmancolor). Music: Jack King. Design: Ted Pettingell. Animation: Harold Whittaker. Commentator: Maurice Denham. Production: Halas and Batchelor. 8 mins.

One of Halas and Batchelor's most amusing and inventive cartoons, poking fun at the extravagances, whims, fancies, and wild absurdities which have arisen throughout cinematic history.

### 1956: Facts of Interest

Ealing studios are sold by Michael Balcon to the B.B.C.

New Elstree studios are bought by the Danziger brothers, prolific producers of supporting features.

The first *New Cinema* programme is held at the National Film Theatre.

The number of cinema closures continues to increase.

*1956: In this still from the Children's Film Foundation serial, FIVE CLUES TO FORTUNE, the fourteen-year-old David Hemmings can be seen (third from left) in his first film appearance.*

# 1957

THE BRIDGE ON THE RIVER KWAI. Script: Pierre Boulle, Carl Foreman, from the former's novel. Direction: David Lean. Photography: Jack Hildyard (Technicolor). Editing: Peter Taylor. Music: Malcolm Arnold. Art Direction: Donald M. Ashton. Players: Alec Guinness, Jack Hawkins, Sessue Hayakawa, William Holden, James Donald, Geoffrey Horne, Andre Morell. Production: Horizon (Sam Spiegel). 161 mins.

The bridge, an important link in Japanese communications, is being built by Japanese prisoners-of-war. Colonel Nicholson, after a confrontation with the Japanese camp commander over a matter of principle, determines that it shall also be a monument to their efficiency and invincibility, regardless of the fact that it is to be used for enemy purposes. Meantime, unknown to him, a small British commando unit is sent out to destroy the bridge. In the confused struggle that follows, the Colonel and others are killed. Nicholson, as he dies, falls on the detonator that destroys his bridge. The film is produced on an epic scale, but it is also a masterpiece of ironic ambiguity. We are presented with, and our sympathies divided between, four protagonists. It is therefore a film likely to be interpreted differently by each individual. To some Nicholson is a fool, to others a hero, to others a traitor, to others a man of vision, to yet others a man of plain commonsense. Thus the confusion and uncertainty of the final moments is seen to be fitting and deliberate: the doctor's final cry of "Madness, madness!" will mean whatever the viewer, in his prejudgement, thinks it ought to mean. It will not convert, because it presents no point of view, and all points of view equally: but it will (and has, ever since its first appearance) promote discussion and a reconsideration of values—and therein lies its own value. In all respects, emotional, cerebral, aesthetic, technical, it is a major work of screen art.

ACROSS THE BRIDGE. Script: Guy Elmes, Denis Freeman, from a story by Graham Greene. Direction: Ken Annakin. Photography: Reginald Wyer. Editing: Alfred Roome. Music: James Bernard. Art Direction: Cedric Dawe. Players: Rod Steiger, David Knight, Maria Landi, Noël Willman, Bernard Lee, Bill Nagy. Production: Rank. 103 mins.

This strange film, full of Graham Greene undertones, is notable for a highly effective—if also somewhat affected—performance by Rod Steiger. He plays Carl Schaffner, a financier who flees to Mexico to escape arrest for fraud. On the way he contrives to exchange identities with a man named Scarff who resembles him, only to find that the latter is wanted by the Mexican police. After revealing who he really is—and leading Scarff to his death—he is himself lured to the bridge on the Mexican-American border by the Scotland Yard inspector who has been hunting him, through means of a pet dog. There, Schaffner meets his own death. The typical Greene use of a thriller plot for a study of grubby desperation is accurately developed in both aspects. The gradual breaking down of the scoundrelly but engaging Schaffner to the state where he will risk his freedom, and lose his life, for a stray dog is presented with subtlety and compelling force by Ken Annakin, echoes of

*1957: The ironically ambiguous climax to THE
BRIDGE ON THE RIVER KWAI, Alec Guinness on
the left.*

*1957: Rod Steiger in ACROSS THE BRIDGE.*

Hitchcock in no way smothering his own individual treatment.

BROTHERS-IN-LAW. Script: Frank Harvey, Jeffrey Dell, Roy Boulting, from the novel by Henry Cecil. Direction: Roy Boulting. Photography: Max Greene. Editing: Anthony Harvey. Music: Benjamin Frankel. Art Direction: Albert Witherick. Players: Ian Carmichael, Richard Attenborough, Terry-Thomas, Miles Malleson, Jill Adams, John Le Mesurier. Production: John Boulting. 94 mins.

The second of a series of comedies, generally starring Ian Carmichael as a well-intentioned but unlucky blunderer, in which the Boulting brothers cast an indulgently satirical eye at sundry British institutions. The first, *Private's Progress*, made fun of military practices. Here it is the law that comes under their caustic scrutiny, from the writings of Henry Cecil, and the trials and tribulations of a young barrister are recorded with wit and a merciful restraint in the presentation of types that can only too easily be broadened into obvious caricature. Following so quickly on the demise of Ealing, the series—though of a style all its own—was doubly welcome as a continuance of one of the happier traditions of the not always happy British film comedy.

TIME WITHOUT PITY. Script: Ben Barzman, from the play *Someone's Waiting*, by Emlyn Williams. Direction: Joseph Losey. Photography: Freddie Francis. Editing: Alan Osbiston. Music: Tristram Cary. Art Direction: Bernard Sarron. Players: Michael Redgrave, Ann Todd, Leo McKern, Peter Cushing, Alec McCowen, Renee Houston. Production: Harlequin (John Arnold, Anthony Simmons). 88 mins.

This is Losey's third British film, but the first

*1957: BROTHERS-IN-LAW, a terrified Ian Carmichael is urged by his client (Brian Oulton) to tell the Judge he is wrong.*

on which he was credited as director by his own name. His two previous features were *The Sleeping Tiger* (1954) and *The Intimate Stranger* (1956). The plot is a suspense drama, in which an alcoholic father returns from a course of treatment in Canada to save his son from execution for murder within twenty-four hours. Eventually he sacrifices his own life, forcing the real murderer to shoot him. Viewed from the standpoint of Losey's later work, this is a minor film. Despite its double-meaning title, it has not much significance beyond its own story of a race against time and a man's redemption of a useless life. It has, however, a few sharp and shrewd comments to make on the typical "protester" (in this case anti-hanging) who is ready to proclaim his beliefs loudly when it suits him, but whose interest shrinks when it is a question of incurring trouble or difficulty, and when the chances for self-exhibitionism are slight.

A KING IN NEW YORK. Script, Direction, Music: Charles Chaplin. Photography: Georges Périnal. Art Direction: Allan Harris. Players: Charles Chaplin, Dawn Addams, Oliver Johnston, Jerry Desmonde, Michael Chaplin, Maxine Audley. Production: Attica (Charles Chaplin). 109 mins.

That Chaplin's first British film should have been accounted so complete a failure as to be hardly ever shown since its first appearance is one of the great disappointments of the period, and the fact that it contains a few sequences as funny

as his best tends to be forgotten. For most of the way, however, there is the sad spectacle of the sincere but unexciting personal thinker finally submerging the inspired universal clown. Even some of the jokes themselves fall flat, and the promising idea of a King seeking refuge in America from a revolution in his own country, and becoming involved in a television commercial world seems lost in the expression of a private bitterness.

SAINT JOAN. Script: Graham Greene, from G. B. Shaw's play. Direction: Otto Preminger. Photography: Georges Périnal. Editing: Helga Cranston. Music: Mischa Spoliansky. Art Direction: Raymond Simm. Players: Jean Seberg, Richard Widmark, Anton Walbrook, Richard Todd, Felix Aylmer, Harry Andrews, Barry Jones, Finlay Currie. Production: Otto Preminger. 110 mins.

Shaw's play has been scripted with great care and ingenuity by Graham Greene. The transition of the Epilogue to the opening is a bold stroke which might not work in the theatre but certainly does so here, and the flashbacks (or flashes forward), though they have been criticised as breaking up the action, serve rather to draw attention to the point of a work which was never intended as a mere chronicle of events. Jean Seberg's very inexperience is turned to advantage, marking her essential innocence and helplessness, despite the strength of her inner faith, as a pawn among the powerful and ruthless men surrounding her: it also serves to modify the hockey-stick bounciness of Shaw's Joan that can become so irritating when given full rein.

THE SMALLEST SHOW ON EARTH. Script: William Rose, John Eldridge. Direction: Basil Dearden. Photography: Douglas Slocombe. Editing: Oswald Hafenrichter. Music: William Alwyn. Art Direction: Allen Harris. Players: Bill Travers, Virginia McKenna, Peter Sellers, Margaret Rutherford, Bernard Miles, Leslie Phillips. Production: British Lion (Launder and Gilliat). 81 mins.

A story about a young couple who inherit a dilapidated flea-pit of a move house and, piqued by the patronising manner of the owner of the flourishing super-cinema nearby, determine to make a go of it, must have instant appeal for any filmgoer. Though not all the possibilities are exploited, the obvious affection with which the story is handled by the director and his photographer and art director make much of the film a nostalgic delight. As the ancient staff (projectionist, box-office manageress, doorman), Sellers, Rutherford and Miles make up a trio of comic eccentrics as rich as anything to be seen anywhere; and the moment when, in the quiet of the night, they settle down to weep gentle tears over the silent *Comin' thro' the Rye* in the empty hall is one of genuine heart-warming pathos. As for the Bijou Cinema itself, squashed under the grimy railway bridge, shaken by every passing train, deserted, dusty, plaster-peeling and poster-tattered, no-one (unless he happens to be interested only in such gross material things as money) could wish for a more enchanting legacy.

## 1957: Facts of Interest

The Cinematograph Act (1957) is passed, under which the Eady Levy becomes statutory.

The National Film Theatre moves to its permanent home under Waterloo Bridge.

The first London Film Festival is held.

# 1958

ROOM AT THE TOP. Script: Neil Paterson, from the novel by John Braine. Direction: Jack Clayton. Photography: Freddie Francis. Editing: Ralph Kempler. Music: Mario Nascimbene. Art Direction: Ralph Brinton. Players: Laurence Harvey, Simone Signoret, Heather Sears, Donald Wolfit, Raymond Huntley, Donald Houston, John Westbrook. Production: Remus. 117 mins.

The story of an unscrupulous young man's ruthless determination to better himself is told with harsh realism against the gritty, grey, stuffy settings of its Northern England background. Famed as the breakthrough to a franker treatment of sex on the screen, it seems mild enough by today's standards, the main step forward being a slightly

1958: ROOM AT THE TOP, Jack Clayton's "sex breakthrough film," with Laurence Harvey, Heather Sears, Ambrosine Philpotts and Donald Wolfit.

self-conscious duologue in which a young girl, after being seduced, says that she enjoyed the proceedings. Even at the time, the censor himself wondered what all the fuss was about. A greater claim to importance lies in the film being the first to present an uncompromisingly disenchanted view of provincial urban life. Sex would doubtless have reached the British screen in time anyway, but municipal corruption and chicanery could well have remained hidden beneath official carpets for long enough. The film aroused new interest in British production abroad and is undoubtedly a key work of the decade, not least in its introduction of Jack Clayton as a feature director, showing an adventurous, accomplished and individual talent.

ORDERS TO KILL. Script: Paul Dehn, from a story by Donald Downes. Direction: Anthony Asquith. Photography: Desmond Dickinson. Editing: Gordon Hales. Music: Benjamin Frankel. Art Direction: John Howell. Players: Paul Massie, Eddie Albert, Irene Worth, Leslie French, James Robertson Justice, Lillian Gish. Production: Anthony Havelock-Allan. 111 mins.

One of the most powerful indictments of war and the war mentality ever screened, Asquith's masterly film concerns an American ex-bomber pilot who is sent to occupied Paris in 1944 to kill an allied agent who is suspected of betraying his associates to the Gestapo. Not even permitted to inquire into the guilt of his victim, he carries out the job, discovers afterwards the man was in fact innocent, is broken by the ordeal, and only re-

1958: *Paul Massie as the ex-bomber pilot given*
ORDERS TO KILL.

covers when it is put to him that there is no such thing as individual responsibility in the circumstances. The gradual change from the pilot's cheery, unthinking acceptance of and training for his mission, to deepening anxiety as the actual time draws near is wonderfully conveyed by Paul Massie. The bomber happily accustomed to killing at a distance shrinks at the thought of having to face what he does. The actual clumsy, fumbling, messy slaying is one of the most horrifying scenes in all cinema. Unfortunately the sequence where he is told by a glib, pseudo-paternal military type that he needn't worry—in wartime, conscience and remorse may be conveniently buried—and so recovers something of his peace of mind, is curiously weaker than the rest, so that the sharp cutting edge of the film is very slightly blunted.

**A NIGHT TO REMEMBER.** Script: Eric Ambler, from the book by Walter Lord. Direction: Roy Baker. Photography: Geoffrey Unsworth. Editing: Sidney Hayers. Music: William Alwyn. Art Direction: Alex Vetchinsky. Players: Kenneth More. Production: Rank. 123 mins.

A painstaking reconstruction of the *Titanic* tragedy, this is mercifully free from pretentious allegory-hunting about man's *hubris* inciting the wrath of the gods, and so on, being content to record the disaster in detail derived from Walter Lord's vivid and carefully documented book. The director lets the courage and cowardice, the panic and stoicism, the efficiency and bungling of that night of disaster speak for themselves without straining after "cinematic" effects. Inevitably this is a group-movie, with a numerous cast presenting cameos rather

223

*1958: The sinking of the Titanic, model work from A*
*NIGHT TO REMEMBER.*

than sustained characterisations, but Kenneth More's Lightoller stands out as the officer from whose viewpoint the events are seen—the personal experiences of officers, crew and passengers, the tragedy of the great doomed ship itself.

**THE INN OF THE SIXTH HAPPINESS.** Script: Isobel Lennart, from Alan Burgess's novel, *The Small Woman*. Direction: Mark Robson. Photography: F. A. Young. Editing: Ernest Walter. Music: Malcolm Arnold. Art Direction: John Fox, Geoffrey Drake. Players: Ingrid Bergman, Curt Jurgens, Robert Donat, Ronald Squire, Noel Hood, Joan Young, Richard Wattis. Production: Twentieth Century-Fox. 159 mins.

An extremely popular and prestigious film, but it is a pity that a true story of such cinematic possibilities as that of a young English servant-girl who became a missionary in China and led a group of Chinese children to safety from the war zone, should have been glamorised and romanticised. A plain and inspiring tale of courage and faith thus becomes an escape thriller, complete with love affair and pretty, slant-eyed tots sweetly singing as they straggle, carefully ragged, over the hills. Ingrid Bergman's sincerity and dedication cannot, and could not be expected to, compensate for her physical difference from the "small woman" of reality. It is obvious throughout that this beautiful and famous Swedish film star will win through. Robert Donat has a striking few minutes in what is, tragically, his last appearance on the screen. A well-made, exciting escape story—but how much more effective had it moved a little closer to the real truth.

**DUNKIRK.** Script: David Divine, W. P. Lipscomb. Direction: Leslie Norman. Photography: Paul Beeson. Editing: Gordon Stone. Music: Malcolm Arnold. Art Direction: Jim Morahan. Players: John Mills, Robert Urquhart, Eay Jackson, Meredith Edwards, Anthony Nicholls. Production: Michael Balcon for M-G-M British. 135 mins.

A spectacular reconstruction made by Michael Balcon for M-G-M (he describes it as perhaps the largest-scale picture with which he had ever been connected), the story sets the experiences of a small party of men against the huge background of the mass evacuation. The treatment of the characters is conventional in the underplayed, anti-heroic manner, but the scenes of the long lines of men across the beach, the sailing of the little boats, the incidents of waiting and enduring and rescue—all these form a worthy tribute to the events they record.

**THE MAN UPSTAIRS.** Script: Alun Falconer. Direction: Don Chaffey. Photography: Gerald Gibbs. Editing: John Trumper. Art Direction: William Kellner. Players: Richard Attenborough, Bernard Lee, Donald Houston, Kenneth Griffith, Virginia Maskell. Production: A.C.T. Films. 88 mins.

This is a neat, taut exercise in suspense, credible and interesting. Richard Attenborough gives one of his best performances as the man in the upstairs lodging room who suddenly becomes violent, tries to kill a policeman, barricades himself in, and refuses to see or talk to anyone. As important as the mystery surrounding the man himself is the varied behaviour of those affected by it, whether intimate, his fiancée, or casual, the other tenants and the crowd in the road outside. In periods when major films are few, a cinema is fortunate if it can fall back on minor productions as good as this.

**CARRY ON, SERGEANT.** Script: Norma Hudis, from R. F. Delderfield's *The Bull Boys*. Direction: Gerald Thomas. Photography: Peter Hennessy. Editing: Peter Boita. Music: Bruce Montgomery. Art Direction: Alex Vetchinsky. Players: William Hartnell, Bob Monkhouse, Shirley Eaton, Eric Barker, Dora Bryan, Charles Hawtrey, Kenneth Williams. Production: Peter Rogers. 83 mins.

The first of the series that, thirteen years later, was to produce its twenty-first *Carry On*, having pursued a relentless course of scatological jokes, bawdy knock-about, "excruciating" puns, stock characterisations and predictable predicaments, to the tune of box-office bells ringing throughout the country. This early effort is not really typical in either humour or dirt, and it is not until number two, *Carry On, Nurse*, that things really get going.

### Short Films and Documentaries

**THE LITTLE ISLAND.** Script and Production: Richard Williams. Colour. Music: Tristram Cary. 33 mins.

Together with George Dunning, Halas and Batchelor, and Bob Godfrey, Richard Williams completes the four most inventive cartoonists in the present-day British cinema. This, his first animated film, took him about three years to make. It reveals a wholly sardonic and cynical view of humanity. Three little men, Truth, Goodness and Beauty, live on a desert island. Here, at least, should perfect peace and harmony reign. On the contrary, Goodness and Beauty are soon at war, while Truth keeps the score on a huge bomb that eventually blows up. The hilarious, doom-laden parable is told with a sustained imagination and technical skill quite outstanding for its time, particularly in view of the picture's unusual length.

## 1958: Facts of Interest

The Odeon and Gaumont cinema circuits are combined.

The Film Industry Defence Organisation is established.

Death of Graham Cutts, Henry Cornelius and Adrian Brunel.

Filippo Del Giudice retires to a monastery.

# 1959

LOOK BACK IN ANGER. Script: Nigel Kneale, John Osborne, from the latter's play. Direction: Tony Richardson. Photography: Oswald Morris. Editing: Richard Best. Music: Chris Barber. Art Direction: Peter Glazier. Players: Richard Burton, Claire Bloom, Mary Ure, Gary Raymond, Edith Evans, Glen Byam Shaw. Production: Woodfall. 101 mins.

In his first feature film Tony Richardson transfers the stage production of Osborne's epoch-marking play more or less straightforwardly to the cinema. Later on the angry young man phase was to be stirred up *ad nauseam* long after its original brief force was spent, but in this picture Richardson incisively and preserves its original score. It is, in fact, one of the most successful of all stage-to-screen transpositions, with only such "opening-up" as can be brought in with relevance, and allowing the abrasive indignation (and the self-pitying petulance) of the theatrical dialogue to boil over unimpeded from an excellent cast. The appearance of Edith Evans as the old cockney Ma Tanner (only spoken of in the play) is a notable addition. No doubt Richardson's feature *début* was made easier by his former knowledge of the play, but apart from his handling of the actors he brings an already assured touch to the handling of the story as a film.

SUDDENLY LAST SUMMER. Script: Gore Vidal, Tennessee Williams, from the latter's play. Direction: Joseph Mankiewicz. Photography: Jack Hildyard. Editing: T. G. Stanford. Music: Malcolm Arnold, Buxton Orr. Art Direction: Oliver Messel.

Players: Katharine Hepburn, Elizabeth Taylor, Montgomery Clift, Albert Dekker, Mercedes McCambridge. Production: Horizon British (Sam Spiegel). 114 mins.

Basing his play on a familiar theatrical plot—the posthumous discovery that a dead man (usually an artist, here a poet) had feet of clay—Tennessee Williams is expectedly not content with mere embezzlement or hidden mistress as the cupboard skeletons, but introduces pimping, homosexuality, cannibalism and presumed insanity as well—in fact, a whole skeleton family. Mankiewicz skilfully re-creates, in this British-based production, the steamy, lurid, hothouse atmosphere of the one-act play, filling the screen with huge carnivorous plants and over-decorated furnishings, and digging down into the abominable revelations so that we have our faces forced into a sequence of yawning pits of corruption, one below the other. Katharine Hepburn, slowly descending in her private lift, suggests unmentionable matters concealed behind a slightly cracked *façade*, and Elizabeth Taylor's long horror story mounts to a highly theatrical climax exactly fitting the unlikely but nastily credible situation which Williams conceived and Mankiewicz flamboyantly delivers.

OUR MAN IN HAVANA. Script: Graham Greene, from his own novel. Direction: Carol Reed. Photography: Oswald Morris (CinemaScope). Editing: Bert Bates. Music: Hermanos Deniz Cuban Rhythm Band. Art Direction: John Box. Players: Alec Guinness, Burl Ives, Maureen O'Hara, Ernie Kovacs, Noël Coward, Paul Rogers, Ralph Richard-

1959: *LOOK BACK IN ANGER*, Tony Richardson's
first feature film, with Claire Bloom, Richard Burton
and Gary Raymond.

son, Duncan Macrae. Production: Kingsmead. 111
mins.

In this story of a mild little vacuum salesman
who, in order to get money to buy his daughter
a horse, allows himself to be used by the British
Government as a spy, with no idea what is re-
quired of him, Greene and Reed between them
have concocted a light satirical fantasy which is
turned, with the utmost skill, into a nightmare
reality. Underlying Greene's thriller surface is one
of his recurrent themes: that innocence, when
allied to ignorance, can breed evil. This more
serious undertone is never more than implied, and
the film can be enjoyed purely on its narrative
level, interpreted by a fine cast and with particularly effective settings and photography. John Box,

the art director, has said that they were faced with
a choice, for economic reasons, between making
the film in Spain in colour, or in Havana in black-
and-white: without hesitation they chose the latter, and the result more than justifies the decision.

TIGER BAY. Script: John Hawksworth, Shelley
Smith. Direction: J. Lee Thompson. Photography:
Eric Cross. Editing: Sidney Hayers. Music: Laurie
Johnson. Art Direction: Edward Carrick. Players:
Horst Buchholz, Hayley Mills, John Mills, Megs
Jenkins, Anthony Dawson. Production: Julian
Wintle-Leslie Parkyn. 105 mins.

The popular theme of a child in danger because
of being in possession of incriminating knowledge
is given a lift here by the tender relationship that

springs up between the small girl and the young Polish seaman who kidnaps her when she discovers him hiding from the police. The ethics of loyalty and betrayal are examined in some depth within the framework of a suspense story. As the doughty, faithful little girl, the young Hayley Mills appears to give an inspired performance, responding with the greatest sensitivity to the director's guiding hand—and no doubt aided by the presence of her father, whose scenes with her have considerable poignance. Horst Buchholz retains sympathy even at his most ruthless. The whole film, exciting and often moving, is beautifully placed in its sea-coast setting.

weight to a murder mystery which is wholly absorbing on its own account.

*1959: Murder and racial tension, Harry Baird and Yvonne Buckingham in SAPPHIRE.*

*1959: Hayley and John Mills in TIGER BAY.*

**SAPPHIRE.** Script: Janet Green, Lukas Heller. Direction: Basil Dearden. Photography: Harry Waxman (Eastmancolor). Editing: John Guthridge. Music: Philip Green. Art Direction: Carmen Dillon. Players: Nigel Patrick, Yvonne Mitchell, Michael Craig, Paul Massie, Bernard Miles, Olga Lindo, Earl Cameron. Production: Michael Relph. 92 mins.

In this original and gripping crime story the hunt for the murderer of a student found dead on Hampstead Heath serves as the basis of a study of underlying causes of racial prejudice and antagonism. The victim is a young Negro girl sufficiently light-skinned to pass for a white, who meets her death on account of her relationship with a white boy. The balance is held with unusual fairness, each "side" appearing as likely to be prejudiced as the other. The social implications give an added

**I'M ALL RIGHT, JACK.** Script: Frank Harvey, John Boulting, Alan Hackney, from the latter's novel, *Private Life*. Direction: John Boulting. Photography: Max Greene. Editing: Anthony Harvey. Music: Ken Hare. Art Direction: Bill Andrews. Players: Ian Carmichael, Peter Sellers, Dennis Price, Margaret Rutherford, Richard Attenborough, Terry-Thomas. Production: Roy Boulting. 105 mins.

In this hilarious free-for-all, possibly the best of the series, the Boulting brothers dare to fire a satirical broadside at that most sacred of all contemporary institutions, the trade unions. The fact that they also let fly at a dozen other targets, including the bosses, has not sheltered them from indignant accusations by the outraged and humourless of having "become jaundiced," "turned sour," and contracted similar unpleasant complaints. Admittedly the broadsides lose some of their force by being fired indiscriminately, but the net result is a lively and appallingly amusing picture of the world we have made for ourselves. Peter Sellers's little-Hitler shop steward is one of his ripest impersonations—even suggesting a little-boy-longing-to-be-loved lurking beneath the grim and glum surface.

**EXPRESSO BONGO.** Script: Wolf Mankowitz,

*1959: I'M ALL RIGHT JACK, Peter Sellers as the shop steward in the Boultings' "satirical broadside."*

from his own play. Direction: Val Guest. Photography: John Wilcox (DyaliScope). Editing: Bill Lenny. Art Direction: Tony Masters. Music/lyrics: Robert Farnon, Val Guest, Norrie Paramor, Bunty Lewis, Paddy Roberts, Julian More, Monty Norman, David Henneker. Players: Laurence Harvey, Sylvia Syms, Yolande Donlan, Cliff Richard, Ambrosine Phillpotts, Meier Tzelniker. Production: Conquest (Val Guest). 111 mins.

As an attempt to bring to the British cinema something of the bite and vigour of a particular type of American musical, this is at least adventurous. The story of a cheap theatrical agent who uses any unscrupulous method to get his teenage client into big-time singing is told with an adroit mixture of fantasy and realism, and the savage, seedy Soho of popular imagination is given brash and vivid life, though softened apparently from the original stage production. It is a filmed musical rather than a film musical, but even so a welcome breath of vulgar life in a hitherto somewhat genteel and moribund form of British cinema.

## Short Films and Documentaries

**WE ARE THE LAMBETH BOYS.** Direction: Karel Reisz. Photography: Walter Lassally. Editing: John Fletcher. Music: Johnny Dankworth. Commentator: Jon Rollason. Production: Leon Clore. 52 mins.

This sympathetic and lively study of the members of a London youth club at work and at play is the second and most lasting of a series sponsored by the Ford Motor Company under the general title *Look at Britain*. In true documentary fashion it strives to capture the spirit of its subject rather than merely report what it sees.

### 1959: Facts of Interest

Bryanston Films is founded by Michael Balcon.

The Columbia Cinema, Shaftesbury Avenue, is opened.

Death of cinema pioneer G. A. Smith (at 96), and Lupino Lane.

# 1960

SATURDAY NIGHT AND SUNDAY MORNING. Script: Alan Sillitoe, from his own novel. Direction: Karel Reisz. Photography: Freddie Francis. Editing: Seth Holt. Music: Johnny Dankworth. Players: Albert Finney, Shirley Anne Field, Rachel Roberts, Hylda Baker, Norman Rossington. Production: Woodfall. 89 mins.

Regarded as yet another "breakthrough" for British cinema, in its brash, uninhibited picture of working-class Midlands life, its absence of patronising comment, and its casual acceptance of extra-marital sex, this film was received with paeans of praise, and has been enormously successful. Its presentation of a totally self-centered, cheerfully amoral, take-what-you-can-get young man as hero is a welcome relief from the petulant denunciations of the angry ones. Nevertheless, its "message" is wholly pessimistic. At the end of the film, when we are led to suppose that he has grown up enough to have developed some sort of responsibility, all that he can do—as his girl points out—is to throw things. All that his awareness of his position teaches him is to want more of the same. Despising his job, and his parents' life, he has absolutely no ambition to replace them by anything different in quality—no ambition, that is, which would require the least effort on his part. He is, in fact, utterly spineless, and the subtle cynicism of Reisz's treatment is that he appears to be attempting to make him likeable—a subtlety deliciously echoed in Finney's performance.

THE ANGRY SILENCE. Script: Bryan Forbes, Michael Craig, Richard Gregson. Direction: Guy Green. Photography: Arthur Ibbetson. Editing: Anthony Harvey. Music: Malcolm Arnold. Art Direction: Ray Simm. Players: Richard Attenborough, Pier Angeli, Michael Craig, Bernard Lee, Alfred Burke, Geoffrey Keen. Production: Beaver (Richard Attenborough, Bryan Forbes). 95 mins.

Richard Attenborough and Bryan Forbes make a notable entry into joint production in this well scripted, realistic and controversial study of a man's fight to work while others assert their right to strike. The film has its rough edges: it undertakes too many thorny problems for its size, many of the less prominent characters appear shadowy and difficult to identify and one of them —the director—is a caricature out of keeping with the rest. The fact that the unofficial strike is brought about by a professional (and mysterious) agitator weakens the points to be made. However, the film's courage and burning sincerity override its incidental failings, and it stands as a horrifying indictment of the sickening violence and calculating cruelty, direct or indirect, to which fundamentally decent men can be incited—only to feel ashamed when it is much too late.

SONS AND LOVERS. Script: Gavin Lambert, T. E. B. Clarke, from D. H. Lawrence's novel. Direction: Jack Cardiff. Photography: Freddie Francis (CinemaScope). Editing: Gordon Pilkington. Music: Lambert Williamson. Art Direction: Tom Morahan, Lionel Couch. Players: Wendy Hiller, Trevor Howard, Dean Stockwell, Mary Ure, Heather Sears. Production: Company of Artists (Jerry Wald). 100 mins.

1960: *THE ANGRY SILENCE, Pier Angeli, Richard Attenborough and Michael Craig.*

The least pretentious and in some ways the best film of a full-length Lawrence (except perhaps for *The Virgin and the Gypsy,* 1970), this is most effective in its family scenes—aided by a superb performance by Wendy Hiller and one almost as good from Trevor Howard. The restrained, straightforward approach tones down the unhealthy underlying hysteria and lightens the steamy, overcharged and often absurd solemnity which is apt to cast a sort of warm sludge over Lawrencian human relationships. Rather too much time is given to these personal problems, to the loss of the background events which are the most brilliant part of the book, but much of the playing is of a quality to make this a matter of less regret than it might have been. As might be expected from Cardiff as director and Francis as cameraman, the photography is exceptional—recording in beautifully shaded black-and-white a convincing Edwardian album of factory, street, farm, canal and woodland.

**THE TRIALS OF OSCAR WILDE (THE MAN WITH THE GREEN CARNATION).** Script: Ken Hughes. Direction: Ken Hughes. Photography: Ted Moore (Technicolor, Technirama). Editing: Geoffrey Foot. Music: Ron Goodwin. Art Direction: Ken Adam, Bill Constable. Players: Peter Finch, John Fraser, Yvonne Mitchell, Lionel Jeffries, Nigel Patrick, James Mason, Emrys Jones, Maxine Audley. Production: Eros/Warwick/Viceroy. 123 mins.

Of the two accounts of the Oscar Wilde *débâcle* that were released within a week of each other, this one must be considered the more successful. (The first was *Oscar Wilde,* directed by Gregory Ratoff, with Robert Morley and John Neville.) It starts with the first night of *Lady Windermere's Fan,* and closes with his departure for Paris after having served his two year sentence. Peter Finch might not seem at first glance the most suitable choice for Wilde (Robert Morley, in the other version, had already portrayed him on stage), but his moving, inwardly tormented performance more than compensates for any physical differences, falling short only as the lionised wit. John Fraser's Lord Alfred is also remarkable, bringing out all the ruthless self-regard and egotism beneath the superficial charm. Where both versions draw almost equal is in making full use of the wonderfully photogenic settings of late Victorian London.

**PEEPING TOM.** Script: Leo Marks. Direction: Michael Powell. Photography: Otto Heller (Eastmancolor). Editing: Noreen Ackland. Music: Brian Easdale. Art Direction: Arthur Lawson. Players: Carl Boehm, Anna Massey, Maxine Audley, Moira Shearer, Esmond Knight. Production: Michael Powell. 109 mins.

A technically brilliant film of horror, *Peeping Tom* was greeted with howls of execration from some quarters on its first appearance. Yet though it deals with perversion, it never suggests that twisted instincts are humorous, nor pleads that they should be tolerated. It does, on the other hand, ask sympathy for the mentally sick son of a sadistic father. Powell himself appears as the man who, for "scientific" reasons, records his small boy's fears—fears which he induces for this very purpose. The actual horrors are treated (in the British version, at least) with considerable restraint. The film is really a penetrating comment on peeping Toms of all kinds—scientific, journalistic, religious, social—or for less high-sounding but franker reasons. We are all, it says in effect, to some extent *voyeurs,* including those of us watching at this moment the horrors in the camera-filled room of the pathological murderer—watching them ourselves through the medium of a camera. Perhaps, after all, the howls of execration are difficult to justify, rather than to understand: we are all sensitive when our own raw spots are touched.

1960: PEEPING TOM, Anna Massey and Carl Boehm in Michael Powell's "technically brilliant film of horror."

THE LEAGUE OF GENTLEMEN. Script: Bryan Forbes, from the novel by John Boland. Direction: Basil Dearden. Photography: Arthur Ibbetson. Editing: John Guthridge. Music: Philip Green. Art Direction: Peter Proud. Players: Jack Hawkins, Nigel Patrick, Roger Livesey, Richard Attenborough, Bryan Forbes, Kieron Moore, Terence Alexander, Norman Bird. Production: Allied Film Makers. 113 mins.

Eight ex-army officers plan a vast bank robbery on strictly military lines. After intensive drill, and a raid on an arms depot for ammunition, the operation is launched—and succeeds. It is not until afterwards, with the booty divided and the League about to depart, that the fatal flaw appears. The often quoted assertion that if you train a soldier to use arms for your own purposes in war you cannot blame him if he uses them for his own purposes in peace has been wittily transferred to the officer class. It is as a slick thriller, however, that the film succeeds, and Bryan Forbes shows his increasing deftness as a scriptwriter. The ironic

closing scene is excellently handled, preceded by a hilarious few moments with Robert Coote as an intrusive, inebriated gentleman—not in the League.

THE ENTERTAINER. Script: John Osborne, Nigel Kneale, from the former's play. Direction: Tony Richardson. Photography: Oswald Morris. Editing: Alan Osbiston. Music: John Addison. Art Direction: Ralph Brinton. Players: Laurence Olivier, Joan Plowright, Brenda de Banzie, Alan Bates, Roger Livesey, Shirley Anne Field. Production: Woodfall. 96 mins.

Instead of using the Northern seaside setting as a background, the film brings it right into the action, thus causing a dichotomy between a naturalistic scene and the heightened dialogue of much of the original play. This is, admittedly, not wholly a disadvantage, as it serves to strengthen the impact of each by contrast with the other. The film's principle justification, however, is the preservation of Olivier's inspired performance as the seedy, desperately bluffing third-rate song and dance man.

VILLAGE OF THE DAMNED. Script: Sterling Silliphant, Wolf Rilla, George Barclay, from John Wyndham's novel, *The Midwich Cuckoos.* Direction: Wolf Rilla. Photography: Geoffrey Faithfull. Editing: Gordon Hales. Music: Ron Goodwin. Art Direction: Ivan King. Players: George Sanders, Barbara Shelley, Martin Stephens, Michael Gwynn, Laurence Naismith, Richard Warner. Production: Ronald Kinnoch. 77 mins.

John Wyndham's chilling story of the mysterious birth to the women in a little English village of alien, flaxen-haired children with strange eyes and super-mental powers has been ably adapted to the cinema screen, particularly remarkable for the unnerving performances the director has obtained from the awesome young strangers. The silly title change from the apt and expressive original can only be deplored. *Children of the Damned,* a parallel rather than a sequel, which followed in 1963, is equally effective.

### Short Films and Documentaries

THE RUNNING, JUMPING, AND STANDING STILL FILM. Direction: Richard Lester. Production: Peter Sellers. 11 mins.

An anarchistic, surrealist romp made by the con-

*1960: Laurence Olivier as Archie Rice in THE EN-
TERTAINER.*

*1960: The sinister alien children in VILLAGE OF
THE DAMNED.*

temporarily popular Goon Show characters from television, impossible to describe, possible only to laugh at, and with an oddly old-fashioned air due not only to the haphazard photography. It was never intended for public release, and yet received an Academy Award nomination.

## 1960: Facts of Interest

The Cinematograph Act (1960) is passed, largely concerned with foreign co-productions.

The Entertainments Duty is abolished.

The number of cinemas drops to about 2,800, and attendances to about 10 million, compared to over 22 million in 1955.

# 1961

THE INNOCENTS. Script: William Archibald, Truman Capote, from Henry James's novel, *The Turn of the Screw*. Direction: Jack Clayton. Photography: Freddie Francis (CinemaScope). Editing: James Clark. Music: Georges Auric. Art Direction: Wilfred Shingleton. Players: Deborah Kerr, Martin Stephens, Michael Redgrave, Pamela Franklin, Megs Jenkins. Production: Jack Clayton. 99 mins.

*The Innocents* opens and closes in darkness. Behind the credit titles we see vaguely a close-up of clasped hands, the meaning of which is not clear until at the end those same hands clasp the dead boy, and are then slowly withdrawn. In between those two shots Clayton has created a work of beauty and horror, elegant and literary and imaginative. The famous ambiguity of James's novella is perfectly balanced—though in fact careful study of the book leaves no doubt that the ghosts and the evil possession were objective realities and no mere figments of a frustrated woman's mind. The mounting sense of indefinable menace, the sexual undertones (e.g. the kiss between the governess and the boy), the sense that every time a door is opened some secret activity within the room is suddenly stilled, the lurking horror and hysteria beneath both the placid, lovely surroundings of Bly and the cool, veiled faces of the children—all this is brought together by Clayton's direction and Francis's photography and developed with increasing power until the dreadful climax is reached. Familiar tricks of suspense such as billowing curtains, ticking clocks, half-seen faces beyond windows, mounting mysterious sounds, have all been given fresh strength by the skill with which they are employed. The total result is arguably the best ghost story—moral or not—that has yet been put on the screen.

A TASTE OF HONEY. Script: Shelagh Delaney, Tony Richardson, from the former's play. Direction: Tony Richardson. Photography: Walter Lassally. Editing: Anthony Gibbs. Music: John Addison. Art Direction: Ralph Brinton. Players: Rita Tushingham, Dora Bryan, Murray Melvin, Robert Stephens, Paul Danquah. Production: Woodfall. 100 mins.

The most successful of Richardson's stage transferences, bringing to the sad, sordid little tale of loneliness a visual poetry which was not possible in the confines of the theatre. The fairground scenes, effective enough though they are, fall into the common-people-at-play category which even at the time were becoming a *cliché*, but the more intimate sequences, whether in the drab, musty rooms or the grey-toned exteriors, preserve and indeed sharpen the bitter-sweet taste of the original. Rita Tushingham's gawky pathos benefits from her inexperience, before the self-conscious gaucherie which was to turn some of her later creations into grotesques. After this theatrical hat-trick, Tony Richardson was to go on to larger-scale, but not necessarily better, things.

WHISTLE DOWN THE WIND. Script: Keith Waterhouse, Willis Hall, from Mary Hayley Bell's novel. Direction: Bryan Forbes. Photography: Arthur Ibbetson. Editing: Max Benedict. Music:

*1961: Pamela Franklin is regarded by an apprehensive
Deborah Kerr in THE INNOCENTS.*

Malcolm Arnold. Art Direction: Ray Simm. Players: Hayley Mills, Alan Bates, Norman Bird, Bernard Lee, Elsie Wagstaff, Alan Barnes. Production: Richard Attenborough. 99 mins.

Three local children find a bearded man hiding in a barn. Their heads being full of Sunday School teachings and Salvation Army preaching (and this taking place before the universal beard revival), they take the man to be Jesus Christ. In fact, he is a murderer on the run. When the net closes, rather than betray their trust he gives himself up and is led away to prison. This potentially embarrassing story is treated with such simplicity, and the attitude of the children is so robustly com-

monsensical, that any such fears are avoided almost throughout. The little boy in particular is saltily sceptical, especially after the man has failed to save a kitten's life. "That's not Jesus—that's just a feller!" Later, when the news of Christ's second coming spreads to other children, allegorical parallels become more strained, but the final moments of the film are intensely moving. The shot of the man outlined against the sky, arms outstretched crucifixion fashion as he is searched for weapons, has been described as a facile *cliché*—but what may appear trite in some circumstances can touch the heart in others. Fine photography of the bleak Northern countryside, incisive direction, down-

*1961: A TASTE OF HONEY, Rita Tushingham and
Murray Melvin in Tony Richardson's film of the play
by Shelagh Delaney.*

*1961: The children in the wintry North England coun-
tryside; a beautiful still from WHISTLE DOWN THE
WIND.*

to-earth performances, and Malcolm Arnold's hauntingly atmospheric music combine to transform what might have been a sentimental experience into something memorably tender and true.

## REACH FOR GLORY. Script: John Kohn, Jud Kinberg, John Rae, based on the latter's novel, *The Custard Boys*. Direction: Philip Leacock. Photography: Bob Huke. Editing: F. Wilson. Music: Bob Russell. Art Direction: John Blezzard. Players: Harry Andrews, Kay Walsh, Michael Anderson, Jnr., Oliver Grimm, Martin Tomlinson. Production: John Kohn, Jud Kinberg. 86 mins.

*Reach for Glory* tells of the effects of war conditions and military propaganda on a group of young boys evacuated from London to live out their bored lives in a "safe area." Fed with stories of the glory of the war hero, the group apply the ethics and manners of the time to their own games and to their encounters with the village children. When one of their gang, only admitted on sufferance, exhibits "cowardice" he is brought before a "court martial" and made to undergo a mock execution. By accident, he is shot and killed. Few films expose so remorselessly and powerfully the ultimate fiendishness, cruelty and futility of the war mentality. Under Leacock's brilliantly sensitive direction, and his superb handling of his young cast, this becomes an accusation and a warning valid for all time. It should be shown as a compulsory accompaniment—and antidote—to every big, bouncing, colorful war epic.

## THE DAMNED. Script: Evan Jones, from H. L. Lawrence's novel. *The Children of Light* (Hammerscope). Direction: Joseph Losey. Photography: Arthur Grant. Editing: Reginald Mills. Music: James Bernard. Art Direction: Don Mingaye. Players: Macdonald Carey, Shirley Anne Field, Viveca Lindfors, Alexander Knox, Oliver Reed, James Villiers. Production: Hammer. 87 mins.

In this mixture of science fiction, monitory parable and motorbike gangs, the main-line story concerns a group of radio-active children who are kept in a cave by a scientist in the hope that they will survive nuclear war and re-populate the world. A young American and his girl come across the children and release them, but in so doing become themselves contaminated. The children are soon rounded up again, and the couple, chased by helicopters, make off in a boat, in which they are last seen drifting, doomed to die from radio sickness. An *avant-garde* sculptress who knows too much is summarily shot, and the children once again sealed in their cave. The film appears to have been badly cut after leaving Losey's hands, and even before this he had to tone down the story. As a warning comment on the ills of today and the expectations of tomorrow the film is understandably confused, but as a science fiction feature which has more to offer than the discovery and destruction of some Blob or Thing, it is uncomfortably impressive.

## VICTIM. Script: Janet Green, John McCormick. Direction: Basil Dearden. Photography: Otto Heller. Editing: John Guthridge. Music: Philip Green. Art Direction: Alex Vetchinsky. Players: Dirk Bogarde, Sylvia Syms, John Barrie, John Cairney, Norman Bird, Peter McEnery. Production: Parkway. 100 mins.

In its day this was considered the last word in adult film-making—perversion (or inversion) considered seriously rather than as an excuse for music hall laughs. Homosexuals are not treated as if they are a persecuted minority; on the other hand, it is demonstrated how the legal position of the time encouraged blackmail of one by another. As in her script for *Sapphire*, Janet Green (in this case with J. McCormick) uses a detective thriller as the basis of a play of social comment. Dirk Bogarde stands out in a generally strong cast. Though the times and the fashions may have passed it by, in its day this was a brave venture, devoid of sensationalism.

## ONLY TWO CAN PLAY. Script: Bryan Forbes, from Kingsley Amis's novel, *That Uncertain Feeling*. Direction: Sidney Gilliat. Photography: John Wilcox. Editing: Thelma Connell. Music: Richard Rodney Bennett. Art Direction: Albert Witherick. Players: Peter Sellers, Mai Zetterling, Virginia Maskell, Richard Attenborough, Kenneth Griffiths, Raymond Huntley. Production: Leslie Gilliat. 106 mins.

Peter Sellers's frustrated librarian may not be the anti-hero of the novel, but it is excellent Sellers, clouded by that ambiguity which marks all his best characterisations in the quieter, less flamboyant style—for example, *Hoffman* and *The*

*1961: Joseph Losey's THE DAMNED, Oliver Reed and the motor-cycle gang.*

*1961: Dirk Bogarde in VICTIM, with Norman Bird.*

*Smallest Show on Earth,* as against *Lolita* and *Dr. Strangelove.* The film is really a series of set pieces in which he finds himself in ever increasingly unfortunate predicaments in pursuit of an affair with an apparently willing but alarming married Norwegian (Mai Zetterling). The funniest of these is a frantic attempt at love-making in a car, interrupted by the arrival of a large and curious cow. No masterpiece, but a film which admirably fulfills its modest function—to entertain.

## Short Films and Documentaries

TERMINUS. Script, Direction: John Schlesinger. Photography: Ken Phipps, Robert Paynter. Editing: Hugh Raggett, David Gladwell, Nicholas Hale. Music: Ron Grainer. Production: British Transport Films (Edgar Anstey). 30 mins.

John Schlesinger came to the cinema from the stage, as actor, and television, as director. *Terminus* is his first significant film, a remarkable half-hour documentary observing Waterloo Station during a period of twenty-four hours, starting and finishing during the quiet moments before the early morning rush. There is no commentary—incidents, faces, objects, vistas being allowed to speak for themselves. Schlesinger has spoken of the valuable experience he gained making this prize-winning sponsored film, in which he was allowed full freedom of treatment.

THE APPLE. Script: Stan Hayward. Direction: George Dunning. Photography: John Williams (Technicolor). Animation: Alan Ball, Jack Stokes, Bill Sewell, Charlie Jenkins, Mike Stuart, Tony Gearty. Editing: Alex Rayment. Music: Ernst Naser. Production: George Dunning. 7 mins.

A comic parable of secret vice is told with the utmost economy of means, brilliant line drawing and perspective, resulting in one of the wittiest of all British cartoon shorts.

## 1961: Facts of Interest

The number of independent productions shows an increase, due to the economic uncertainties in the industry.

Walton studios are closed.

Jack Greenwood starts production of second-feature Edgar Wallace films, completing twenty-five in as many months.

The Cameo, Windmill Street, London, one of the earliest news theatres, closes, to reopen as the Cameo-Moulin, showing Continental films, with a bias towards sex.

The Coliseum Theatre, St. Martin's Lane, London, starts screening M-G-M productions with a revival of *Gone with the Wind.*

Death of Filippo Del Giudice.

# 1962

LAWRENCE OF ARABIA. Script: Robert Bolt. Direction: David Lean. Photography: F. A. Young (Technicolor, Super Panavision 70). Editing: Anne V. Coates. Music: Maurice Jarre. Art Direction: John Box. Players: Peter O'Toole, Alec Guinness, Anthony Quinn, Jack Hawkins, Omar Sharif, Jose Ferrer, Claude Rains, Anthony Quayle. Production: Horizon Pictures (G.B.) (Sam Spiegel). 222 mins.

Robert Bolt has stated how he waded through a mass of authorities who all contradicted one another and eventually retired to *The Seven Pillars of Wisdom* even though it contained passages of dubious authenticity, taking the reasonable line that either certain things happened or Lawrence in some way wished them to happen: he then asked himself, "Supposing them to be true, what sort of individual was he whose life could contain so many irreconcilables?" Thus it is irrelevant to criticise a script which was never intended as a strictly historical record, for not being one. Aqaba may not have been entered in such a cinematogenic fashion, but it is all very exciting to watch. Peter O'Toole, though physically all wrong for the role, manages to convey something of the hysterical, unbalanced, slightly less than admirable qualities of the almost mythical figure—and also, like most mythical figures, remains indefinite, a shadow. What stay in the memory are the unsurpassed visual qualities, above all the justly famous approach of the single horseman through the mirage. One great mystery, though, still remains unsolved—just what did the Turks do to Lawrence on that fateful occasion at Deraa that changed his life?

A KIND OF LOVING. Script: Willis Hall, Keith Waterhouse, from Stan Barstow's novel. Direction: John Schlesinger. Photography: Denys Coop. Editing: Roger Cherrill. Music: Ron Grainer. Art Direction: Ray Simm. Players: Alan Bates, June Ritchie, Thora Hird, Bert Palmer, Gwen Nelson. Production: Joseph Janni. 112 mins.

In this admirable first feature, John Schlesinger draws a truer picture of Northern life, from Stan Barstow's equally admirable book, than any yet put on film, embellishing the quite ordinary story of a young man caught into an unwelcome marriage because of his girl becoming pregnant, with a constant series of small, subtle touches. The engaging (and unwillingly engaged) Vic is brought delightfully to life by Alan Bates, and Thora Hird manages to evoke a shred of sympathy for a selfish, jealous, embittered woman. Most refreshing of all, present in the book and preserved in the film, is the sense that life has something to offer at all levels, and the substitution of a tough, mature unresigned acceptance of imperfection in place of the childish petulance of the pipedream.

THE LONELINESS OF THE LONG-DISTANCE RUNNER. Script: Alan Sillitoe, from his short story. Direction: Tony Richardson. Photography: Walter Lassally. Editing: Anthony Gibbs. Music: John Addison. Art Direction: Ted Marshall, Ralph Brinton. Players: Tom Courtenay, Michael Redgrave, James Bolam, Avis Bunnage, James Fox, Alec McCowen, Julia Foster. Production: Woodfall. 104 mins.

Tony Richardson's sense of freedom in his first feature away from the confines of a stage adapta

*1962: Desert scene—a quieter moment from David Lean's spectacular LAWRENCE OF ARABIA.*

*1962: Husband, daughter, mother-in-law; Alan Bates, Thora Hird and June Ritchie in A KIND OF LOV-ING.*

tion has perhaps led him to a certain over-indulgence in camera pyrotechnics in this long version of a short story: without doubt, though, the run itself, intercut with memory flashbacks and photographed from a multiplicity of angles, reflections, subjective shots, is very exciting to watch. The petty thief non-hero has been considerably softened from the story, but he is still the feeble little would-be rebel, who expects other people (his mother, for instance) to abide by standards he himself affects to despise, and whines when he has to face the consequences. The caricaturing of the Establishment is evidently intended as a subtle and amusing double-bluff—the old trick of reversing an apparent position in an argument by overstating to absurdity the alleged defects of the other side. It works very well, showing all too clearly that the fault is not, in fact, in Society, but in the runner himself, that he is an underling. It is this ingenious ambiguity that lifts an erratic but intriguing film out of the by then increasingly tedious angry young man rut. Michael Redgrave as the Borstal Governor gives an exceedingly subtle portrayal in what appears an eccentric piece of casting, and Tom Courtenay is unselfishly excellent as the weak, unpleasant runner.

**TERM OF TRIAL.** Script: Peter Glenville, from James Barlow's novel. Direction: Peter Glenville. Photography: Oswald Morris. Editing: James Clark. Music: Jean-Michel Demase. Art Direction: Antony Woolard. Players: Laurence Olivier, Simone Signoret, Sarah Miles, Hugh Griffith, Terence Stamp, Roland Culver, Frank Pettingell, Barbara Ferris. Production: Romulus. 130 mins.

Another "realistic" North country film, this is less an examination of a community than an intimate study of character, though existence in a grimy secondary-modern school is shown to be nasty, brutish, though not—unhappily—short. Laurence Olivier gives a muted performance of great sensitivity as the schoolmaster who refuses to seduce one of his pupils, and is then spitefully accused by her of attempting to do so, and Sarah Miles beneath her innocent sexuality reveals a glimpse of *The Servant* to come. The cynical story of a decent but weak man brought to degradation by his own high principles and only able to regain a measure of respect when he betrays them and lies to his wife, is directed by Peter Glenville with his usual unobtrusive skill with actors, concentrating on the characters and letting the background of school life make its own grubby impression.

**THE L-SHAPED ROOM.** Script: Bryan Forbes, from the novel by Lynn Reid Banks. Direction: Bryan Forbes. Photography: Douglas Slocombe. Editing: Anthony Harvey. Music: John Barry; Brahms's First Piano Concerto. Art Direction: Ray Simm. Players: Leslie Caron, Tom Bell, Brock Peters, Cicely Courtneidge, Bernard Lee, Avis Bunnage. Production: Romulus. 142 mins.

Though he has to hand a rather too conveniently assorted group of unusual lodgers, Bryan Forbes makes of this story of contemporary bed-sitter life a moving study of loneliness. The atmosphere of the grubby Notting Hill Gate boarding house is so strongly captured that the viewer can almost smell the mustiness as he mounts the stairs to the L-shaped room at the top. The simple, open-ended story is told with a sort of tough compassion very typical of its director and writer, and the final scene, with the room taken over by a new girl in much the same predicament as the one we have come to know, extends its significance from a particular case to a wider world of solitude and despair, saved from being merely depressing by the knowledge that the compassion is also part of that same world.

**DR. NO.** Script: Richard Maibaum, Johanna Harwood, Berkely Mather, from Ian Fleming's novel.

2: Tom Courtenay, second from left, "unselfishly
llent" as the feeble non-hero in THE LONELI-
SS OF THE LONG-DISTANCE RUNNER.

1962: THE L-SHAPED ROOM, Leslie Caron and
Cicely Courtneidge in Bryan Forbes's sensitive study
of loneliness.

Direction: Terence Young. Photography: Ted Moore (Technicolor). Editing: Peter Hunt. Art Direction: Syd Cain, Ken Adam. Players: Sean Connery, Ursula Andress, Joseph Wiseman, Jack Lord, Zena Marshall, Bernard Lee. Production: Harry Saltzman, Albert Broccoli. 105 mins.

The first Bond, an obvious dam-buster to let loose a flood, had not yet developed the grotesqueries and bizarreries of those that were to follow. Without the exaggerations of absurdity (at least until the grand finale), the relative realism makes the brutalities and destruction less easy to accept, despite the overall black comedy approach. Bond too, contemporarily described as wooden and boorish, is not yet the man that repeated excess of sex and sadism is to make him. Follow-ups include *From Russia with Love* (1963), *Goldfinger* (1964), *Thunderball* (1965), *You Only Live Twice* (1967), *On Her Majesty's Secret Service* (1969)—the last featuring a different and less successful Bond—*Diamonds are Forever* (1971), marking Connery's return, with more in the pipeline.

*1962: DR. NO; Sean Connery, Ursula Andress and John Kitzmiller run through the radioactive swamp in the first Bond film.*

**LOLITA.** Script: Vladimir Nabokov, from his own novel. Direction: Stanley Kubrick. Photography: Oswald Morris. Editing: Anthony Harvey. Music: Nelson Riddle, Bob Harris. Art Direction: William Andrews. Players: James Mason, Sue Lyon, Peter Sellers, Shelley Winters, Diana Decker, Jerry Stovin. Production: J. B. Harris. 153 mins.

Since Vladimir Nabokov made his own adaptation he was presumably a consenting party to the total negation of his novel by the up-ageing of Lolita from a guileful, gullible twelve-year-old to a knowing, self-aware teenager: a negation completed by the miscasting of the generally excellent Shelley Winters as the genteel, suburban culture-vulture Mrs. Haze, the destruction of the glorious mystery of Quilty by the reshaping of the story, and the probably inevitable loss of the coruscating literary style. All that remain are the final confrontation with Lolita (when, perversely, she looks too young) and James Mason's admirable Humbert Humbert. It may be after all that *Lolita* cannot adequately be filmed.

**Short Films and Documentaries**

**THE WAR GAME.** Script: Mai Zetterling, David Hughes. Direction: Mai Zetterling. Photography: Brian Probyn, Christopher Menges. Editing: Paul Davies. Players: Ian Ellis, Joseph Robinson. Production: Mai Zetterling. 15 mins.

Not to be confused with Peter Watkins's more widely known film of the same name, this excellent little dramatic parable of two boys playing a game that threatens at any moment to turn into a real conflict increases regret that the short fiction feature is now almost totally barred from the commercial cinema. Using only natural sounds (without music or dialogue), and coaxing totally unself-conscious performances from their two young players, Mai Zetterling and David Hughes have between them created a miniature of film art.

**THE FLYING MAN.** Script: Stan Hayward. Direction, Photography, Animation: George Dunning (Eastmancolor). Music: Ron Goodwin. Production: George Dunning. 2¾ mins.

With even more originality than in *The Apple*, Dunning here uses indeterminate water-colour shapes rather than clear outlines to tell his little tale of a flying man, verging constantly on the abstract yet always clear in their narrative purpose.

**1962: Facts of Interest**

J. Arthur Rank retires from the industry, and is succeeded as Chairman by John Davis.

246

The Pilkington Report is issued, rejecting pay-TV and leading to considerable discussion.

The Odeon, Haymarket, London, opens on the site of the former Capitol and Gaumont.

The rebuilt Empire, Leicester Square, opens.

The number of British cinemas is registered as 2,421.

# 1963

THE SERVANT. Script: Harold Pinter, from the novel by Robin Maugham. Direction: Joseph Losey. Photography: Douglas Slocombe. Editing: Reginald Mills. Music: John Dankworth. Art Direction: Richard Macdonald, Ted Clements. Players: Dirk Bogarde, Wendy Craig, Sarah Miles, Catherine Lacey, Richard Vernon. Production: Joseph Losey, Norman Priggen. 115 mins.

The film by which Joseph Losey came into his own as a British director, examining the master-servant, power-corruption relationship in all its aspects. Far more than a facile attack on a class-conscious society (a view which has sometimes been given undue prominence) it is really a retelling of the Faust story, with Dirk Bogarde superb as the man who arrives in answer to the effete young aristocrat's summons and, by obeying his every whim, and encouraging all the baser side of his nature. destroys him—and reverses their positions. As important as the characters is the Chelsea house which follows and reflects the descent into hell. Together with Polanski, Losey is unsurpassed in bringing his audience with him into the rooms and houses which are so vital a part of his vision. A brilliant interpolation is the scene in a restaurant, where two or three varieties of domination are briefly and subtly exemplified. Only in the final sequence does the film lose its grip and come perilously close to a sort of black-magic-horror-melodrama. Utter depravity is apparently impossible to represent on the screen without seeming ludicrous—as orgy-makers from Stroheim to Fellini and Russell have surely found.

THIS SPORTING LIFE. Script: David Storey, from his novel. Direction: Lindsay Anderson. Photography: Denys Coop. Editing: Peter Taylor. Music: Roberto Gerhard. Art Direction: Alan Withy. Players: Richard Harris, Rachel Roberts, Alan Badel, William Hartnell, Colin Blakely, Vanda Godsell. Production: Julian Wintle/Leslie Parkyn (Karel Reisz). 134 mins.

Lindsay Anderson's first feature, the tragedy of a man and a woman, both containing within their own tormented natures the seeds of self-destruction, brought together in an intimacy which can only lead to that destruction becoming mutual, is a distinguished and impressive debut. The Northern setting is thankfully free from *cliché*, both in detail and in general atmosphere, and the brutish sporting background—muddied oafs in the field—is horrifyingly well done. The exploitation, the dirty dealing, the sly, arrogant promoters and the pathetic or contemptible hangers-on are drawn with a quite beastly power. The struggle between the two protagonists—both heartbreaking and infuriating—mounts inevitably to its climax, and the final scenes of the woman's death in the bare, white hospital room are as desolate as anything on film. The famous shot of the spider on the wall has been criticised as melodramatic, and referred to out of context can be made to sound so, but when seen in the course of the action the effect is shattering.

TOM JONES. Script: John Osborne, from Henry Fielding's novel. Direction: Tony Richardson. Photography: Walter Lassally (Eastmancolor). Editing: Anthony Gibbs. Music: John Addison. Art Direction: Ted Marshall. Players: Albert Fin-

*1963: THE SERVANT, Sarah Miles and Robin Fox in Joseph Losey's study of corruption.*

*1963: Richard Harris and Rachel Roberts as the tormented, self-destroying couple in Lindsay Anderson's powerful first feature, THIS SPORTING LIFE.*

ney, Susannah York, Hugh Griffith, Edith Evans, Joan Greenwood, Diane Cilento, George Devine, Joyce Redman. Production: Woodfall. 128 mins.

Rowdy, bawdy, roistering, uproarious, lusty, romping, full-blooded, rollicking, salacious, brawling—all these adjectives have already been applied to *Tom Jones*. Missing is the humanity, the urbanity, the grace, even the geniality (in this fiercely, determinedly jovial film) of the great original—except perhaps in those moments when Miss Western, as brought to life by Edith Evans, moves across the screen. The famous sexual-eating sequence, the hunting sequence—all the set pieces in fact, come off splendidly, and everyone works extremely hard: and yet—what we are always conscious of is a lot of good, popular actors and actresses going at it hammer and tongs in very photogenic (and beautifully photographed) costumes against very photogenic (and beautifully photographed) settings. A field day, in fact—but not for Fielding.

**BILLY LIAR.** Script: Keith Waterhouse, Willis Hall. Direction: John Schlesinger. Photography: Denys Coop. Editing: Roger Cherrill. Music: Richard Rodney Bennett. Art Direction: Ray Simm. Players: Tom Courtenay, Julie Christie, Wilfred Pickles, Mona Washbourne, Finlay Currie, Rodney Bewes, Helen Fraser. Production: Joseph Janni. 98 mins.

Bill Fisher, though as feeble a type as the long-

distance runner of Tom Courtenay's previous film, is a good deal more attractive, having at least the courage of his imagination. He is also both amusing and pathetic, dreaming up his fantasies in his dreary Northern (once again) home town, and attempting without much success to keep his love and his home lives in some semblance of order. Schlesinger combines the fantasy and the reality for the most part with imaginative skill—though oddly enough the former seems more effective when we merely see Billy enacting it to himself on the bare stage of a theatre. The feckless antihero, however, has severe limitations as a lasting object of interest, and by this time they are beginning to become apparent. Nobody is less worth listening to than a compulsive liar.

**THE CARETAKER (THE GUEST).** Script: Harold Pinter, from his own play. Direction: Clive Donner. Photography: Nicolas Roeg. Editing: Fergus McDonell. Effects scored by: Ron Grainer. Art Direction: Reece Pemberton. Players: Donald Pleasence, Alan Bates, Robert Shaw. Production: Michael Birkett. 105 mins.

The film was made chiefly in the attic of a Hackney house deliberately overcrowded with rubbish to such an extent that technicians and cameramen had scarcely room to move. This in itself would not necessarily have ensured the cluttered, claustrophobic atmosphere of the original: Clive Donner has triumphantly obtained the desired effect by the mobility of his camera threading its way among the piles of obstacles. The acting, however, is here the thing, and the preservation of three such performances without directorial gimmickry is a matter for which we may be truly thankful.

**THE HAUNTING.** Script: Nelson Gidding, from a novel by Shirley Jackson. Direction: Robert Wise. Photography: David Boulton (Panavision). Editing: Ernest Walter. Music: Humphrey Searle. Art Direction: Elliot Scott. Players: Julie Harris, Claire Bloom, Richard Johnson, Russ Tamblyn, Fay Compton, Lois Maxwell. Production: Robert Wise. 112 mins.

After making a directorial *début* in one of Val Lewton's best horror productions, *The Curse of the Cat People,* and following it up with the equally impressive *Body Snatcher* starring Boris

*1963: BILLY LIAR, Tom Courtenay indulging in one
of his fantasies.*

*1963: The sinister staircase in Robert Wise's THE
HAUNTING. Julie Harris and Richard Johnson are
on it.*

Karloff, Robert Wise here returns to the genre with a British feature (though set in Boston) concerning a sinister house and a group of people gathered there. After very effectively leading us to believe that the house itself resents its visitors, however, he makes a U-turn and goes on to suggest that the menacing manifestations emanate from the subconscious frustrations of one of the female guests. This *volte-face* considerably dispels the chilling fear conjured up by the idea of the house itself as an evil entity. Apart from his, however, *The Haunting* is a good and unusual example of its school. Little horrific is seen, much is imagined—according to the master's dictum. The sound effects add up to a symphony of terror in themselves. The sinister nooks and corners of the distorted rooms are a credit to the art director, Elliot Scott, in particular the library with its spiral staircase which, with apparent intent, shakes and gradually disintegrates while two of the characters are standing at the top.

THE VICTORS. Script: Carl Foreman, from Alexander Baron's book, *The Human Kind*. Direction: Carl Foreman. Photography: Christopher Challis (Panavision). Editing: Alan Osbiston. Music: Sol Kaplan. Art Direction: Geoffrey Drake. Players: George Hamilton, George Peppard, Eli Wallach, Vincent Edwards, Rosanna Schiaffino, Romy Schneider, Jeanne Moreau, Melina Mercouri, James Mitchum. Production: Open Road (Carl Foreman). 175 mins.

Carl Foreman's one-man act, as scriptwriter, director and producer, is a very long, expensively cast and mounted anti-war epic that suffers to some extent from over-emphasis because of his desire that no point made should be missed, but even so it is often impressive and grim. What degree of influence such comments on past wars have on present thinking and future action may be questioned, but they should surely be made. Foreman has stated the need he felt for "a completely personal statement based on complete responsibility," and there can be no doubt of the sincerity of a project on which so much was staked.

JASON AND THE ARGONAUTS. Script: Jan Read, Beverley Cross. Direction: Don Chaffey. Special visual effects: Ray Harryhausen. Photography: Wilkie Cooper (Technicolor). Music: Bernard Herrmann. Art Direction: Geoffrey Drake, Herbert Smith, Jack Maxsted, Tony Sarzi Braga. Players: Todd Armstrong, Nancy Kovack, Gary Raymond, Laurence Naismith, Honor Blackman, Nigel Green. Production: Charles Schneer. 103 mins.

This first-class fantasy shows just how great an advance has been made in model animation, even from the times of *King Kong*. The harpies, the bronze Titan, above all the heroes' fight against armed skeletons (a sequence which, lasting a few minutes, took over five months to complete) are all superb examples of Harryhausen's work. Combined with gaily coloured backgrounds of Mount Olympus and legendary islands and seas, a bunch of handsomely stalwart Argonauts conversing in acceptably mythical speech, and an outsize wooden prow in the shape of Honor Blackman dispensing good advice when consulted, Harryhausen's models complete an enchanted hundred minutes, with roots far back in the silent days.

**Short Films and Documentaries**

THE SIX-SIDED TRIANGLE. Script, Direction: Christopher Miles. Photography: David Watkin. Editing: Peter Musgrave. Music: Michael Dress. Piano: Arthur Dulay. Art Direction: Bernard Sarron. Players: Sarah Miles, Nicol Williamson, Bill Meilen. Production: Christopher Miles. 30 mins.

A really hilarious short film, dealing with the eternal triangle as it might be depicted on the films of six different countries, starting with silent America. The idea is not new, nor are some of the gags, but the whole thing is directed with such aplomb and played with such wit and sense of parody that the result is as fresh as it is funny. Sweden, with wildly exaggerated and splurging soundtrack; and France, all beds and high-angle shots, probably come off best, but each viewer will have his or her own first choice.

AUTOMANIA 2000. Script: Joy Batchelor. Direction: John Halas. Animation: Harold Whitaker (Eastmancolor). Art Direction: Tom Bailey. Music: Jack King. Narrator: Edward Bishop. Production: Halas and Batchelor. 10 mins.

One of Halas and Batchelor's most imaginative and ominous cartoons, envisaging a world so cluttered with automobiles that people live perma-

*1963: SIX-SIDED TRIANGLE, Nicol Williamson and Sarah Miles in the hilarious silent Sheikh film parody.*

nently immured in their vehicles and are fed by helicopters. Eventually a scientist invents a car which can reproduce itself—this it continues to do until everything is submerged.

## 1963: Facts of Interest

Unemployment in the industry increases as production drops.

The London Coliseum opens as London's second Cinerama Theatre: this is followed by openings in the provinces and Scotland.

Circlorama, with eleven co-ordinated projectors, opens in Piccadilly, London.

Death of Robert Hamer.

# 1964

DOCTOR STRANGELOVE, OR HOW I LEARNED TO STOP WORRYING AND LOVE THE BOMB. Script: Stanley Kubrick, Terry Southern, Peter George, from the latter's novel, *Red Alert.* Direction: Stanley Kubrick. Photography: Gilbert Taylor. Editing: Anthony Harvey. Music: Laurie Johnson. Art Direction: Ken Adam. Players: Peter Sellers, Sterling Hayden, Keenan Wynn, George C. Scott, Slim Pickens, Peter Bull. Production: Hawk. 94 mins.

An ebullient piece of sustained black comedy, *Doctor Strangelove* marks the change of treatment in anti-war and similar films, from *All Quiet on the Western Front* to *The Victors,* using grim ridicule—a mixture of wild farce and stark pessimism—which would not have been possible a few years previously. The triple appearance of Sellers in brilliantly comic music hall sketches rather than characterisations further removes the film's approach from the realistic and earnest admonishments of war tragedies aimed primarily at the emotions: and conscious admiration of an actor's virtuosity increases the feeling of detachment from the events depicted. The magnificent warroom setting appears as a take-off of the Round Table of King Arthur—knights without chivalry, puppets in power, an enclosed circle of fools, shut away from reality, given a trust they can only betray by a populace as foolish as themselves. In more than its context and immediate relevance this is a key film of its time—a time when the "never-let-it-happen-again" determination of yesterday's productions was replaced by the "well-it's-bound-to-come-whatever-we-do-so-let's-all-have-a-giggle" hopelessness of today's.

GUNS AT BATASI. Script: Robert Hollis, from hi own novel. Direction: John Guillermin. Photog raphy: Douglas Slocombe. Editing: Max Bennett Music: John Addison. Art Direction: Mauric Carter. Players: Richard Attenborough, Flor Robson, Mia Farrow, Jack Hawkins, John Leyton Earl Cameron, Cecil Parker. Production: Twenti eth Century-Fox. 103 mins.

In two of the best British films of the yea Richard Attenborough adds to his growing repu tation as a character actor. In *Guns at Batasi* h appears as a Regimental Sergeant Major of mixed Anglo-African company in a newly inde pendent African State. When rebellion breaks ou in the capital a sequence of events leads to a sit uation in which, by following what he consider his duty, he commits a political blunder that re sults in his being moved from the country. Atten borough gives an astonishing and masterly por trayal of the "simple soldier" in conflict wit political expediency and guile quite beyond hi comprehension, stubbornly, bravely, honestly an absurdly doing his job as he sees it. The climacti moment when, in a confused and frustrated fury he smashes the Royal portrait and reacts in horro at his self-betrayal is genuinely moving. Th black-and-white photography is exceptional, par ticularly in its use of the wide parade-ground spaces.

SEANCE ON A WET AFTERNOON. Script, Di rection: Bryan Forbes. Photography: Gerry Tur pin. Editing: Derek York. Music: John Barry. Ar Direction: Ray Simm. Players: Richard Atten borough, Kim Stanley, Mark Eden, Nanette New

1964: *DOCTOR STRANGELOVE, the remarkable war-room setting.*

nan, Judith Donner, Patrick Magee, Gerald Sim. Production: Allied Film Makers/Beaver. 116 mins.

Sinister goings-on in dull, respectable suburban streets have long been a staple fare of British stage and screen, partly perhaps because real-life counterparts have more than once hit the headlines. Seldom, however, has so gripping and finely acted an example as this come to the cinema. Richard Attenborough appears as the mild little husband of a professional medium who has never acknowledged the fact that their child was stillborn: she persuades him to kidnap a child and demand ransom, intending to reveal the whereabouts of both in a seance and build up her mediocre reputation. Until that day comes, the child will be led to suppose she is in hospital, and to that end a room in the house is specially prepared. This—to

put it mildly—unlikely plot, is made horribly convincing by the director and his two stars. The scenes between the pathetic, tormented couple in their cluttered Victorian house—she on the verge of insanity and he trying desperately both to dissuade and humour her—and the final revelatory seance, are deeply affecting.

KING AND COUNTRY. Script: Evan Jones, from the play, *Hamp,* by John Wilson and a story by J. L. Hodson. Direction: Joseph Losey. Photography: Denys Coop. Editing: Reginald Mills. Music: Larry Adler. Art Direction: Peter Mullins. Players: Dirk Bogarde, Tom Courtenay, Leo McKern, Barry Foster, James Villiers, Peter Copley. Production: Norman Priggen, Joseph Losey. 86 mins.

*King and Country* is concerned with the execu-

1964: Contrasting characterisations—Richard Atten-
borough (a) as the "simple soldier" in GUNS AT
BATASI and (b) as the "mild little husband," with
Kim Stanley, in SEANCE ON A WET AFTERNOON.

(a)

(b)

tion of a private soldier for desertion during the First World War. The victim is a wretched little inarticulate cypher: the officers who condemn him to death are, most of them, fundamentally decent men—but all are caught in the same trap, like the rats that figure so largely in the film, and all consent to an obviously disgusting act because all bow to the same rules of conduct, and are able to shelve responsibility while doing so. Rules of conduct, moreover, that are man-made. It is thus wrong to say, as has been said, that Losey's theme in this great and tragic film, is inevitability. Indeed, to suggest this is in itself a shelving of responsibility. Even Hamp's own situation is not inevitable, for he was not conscripted, but (egged on by the women at home) volunteered—and stayed until his nerve broke. Had he lost his sight or his legs rather than his nerve he would have been labelled a hero. The performances of both Bogarde and Courtenay rank high among any during the whole decade.

BECKET. Script: Edward Anhalt, from the play by Jean Anouilh. Direction: Peter Glenville. Photography: Geoffrey Unsworth (Technicolor, Panavision 70). Editing: Anne Coates. Music: Laurence Rosenthal. Art Direction: John Bryan, Maurice Carter. Players: Richard Burton, Peter O'Toole, Donald Wolfit, John Gielgud, Martita Hunt, Pamela Brown, Sian Phillips. Production: Paramount/Keep Films (Hal Wallis). 149 mins.

To look on this colourful pageant as a "valuable history lesson," as has been advised, would be to court more examination failures than most teachers would care to contemplate. The play, which the film follows closely, was not intended as a factual chronicle but rather as a witty historical conceit—totally ignoring such inconvenient details as that of Becket being Henry's senior by some dozen years. Burton suggests the change from roistering King's companion to austere and inflexible prelate with considerable power, and Peter O'Toole's Henry is theatrically effective.

1964: *KING AND COUNTRY, Dirk Bogarde and Tom Courtenay in Joseph Losey's shattering picture of the filthiness of war.*

Costumes and sets look magnificent, and on the whole are the most "historical" things in the production.

**A HARD DAY'S NIGHT. Script: Alun Owen.** Direction: Richard Lester. Photography: Gilbert Taylor. Editing: John Jympson. Music: John Lennon, Paul McCartney. Art Direction: Ray Simm. Players: John Lennon, Paul McCartney, George Harrison, Ringo Starr, Wilfrid Brambell, Norman Rossington. Production: Walter Shenson. 85 mins.

With just enough story to link the songs together and afford a modicum of characterisation, Richard Lester has made a most enjoyable film out of apparently intractable material—enjoyable even by those in whom the Beatles do not induce hysteria. The treatment is wildly imaginative but the gimmickry is disciplined, and the whole thing

is a good deal more acceptable than its successor, *Help!* (1965), in which a silly and superfluous plot becomes so forcedly funny as to end up merely tiresome.

**THE MASQUE OF THE RED DEATH. Script:** Charles Beaumont, R. W. Campbell, from Edgar Allan Poe. Direction: Roger Corman. Photography: Nicolas Roeg (Technicolor). Editing: Ann Chegwidden. Music: David Lee. Art Direction: Robert Jones. Players: Vincent Price, Hazel Court, Jane Asher, Skip Martin, Patrick Magee, Nigel Green, John Westbrook. Production: Alta Vista/Anglo Amalgamated. 86 mins.

**THE TOMB OF LIGEIA. Script:** Robert Towne, from Edgar Allan Poe. Direction: Roger Corman. Photography: Arthur Grant (Eastmancolor). Editing: Alfred Cox. Music: Kenneth V. Jones.

*1964: Vincent Price in Roger Corman's THE MASQUE OF THE RED DEATH.*

Art Direction: Colin Southcott. Players: Vincent Price, Elizabeth Shepherd, John Westbrook, Oliver Johnston, Derek Francis. Production: Alta Vista. 81 mins.

Roger Corman was already known for his American Poe films, but it was in these two British productions that his work in the field reached its highest peak, partly, it seems, because of a larger budget being available. Both are remarkable for their flair and panache, the great beauty of their settings and colour, and the bravura performances of the masterful and sardonic Vincent Price. *The Masque* is the weightier of the two, a brilliant parable of good and evil rising at times to poetic

mystery; but *Ligeia* is also full of imaginative originality, including a superbly treated nightmare sequence. These are unquestionably the two British horror films of the year.

## Short Films and Documentaries

SCENE NUN, TAKE ONE. Script: Maurice Hatton, Michael Wood. Direction: Maurice Hatton. Photography: David Muir, Ian Macmillan. Editing: Nicholas Hale. Music: Kenny Graham. Player: Susannah York. Production: Maurice Hatton. 26 mins.

A young actress playing a nun in a film has a tiff with her director, goes off in annoyance, and is taken by the public she encounters for the genuine article. The ensuing developments have a gaiety and warmth largely due to Susannah York's enchanting presence. A moral is offered at the end: "When you're pretending to be something you're not, make sure the others are pretending too," but in truth this delightful little movie needs no justification other than its own tonic qualities.

## 1964: Facts of Interest

Michel Balcon gains control of British Lion and plans an ambitious programme of British films.

The Academy Cinema, Oxford Street, London, opens its Academy 3 as a private cinema club—later to become public. Academy 2 is to open in 1965, making the group a pioneer triplet.

# 1965

DARLING. Script: Frederick Raphael. Direction: John Schlesinger. Photography: Ken Higgins. Editing: James Clark. Music: John Dankworth. Art Direction: Ray Simm. Players: Dirk Bogarde, Laurence Harvey, Julie Christie, Roland Curram, Alex Scott. Basil Henson. Production: Joseph Janni. 127 mins.

It is important to remember, in considering this film, that the story is told in the framework of an interview for a woman's magazine—hence the events are seen, or at least recounted, from "Darling's" own viewpoint. The blaming of society for her actions or character are thus seen merely as a spoilt, petty, amoral, self-centered and often tedious young woman's attempts at self-justification, rather than an objective appraisement of a state of affairs which might have made her what she unfortunately is. At times, admittedly, the adopted convention seems strained to accommodate a mature and compassionate vision quite out of her range. On the whole, however, the film is thus a sort of double bluff. Darling herself is frankly a bit of a bore—worthless characters are seldom worth watching—and it is in the often brilliant incidental episodes that most of the interest lies. The sum of the parts is greater than the whole. One of the most interesting things about the film in its entirety, in fact, is how uninteresting its central character is.

THE SPY WHO CAME IN FROM THE COLD. Script: Paul Dehn, Guy Trosper, from the novel by John Le Carré. Direction: Martin Ritt. Photography: Oswald Morris. Editing: Anthony Harvey.

Music: Sol Kaplan. Art Direction: Edward Marshall. Players: Richard Burton, Claire Bloom, Oskar Werner, Peter Van Eyck, Sam Wanamaker, Cyril Cusack, Beatrix Lehmann. Production: Martin Ritt. 112 mins.

This is generally regarded as having inaugu-

*1965: Julie Christie as DARLING.*

1965: *THE SPY WHO CAME IN FROM THE COLD*, Claire Bloom and a disenchanted Richard Burton.

rated the realistic school of espionage movies—the reverse side of the Bond coin. Whether the events really add up to a much more accurate account of the grubby business may be open to question, but the grey gritty photography, and Burton's grey, gritty face, the low-toned performances, the dreary settings, the deliberately cool revelation of the many plot twists—all certainly give an *illusion* of reality. Burton's bitter denunciation rings true. The atmosphere of tired, dogged, disillusioned purposefulness is almost as strong as in *The Third Man,* and even more depressing in that—unlike the earlier film—it cannot be set down to the exhaustion following a disastrous but past war, but to the hopeless continuation of a present and apparently permanent one.

REPULSION. Script: Roman Polanski, Gerard Brach. Direction: Roman Polanski. Photography: Gilbert Taylor. Editing: Alastair McIntyre. Music: Chico Hamilton. Art Direction: Seamus Flannery.

Players: Catherine Deneuve, Yvonne Furneaux, John Fraser, Ian Hendry, Patrick Wymark, Helen Fraser, Valerie Taylor, James Villiers, Hugh Fuchter. Production: Compton-Tekli (Gene Gutowski). 104 mins.

In this complex and cleverly constructed film, his first in English, Polanski charts the disintegration of a mind—from withdrawn moodiness to maniacal killing and final complete collapse. Carol Ledoux, a strangely silent and unresponsive Belgian girl, shares a flat with her sister, and works in a South Kensington beauty salon. Her sister, who is carrying on an affair with a married man, goes away with him for a fortnight, leaving Carol alone: when they return it is to find the flat a shambles, two men dead, and Carol lying inert on the floor. Particularly subtle is the way in which we are gradually drawn into closer and closer involvement with Carol: the very opening shot establishes how close that involvement is to be, and the lead up to the moment when, as distinct from looking *at* her, we begin to look *with* her, is most cunningly contrived. The same applies to the main set—by constant small touches Polanski ensures that we shall feel as closed up as she does in the dingy little Earls Court apartment. The final shot travels slowly round the living-room, then up to and right into one small part of an all-important family group. This brilliantly rounds off a wholly brilliant film; resolving, if not fully explaining, all the horror that has taken place, as the last chord of Chico Hamilton's highly atmospheric score is itself resolved to harmony. The film was passed uncut by the censor (a triumph for the time) because of professionally confirmed authenticity in its study of an abnormal condition.

**THE KNACK.** Script: Charles Wood, from Ann Jellicoe's play. Direction: Richard Lester. Photography: David Watkin. Editing: Anthony Gibbs. Music: John Barry. Art Direction: Assheton Gorton. Players: Rita Tushingham, Ray Brooks, Michael Crawford, Donal Donnelly. Production: Woodfall. 84 mins.

Nothing in Richard Lester's film version of the play about a young man's anxiety to learn the knack of collecting girls quite comes up to the wonderful opening fantasy wherein the whole house and staircase teems with blondes all clad in white, mystic, wonderful. Nevertheless, and despite complaints that extensions and camera tricks have coarsened the play's subtlety, the rest is full of delights—the transporting of the bed (though it goes on too long), Rita Tushingham crying "Rape!" to disconcerted onlookers, the miraculous

*1965: REPULSION, Catherine Deneuve as Carol being guided past the workman (Mike Pratt) who will figure in her hallucinations. Director Roman Polanski can be glimpsed behind her.*

white room, the brisk and witty direction, Michael Crawford's engaging performance. The film, in fact, is fun—a quality these days rare enough to be treasured.

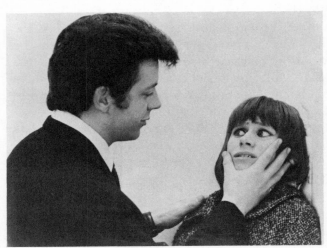

*1965: Ray Brooks and Rita Tushingham in THE KNACK.*

FOUR IN THE MORNING. Script, Direction: Anthony Simmons. Photography: Larry Pizer. Editing: Fergus McDonell. Music: John Barry. Art Direction: Bernard Sarron. Players: Judi Dench, Ann Lynn, Brian Phelan, Norman Rodway, Joe Melia. Production: West One (John Morris). 94 mins.

*Four in the Morning* comprises two interwoven but unconnected stories—one about a married couple, the other a casual encounter—linked by an episode, the discovery of a dead girl in the river. Its original intention was to be a lyrical documentary about the River Thames, but Simmons then decided to develop the story, basing it on an old Victorian poem about a drowned girl. The narratives were shot separately, with an interval of some two months, and further delays were caused by other commitments of the cast. The result shows no sign of any such broken schedule. The underlying interrelationships and contrasts between the two main stories are most subtly suggested; the ending is brilliantly and disturbingly ambiguous. Depressing though the subjects may appear, the final effect is inspiring rather than otherwise, on account of the sympathy and insight

with which they are treated, and the closeness of our own involvement. Films such as this can only be regarded with a mixture of delight and despair: delight at the thought that independent producers without much money to spare have the faith and enthusiasm to make them—despair at an industrial set-up that results in their encountering such difficulty in achieving the recognition they deserve.

THE NANNY. Script: Jimmy Sangster, based on Evelyn Piper's novel. Direction: Seth Holt. Photography: Harry Waxman. Editing: Tom Simpson. Music: Richard Rodney Bennett. Art Direction: Edward Carrick. Players: Bette Davis, Wendy Craig, Jill Bennett, James Villiers, William Dix, Pamela Franklin. Production: Hammer. 93 mins.

FANATIC (DIE, DIE, MY DARLING). Script: Richard Matheson, from Anne Blaisdell's novel, *Nightmare*. Direction: Silvio Narizzano. Photography: Arthur Ibbetson (Technicolor). Editing: James Needs. Music: Wilfred Josephs. Art Direction: Peter Proud. Players: Tallulah Bankhead, Stefanie Powers, Peter Vaughan, Maurice Kaufman, Yootha Joyce, Donald Sutherland. Production: Hammer. 96 mins.

Two distinguished American actresses graced the Hammer studios during the year. *The Nanny* is the more realistic of these productions—though the difference is only relative. Bette Davis appears, unusually restrained for the most part, as a children's nurse who arrives at a neurotic family's house to look after an unbalanced little boy. She is also in a distinctly shaky mental condition herself, which doesn't help matters. Jill Bennett's crawling, gasping death by heart attack (post-synchronised) is a *tour-de-force*. Tallulah Bankhead in *The Fanatic* rules over a country household consisting of a dour housekeeper, an oversexed handyman, a mad gardener, and obsessive memories of her dead son. When the latter's erstwhile fiancée makes a courtesy call on the occasion of her engagement to someone else the old lady regards her as permanently part of the family. When she tries to leave she is locked in the attic, starved, physically maltreated by the housekeeper, and given lessons in moral uplift. Both films are expertly made essays in horror, and both ladies appear to enjoy themselves tremendously.

*1965: Judi Dench and Norman Rodway, superb as the disillusioned married couple in FOUR IN THE MORNING.*

## 1965: Facts of Interest

Rank opens "twin Odeons" in Nottingham, claimed to be the world's first automated cinema project.

The number of British cinemas is put at 1,971, of which Rank owns 329, A.B.C. 267, Essoldo 145 and Star 107. Ninety-two were closed during the year ended July 1965.

Death of H. Bruce Woolfe.

# 1966

A MAN FOR ALL SEASONS. Script: Robert Bolt, based on his own play. Direction: Fred Zinnemann. Photography: Ted Moore (Technicolor). Editing: Ralph Kemplen. Music: Georges Delerue. Art Direction: John Box, Terence Marsh. Players: Paul Scofield, Robert Shaw, Wendy Hiller, Leo McKern, Orson Welles, Susannah York, John Hurt, Nigel Davenport. Production: Fred Zinnemann. 120 mins.

*A Man for All Seasons* concerns itself almost exclusively with Thomas More's stand against Henry's demand for a divorce in order to marry Anne Boleyn. In an account which deals with only a particular part (albeit the most important one) of a man's life, it is irrelevant to complain that only part of his character is revealed. This holds good even if, by excluding some of his poorer traits, it presents him as a more remote, less human, figure. Bolt and Zinnemann are here aiming for a distillation rather than a re-creation of history. Bolt has, for instance, said that he quite deliberately made the King several years younger than he in fact was at the time, because what he felt to be essential about his relationship with More was something which was much more obvious when the King was in his earlier years. With only two hours in which to present a historical character it is obvious that a writer, a film-maker, a dramatist, will emphasise those qualities which most interest him. In this light, *A Man for All Seasons* is a work of the greatest integrity, dignity, humanity and dramatic power, beautiful to look at and almost flawlessly performed, with Scofield's portrayal gaining from a medium able to reproduce every subtle nuance of voice and expression.

ALFIE. Script: Bill Naughton, from his own play. Direction: Lewis Gilbert. Photography: Otto Heller (Technicolor). Editing: Thelma Connell. Music: Sonny Rollins. Art Direction: Peter Mullins. Players: Michael Caine, Shelley Winters, Millicent Martin, Julia Foster, Jane Asher, Shirley Anne Field, Vivien Merchant. Production: Lewis Gilbert. 114 mins.

Despite the fact that *Alfie* in its elaborate and broadened screen version has lost some of the simple point and pathos of the original, it remains an entertaining and sometimes touching film. The young man who believes in making the most of his own life regardless of other people's was never a very satisfying protagonist, and even by this time was about played out: still, his little entanglements are amusingly related, with the help of half-a-dozen excellent actresses, and Michael Caine achieves the considerable feat of making us feel an occasional pang of sympathy for Alfie when, suddenly and belatedly, he begins to wonder whether his life with the girls was really so worth while after all.

CUL-DE-SAC. Script: Roman Polanski, Gerard Brach. Direction: Roman Polanski. Photography: Gilbert Taylor. Editing: Alastair McIntyre. Music: Komeda. Art Direction: Voytek. Players: Donald Pleasence, Françoise Dorléac, Lionel Stander, Jack MacGowran, William Franklin, Robert Dorning, Jacqueline Bisset. Production: Compton-Tekli (Gene Gutowski). 111 mins.

The basic plot of *Cul-De-Sac* (Polanski's favourite of his own films to date, though not all would agree with him here) is the conventional

*1966: A MAN FOR ALL SEASONS, Orson Welles as Cardinal Wolsey.*

*1966: ALFIE and one of his numerous girls, Michael Caine and Julia Foster.*

thriller of criminals breaking into a lonely house and terrifying the occupants. But the plot is the least part of this film which demonstrates—in grim comedy and hilarious tragedy—that escapism is no escape. All the characters are seeking to escape from something—all are thrown together in a blind alley where reason itself breaks down, where nothing and nobody reacts as might be expected. The atmosphere of a sort of mad, blundering confusion is sustained and developed with light-handed skill, and the island castle setting—up-

*1966: CUL-DE-SAC, Lionel Stander and Donald Pleasence in Roman Polanski's surrealistic-style black farce.*

turned boat hen-house, endless stone ramps, inundated causeway, long blank beach—contributes much to overall strangeness of this blackest of farces.

**THE FAMILY WAY.** Script: Bill Naughton, from his own play, *All in Good Time.* Direction: Roy Boulting. Photography: Harry Waxman (Eastmancolor). Editing: Ernest Hosler. Music: Paul McCartney. Art Direction: Alan Withy. Players: Hayley Mills, Hywel Bennett, John Mills, Marjorie Rhodes, Murray Head, Avril Angers, John Comer. Production: John Boulting. 114 mins.

Hayley Mills "grows up" in this pleasant, sharp little comedy of a young married couple's early sexual difficulties (or rather, the bridegroom's inability to consummate). The film has no serious suggestions to make—other than the advisability of making sure the honeymoon accommodation is secure—and in fact the characters developed most in depth are the parents. The North country setting is evident in the reactions of those concerned to their situation rather than in the situation itself, which could occur anywhere—well, almost. Roy Boulting keeps things moving efficiently along, and the result is a warm, sincere little movie with sufficient salty truth and humour to prevent it lapsing into sentimentality.

**FAHRENHEIT 451.** Script: François Truffaut, Jean-Louis Richard, from Ray Bradbury's story. Direction: François Truffaut. Photography: Nicolas Roeg (Technicolor). Editing: Thom Noble. Music: Bernard Herrmann. Art Direction: Syd Cain. Players: Julie Christie, Oskar Werner, Cyril Cusack, Anton Diffring, Bee Duffell. Production: Lewis M. Allen. 112 mins.

Truffaut's first, and to date only, British film has not been altogether favourably received, but had it appeared under a less illustrious name, and expectations less highly raised, its reception might have been kinder. The chill story of a future in which the printed word is forbidden, books outlawed and burnt because of their power to encourage independent thought, is told with suitable coolness, photographed by Roeg in equally suitable picture-book colouring. Few sights are more paradoxically sinister than that of the little bright red fire-engine gliding toy-like across the landscape on its mission of destruction.

*1966: Hayley Mills contemplates her new husband in*
THE FAMILY WAY.

*1966: FAHRENHEIT 451, Oskar Werner and Julie Christie.*

**IT HAPPENED HERE.** Script, Direction: Kevin Brownlow, Andrew Mollo. Photography: Peter Suschitsky, Kevin Brownlow. Editing: Kevin Brownlow. Music: Jack Beaver. Art Direction: Andrew Mollo. Players: Pauline Murray, Sebastian Shaw, Fiona Leland, Honor Fehrson. Production: Kevin Brownlow, Andrew Mollo. 99 mins.

Ten years in the making, launched when the producers/directors were barely out of school, this film of an imaginary occupation of England by the Nazis is a monument to endurance and ingenuity: but it does not need the prop of an interesting production story to hold it up. It stands firmly on its own feet, telling a bleak tale in cold, uncompromising absolutely convincing espisodes, shot and played with newsreel immediacy and reality. The result is a frightening and thought-provoking essay in the what-might-have-been.

**ONE MILLION YEARS B. C.** Script: Michael Carreras, based on a story by Mickell Novak, George Baker and Joseph Frickert. Direction: Don Chaffey. Photography: Wilkie Cooper (Technicolor). Special visual effects: Ray Harryhausen. Editing: James Needs, Tom Simpson. Music: Mario Nascimbene. Art Direction: Robert Jones. Production: John Richardson, Raquel Welch, Percy Herbert, Robert Brown, Martine Beswick. Production: Hammer. 100 mins.

Hammer celebrated their one-hundredth production in flamboyant style, presenting not the super-horror film that might have been expected,

*1966: One of Ray Harryhausen's impressive models in* ONE MILLION YEARS B.C., *the film marking Hammer's first century.*

but a sort of pre-history comic strip with Raquel Welch as an early Jane. The swirling, coloured opening is most effective, as are most of the Dynamation monsters—the least successful is the lizard who really is a lizard, and shows much less liveliness than Harryhausen's little models. The human cast has a whale of a time running around in matted hair and not much else, gnawing bones, looking wild-eyed at nature's manifestations, conversing in grunt-and-monosyllable dialogue, stuffing in caves and fighting for scraps: or alternatively, if they are fortunate enough to have been born blond, cavorting by the sea. It is all done in Hammer's best manner, with Don Chaffey never putting a Triceratops' foot wrong.

## 1966: Facts of Interest

The Monopolies Commission reports that monopoly conditions prevail in the supply of films to exhibitors, but recognise that radical changes in the industry's structure, such as the introduction of a third circuit, might do more harm than good.

The rebuilt Marble Arch Odeon, London, opens, with the first cinema moving-staircase in Britain. The cinema originally on the site, the Regal, opened in 1928, with Al Jolson in *The Singing Fool*.

# 1967

BLOW-UP. Script: Michelangelo Antonioni, To-nino Guerra, from a short story by Julio Cortazar. Direction: Antonioni. Photography: Carlo Di Palma (Eastmancolor). Editing: Frank Clarke. Music: Herbert Hancock. Art Direction: Assheton Gorton. Players: David Hemmings, Vanessa Redgrave, Sarah Miles, Peter Bowles, John Castle, Jane Birkin, Gillian Hills, Verushka, Susan Brodrick. Production: Carlo Ponti-M.G.M. 111 mins.

The main theme of *Blow-up* is individual responsibility and the ease with which it is possible to avoid that responsibility in a world where the borderline between reality and illusion is ever less clearly defined. The chief medium of self-deception in Antonioni's brilliant film is his own instrument of communication, the camera. Thomas, the fashion photographer, is brought face to face with reality as a result of entering the strangely sinister, pale-green, tree-rustling little park (a triumph of location work), where he witnesses, or at least records with his camera unwittingly, a murder. Because of the indeterminate quality of his evidence, and by taking advantage of intervening distractions (such as a roll in purple paper with two pretty teenagers) he is able to avoid commitment, eventually renouncing reality altogether and, a tiny dot on the green lawn by the tennis court, dissolving into nothingness himself. The amount of argument that has arisen over the fundamentally irrelevant question as to whether there actually *has* been a murder (it is shown clearly enough that there has), is a measure of the director's success in extending the significance of Thomas's predicament beyond the confines of the screen, to involve us all. It is impossible in so brief a comment to do justice to this complex, tantalising, thought-provoking, beautiful and wholly engrossing masterpiece, a triumphant success for the director's first British production.

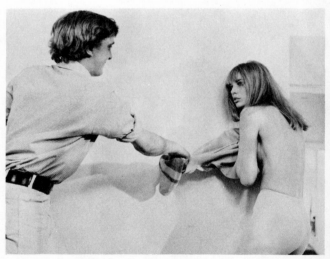

*1967: BLOW-UP, David Hemmings and Jane Birkin at the start of the "roll in the purple."*

ACCIDENT. Script: Harold Pinter, from Nicholas Mosley's novel. Direction: Joseph Losey. Photography: Gerry Fisher (Eastmancolor). Editing: Reginald Beck. Music: John Dankworth. Art Direction: Carmen Dillon. Players: Dirk Bogarde, Stanley Baker, Jacqueline Sassard, Michael York, Vivien Merchant, Delphine Seyrig. Production: Joseph Losey, Norman Priggen. 105 mins.

270

Losey's study of the rivalries and animosities in university life, between tutors, pupils and wives, brought to a head by the presence of an almost totally uncommunicative Austrian girl, shows that aristocrats of both intellect and class can behave as stupidly and bady as anyone else (if such a thing needed proof), and are as liable to the accidents of chance. The theme, as in *Blow-up,* is individual responsibility, in this case emphasising the unforeseen—or accidental—effects that anything we say or do may have on our own, or anyone else's life. Apart from an odd touch of smugness this is a haunting, compelling film, marred in parts by seemingly wilful and arbitrary obscurity in both script and direction—tricks with time sequences, with the soundtrack, that add nothing to the significance of the film.

HALF A SIXPENCE. Script: Beverly Cross, from H. G. Wells's novel *Kipps* and his own musical play. Direction: George Sidney. Photography: Geoffrey Unsworth (Technicolor, Panavision). Editing: Bill Lewthwaite, Frank Santillo. Music: David Heneker. Art Direction: Peter Murton. Players: Tommy Steele, Julia Foster, Cyril Ritchard, Penelope Horner, Elaine Taylor, Grover Dale, James Villiers. Production: Charles H. Schneer, George Sidney. 146 mins.

Here at last, and worth waiting for, is a wholly successful large-scale British musical (by an American director). Even though this is the film version of a musical version of a play of a novel, Kipps is still Kipps. The sets are stunning, the big numbers, particularly "Banjo" and "Rain," are exhilarating, and the whole two-and-a-half hours swings by with a verve and a dash which equals any other musical yet made. Tommy Steele brings all the charm of his stage performance to the screen, Julia Foster—with little experience as either singer or dancer—is delightful, George Sidney's practised hand is in firm control, it all goes, in fact, with a flash, a bang, and a wallop.

OUR MOTHER'S HOUSE. Script: Jeremy Brooks, Haya Harareet, from Julian Gloag's novel. Direction: Jack Clayton. Photography: Larry Pizer (Metrocolor). Editing: Tom Priestley. Music: Georges Delerue. Art Direction: Reece Pemberton. Players: Dirk Bogarde, Margaret Brooks, Pamela Franklin, Mark Lester, Sarah Nicholls, Yootha Joyce. Production: Heron/Filmways (Jack Clayton). 105 mins.

Throughout their mother's long illness seven young children, brought up in the strictest religious training, have lived with her in a rambling, decaying house alone save for a sluttish daily help. Thinking, when she dies, they will be taken away to an orphanage, the children hide the mother's body in the garden and set up a sort of chapel which they decorate with her personal relics. There they gather at night and, through the mediumship of one of the girls, "communicate" with their mother to learn her will. This seemingly improbable situation is made entirely credible by Clayton's tactful handling. Particularly striking are the

*1967: Stanley Baker and the enigmatic Jacqueline Sassard in ACCIDENT.*

*1967: The title number routine from the exhilarating HALF A SIXPENCE, Julia Foster and Tommy Steele.*

*1967: FAR FROM THE MADDING CROWD, Terence Stamp as Sergeant Troy and Julie Christie as Bathsheba.*

formidable scenes of the children coldly quoting Biblical texts at one another and ruthlessly putting into practice the teachings as they interpret them. The closing moments are poignant, when—after their private world has been broken into by their disreputable father who has driven one of the girls to kill him—they slowly leave the house. Throughout the film the director shows his sensitivity in creating this strange, haunting film without once resorting to the easy sentimentality of conventional childish charm.

## FAR FROM THE MADDING CROWD.

Script: Frederic Raphael, from Thomas Hardy's novel. Direction: John Schlesinger. Photography: Nicolas Roeg (Technicolor, Panavision, 70 mm). Editing: Malcolm Cooke. Music: Richard Rodney Bennett. Art Direction: Roy Smith. Players: Julie Christie, Terence Stamp, Peter Finch, Alan Bates, Fiona Walker, Prunella Ransome, Alison Leggatt. Production: Joseph Janni. 168 mins.

Hardy has generally proved intractable material for transferring to another medium: Schlesinger has gone at least some way towards succeeding. Hardy's countryside is fixed most beautifully in Roeg's photography, his villagers and village life re-created without patronage and with apparent authenticity, his main characters, particularly as played by Alan Bates and Peter Finch, are convincing and their fate concerns us. The trouble seems to be that except for a few moments of grandeur the events are seen from ground level. Storms and sunshine and chance and fate are seen to have their effects on the lives of the little people, but the brooding majesty—the sense of Destiny acting through nature—is absent.

## DUTCHMAN.

Script: the play by LeRoi Jones. Direction: Anthony Harvey. Photography: Gerry Turpin. Editing: Anthony Harvey. Music: John Barry. Art Direction: Herbert Smith. Players: Shirley Knight, Al Freeman, Jnr. Production: Gene Persson. 56 mins.

LeRoi Jones's short, pithy play is a parable of three-fold confrontation—class, sex, race. In transferring it from the stage, Anthony Harvey (well-known as an editor but here making his *début* as director) has used the film medium to enlarge its significance from a particular encounter to a universal allegory; the same subway station recurs more than once, the arrival of the other passengers is concealed until a dramatic moment when the camera draws back from the protagonists to reveal the coach filled with unnoticed and unnoticing people. At the same time he uses close-up to suggest the claustrophobic confrontation between the couple. It is a film of compelling power, photographed in harsh black-and-white, unrelenting, pared to the bone.

*1967: DUTCHMAN, Shirley Knight and Al Freeman Jr. in Anthony Harvey's taut version of the play by LeRoi Jones.*

## 1967: Facts of Interest

Large sales of films to television causes anxiety to distributors but is recognized as an integral part of film production economics.

The Odeon, St. Martin's Lane, London, is opened, with a "floating screen."

The British Film Institute launches its first Regional Theatres.

Death of Maurice Elvey.

1967: *Boris Karloff and Catherine Lacey in THE SORCERERS, directed by Michael Reeves. Reeves died at the age of twenty-five after completing three films, of which this is the most noteworthy. In it he already shows promise that, but for his early death, he might have become a master of suspense.*

1967: *An eerie moment from THE SHUTTERED ROOM, a superior exercise in horror directed by David Greene, with a really credible and terrifying "thing-in-the-attic" and a tension sustained through-out. The understandably apprehensive girl is Carol Lynley, being ogled by Oliver Reed.*

# 1968

IF. . . . Script: David Sherwin, based on the scenario *Crusaders,* by David Sherwin and John Howlett. Direction: Lindsay Anderson. Photography: Miroslav Ondricek (Eastmancolor and monochrome). Editing: David Gladwell. Music: Marc Wilkinson: "Sanctus" from the *Missa Luba.* Art Direction: Jocelyn Herbert. Players: Malcolm McDowell, David Wood, Richard Warwick, Robert Swann, Christine Noonan, Hugh Thomas, Rupert Webster, Peter Jeffrey, Arthur Lowe, Mary Macleod, Geoffrey Chater, Graham Crowden, Mona Washbourne. Production: Memorial (Michael Medwin, Lindsay Anderson). 111 mins.

*If.* . . . starts as a realistic and perfectly straightforward picture of British public school life, until gradually the fantastic starts to seep in, as when the Housemaster's wife, until now an ordinary if somewhat dumb and enigmatic figure, is suddenly seen wandering along the deserted corridors in the nude. As the surreal takes over the satirical attack on the Establishment, which the school is in microcosm, intensifies. The film suggests the necessity of revolt against irresponsible authority. As Lindsay Anderson points out in his notes to the published script, the three boys and the girl are traditionalists, neither anti-heroes nor drop-outs. The film's irony lies in the realisation of the futility of the revolting gesture, if only because in so short a time those concerned will have grown into positions of authority themselves. Hence the holocaust at the end is, in Lindsay Anderson's words, plainly metaphorical. It is also, ultimately, purposeless. The "god" appears to be thrown down and bodies fall about, but nothing has really happened at all.

The final shot is of the leader of the revolutionaries firing direct at the audience—but they leave the theatre unharmed. The ultimate pessimism of this exciting and totally non-depressing film is in its title: the challenging word IF—but all that follows is a row of dots . . .

2001—A SPACE ODYSSEY. Script: Stanley Kubrick, Arthur C. Clarke, from the latter's story, *The Sentinel.* Direction: Stanley Kubrick. Photography: Geoffrey Unsworth (Metrocolor, Super Panavision, presented in Cinerama). Editing: Ray Lovejoy. Music: Richard Strauss, Johann Strauss, Aran Khachaturian, György Ligeti. Art Direction: Tony Masters, Harry Lange, Ernie Archer, John Hoesli. Special effects: Wally Veevers, Douglas Trumbull. Players: Keir Dullea, Gary Lockwood, William Sylvester, Daniel Richter, Douglas Rain, Leonard Rossiter. Production: Stanley Kubrick. 141 mins.

The most ambitious of all essays in science fiction, extending from pre-history to the last syllable of recorded time, turns, paradoxically, back to religion. As a rule in such films, though he may speak in an awed voice of "meddling in something beyond our limited knowledge," when he has stupidly let loose some unimaginable catastrophe or blob-shaped monster, man is pictured as master of what he does. In *2001,* from ape to astronaut, he is pushed ahead by a mysterious booster, on which he is dependent for each stage of his "progress." All he seems anxious to do, all the use he derives from his slab-given gifts, is to move his body from one place to another ever further away

*1968: IF. . . . , The schoolboy revolution in full force.*

and at ever increasing speed—as if locomotion was the highest aim of human existence. It is thus a deeply pessimistic film, its essentially nihilistic lesson wrapped up in some of the most beautiful artificial images ever put on the screen. Scene after scene catches the breath with the delight of a child watching a sparkler, and serves to conceal the bitter medicine we are asked to swallow.

## DANCE OF THE VAMPIRES (THE FEARLESS VAMPIRE KILLERS).

Script: Gerard Brach, Roman Polanski. Direction: Roman Polanski. Photography: Douglas Slocombe (Metrocolor, Panavision). Editing: Alastair MacIntyre. Music. Komeda. Art Direction: Wilfred Shingleton. Players: Jack MacGowran, Roman Polanski, Sharon Tate, Alfie Bass, Ferdy Mayne, Terry Downes, Iain

Quarrier, Fiona Lewis. Production: Cadre Films/Filmways (Gene Gutowski). 107 mins.

To dismiss this as no more than a parody of a horror film is very much to underrate it. A parody has no existence except by courtesy of the original it parodies, whereas this enchanting movie, hilarious, horrific, and tender by turns, full of underlying meanings and visually dazzling, exists altogether in its own right. In it are to be found many of the Polanski preoccupations developed in his other films—the master-servant relationship, the solitude and loneliness of human beings, no-one in the last resort much help to anyone else, the only really effective community that of the wicked: as the black magic devotees in *Rosemary's Baby,* so the vampires here. It is also a devastating picture of the catastrophic arrogance of the "scientist"—

276

the half-informed do-gooders, the "progressives" who claim they know what is best for other people. There is one moment when the good Professor— who by his muddling lets loose the vampiric evil throughout the world—looks every bit as wicked as the Count himself. But while this refutes suggestions that the film is no more than a joke and a wonderfully successful parody, that it is the odd man out in Polanski's work to date, it is, of course, the humour and visual beauty that are its most immediate delights. And call him "von Krolock" or anything else, Ferdy Mayne, with his black-velvet voice and imposing presence, is the most impressive Dracula of them all.

*1968: Roman Polanski (who also directed), Jack Mac-Gowran, and Ferdy Mayne as chief vampire, in DANCE OF THE VAMPIRES.*

**THE BOFORS GUN.** Script: John McGrath, from his own play. Direction: Jack Gold. Photography: Alan Hume (Technicolor). Editing: Anne Coates. Art Direction: Terence Knight. Players: Nicol Williamson, Iam Holm, David Warner, Richard O'Callaghan, Barry Jackson, Peter Vaughan. Production: R. A. Goldston, Otto Platchkes. 105 mins.

This is another film which, owing to the present distribution system, shamefully few people have had a chance of seeing. It is also another first feature by a director whose work has so far been confined to television. The events of a single climactic night among the members of a guard squad in a British army camp in Germany during the Fifties are depicted with taut, economical, uncompromis-

ing realism—events which culminate in one man's suicide and the ruin of another's career. Superbly acted by its small cast, reproducing the claustrophobic atmosphere of men cooped up in a small army hut with all their hostility and frustration and boredom simmering until they boil over, the action mounts unrelentingly from quiet start to shattering finish. Nicol Williamson is superb as the violent Irishman who deliberately destroys himself in order to vent his malice on others, and David Warner is equally impressive as the Lance Bombardier whose indecision leads to tragedy.

**OLIVER!** Script: Vernon Harris, from Lionel Bart's musical based on Charles Dickens's *Oliver Twist.* Direction: Carol Reed. Photography: Oswald Morris (Technicolor, Panavision 70). Editing: Ralph Kemplen. Music: Lionel Bart. Art Direction: John Box. Players: Ron Moody, Shani Wallis, Oliver Reed, Harry Secombe, Mark Lester, Hugh Griffith, Jack Wild, Joseph O'Conor. Production: Romulus. 146 mins.

*Oliver Twist,* written by Dickens in burning indignation at the evils of the time, is, in the words of Edgar Johnson, "a sulphurous melodrama in which horror is fused with angry pathos." Here we are presented with a huge "Victorian" musical (with very un-Victorian music) in which the starved and stunted children heartily sing and dance, whores are healthy, rosy and wholesome as brown bread (and also sing and dance), pimps, receivers and thieves are sprightly men and lads (and also sing and dance), and all this—stealing, murdering, whoring, abduction, exploitation—is dished up as a suitable family U certificate treat. *Oliver!* is a pretty, lively spectacle with some truly magnificent sets. It has been loaded with Oscars.

**CHARLIE BUBBLES.** Script: Shelagh Delaney. Direction: Albert Finney. Photography: Peter Suschitsky (Technicolor). Editing: Fergus McDonell. Music: Musha Donat. Art Direction: Edward Marshall. Players: Albert Finney, Billie Whitelaw, Colin Blakely, Liza Minelli, Timothy Garland, Richard Pearson, John Ronane. Production: Memorial/Universal (Michael Medwin). 89 mins.

Another praiseworthy first feature that has had a considerable struggle to reach the screen at all (in Britain, that is—in America it had had some success before being shown elsewhere), *Charlie*

*Bubbles* concerns a successful modern writer who finds both affluence and fame unsatisfying and sets out to discover, and recover, himself in the small farmhouse where his ex-wife and his son have been parked. Finney combines direction and performance with the utmost confidence and the story of his doomed odyssey is—except for an amusing but out-of-key bit of escapist fantasy at the final moment—convincing and ironically discerning.

THE LION IN WINTER. Script: James Goldman, from his own play. Direction: Anthony Harvey. Photography: Douglas Slocombe (Eastmancolor, Panavision). Editing: John Bloom. Music: John Barry. Art Direction: Peter Murton. Players: Katharine Hepburn, Peter O'Toole, Jane Merrow, John Castle, Anthony Hopkins, Nigel Terry, Timothy Dalton, Nigel Stock. Production: Joseph Levine, Martin Poll. 134 mins.

The pleasures of this film lie almost wholly in the externals—all Douglas Slocombe's exquisite photography, much of John Barry's Music, most of the performances, many of Anthony Harvey's illuminating directorial asides. The script is superior fustian, in which the author himself does not appear to believe, judging from the passages of glib, music hall repartee, and his throw-away (or give-away) lines at the end of a tense scene—"Well, what family doesn't have its ups and downs"— just in case we start to believe in what we are being shown. But if we don't believe it, why bother? Admittedly belief is frequently difficult: the film hovers uncertainly between historical reconstruction, family drama in costume, and retrospective sophisticated comment *à la Becket*, and falls between three stools.

OEDIPUS THE KING. Script: Michael Luke,

*1968: Richard Johnson as Creon and Christopher Plummer as Oedipus in Philip Saville's and Michael Luke's impressive OEDIPUS THE KING.*

1968: Oskar Werner and Barbara Ferris, who both give performances of great sensitivity in Kevin Billington's INTERLUDE, a modern re-hash of the INTERMEZZO situation; the director, in his first feature, succeeds in telling a romantic story in terms of reality, with genuine rather than contrived motivation and an avoidance of cliché in both character and situation.

*1968: THE YELLOW SUBMARINE, the Beatles as portrayed in a brilliantly imaginative pop and op art film, the first full-length British animated feature since ANIMAL FARM.*

Philip Saville, based on Paul Roche's translation of the play by Sophocles. Direction: Philip Saville. Photography: Walter Lassally (Technicolor). Editing: Paul Davies. Music: Yannis Christou. Art Direction: Yannis Migadis. Players: Christopher Plummer, Lilli Palmer, Richard Johnson, Orson Welles, Cyril Cusack, Roger Livesey, Donald Sutherland. Production: Michael Luke. 97 mins.

In this extremely impressive staging of the tragedy Philip Saville and Michael Luke had the interesting idea of turning the Greek theatre at Dodona inside out, as it were, using the whole of it, including the auditorium, to represent the Theban Palace, moving out into the neighbouring countryside when necessary. The thorny problem of treating the Chorus has been very satisfactorily solved and the whole presentation is straightforward and free from gimmickry. The flashbacks of the killing of Laius—the only occasions on which the film medium is obviously brought into use to break up the play—are extraneous, but are fitted unobtrusively into their context and serve a useful purpose of illustration and clarification. Not the least contribution of the power of the film is the brilliantly dramatic percussive score. All in all, this is arguably the most successful filming of a Greek classical tragedy to date (1971)—largely because we feel we are being shown Sophocles in a new medium, and not what some director thinks he can make out of Sophocles in that medium.

## Short Films and Documentaries

THE WHITE BUS. Script: Shelagh Delaney. Direction: Lindsay Anderson. Photography: Miroslav Ondricek. Editing: Kevin Brownlow. Music: Misha Donat. Players: Patricia Healey, Arthur Lowe, John Sharp, Julie Perry, Anthony Hopkins.

Production: Lindsay Anderson. 41 mins.

This film was made some two years before its release, thus well preceding *If. . . .* It was to have been part of a three-episode project with Peter Brook and Tony Richardson. An incident rather than a story, it deals with a girl typist's trip from London to re-visit her North country home town, her drive on a white bus taking tourists around and led, strangely, by the Mayor and his mace bearer. The film is an ambiguous mixture of fantasy and realism, intriguing to watch but difficult to interpret.

## 1968: Facts of Interest

John Player Lectures are inaugurated at the National Film Theatre.

Death of Anthony Asquith.

# 1969

OH! WHAT A LOVELY WAR. Script: based on the Joan Littlewood Theatre Workshop production from the radio feature, *The Long Long Trail* by Charles Chilton. Direction: Richard Attenborough. Photography: Gerry Turpin (Technicolor, Panavision). Editing: Kevin Connor. Music: Alfred Ralston: popular songs of the period. Art Direction: Don Ashton, Harry White. Players: John Mills, Ralph Richardson, John Gielgud, Laurence Olivier, Michael Redgrave, Jack Hawkins, John Clements, Kenneth More, Vanessa Redgrave, Paul Daneman, Joe Melia, Kim Smith, Cecil Parker, Mary Wimbush, Wendy Allnutt, Corin Redgrave, Susannah York, Dirk Bogarde, Gerald Sim, Malcolm McFee, Maurice Roeves, Colin Farrell. Production: Brian Duffy, Richard Attenborough. 144 mins.

The greatness of Richard Attenborough's achievement has been widely acclaimed, and need be only noted and endorsed here. The task of transferring a radio documentary via pier-head concert party show to large-scale wide-screen musical (for that is what the film essentially is) has been triumphantly carried out. An imaginative reconstruction of a tragic piece of recent history, the film makes its blasting attack on war primarily by revealing the bitterness, waste, futility and evil underlying what are now regarded as cosily nostalgic songs. It shows the unbridgeable gap between the experiences of those at the front, and those at home to whom the war was viewed as if through the peepshows, penny-in-the-slot machines and miniature railways of the seaside pier; between the men, and their officers and top brass (isolated in their ivory helter-skelter tower play-

ing their games of war and more concerned with their own careers than the lives they control); between the rulers, statesmen and politicians stylishly played by instantly recognisable famous film stars, and the Smith-anonymous, deliberately unmemorable figures dying in shell-holes. One of the most subtle and brilliant inventions is that of the beach-photographer figure of destiny (played by Joe Melia) who in the early stages links the various parts and speaks direct to the audience, later merging more into the background, with a more active and mysterious hand in the fate of the characters and the world itself. *Oh! What a Lovely War* is a memorial and a summing-up, a revelation

*1969: OH! WHAT A LOVELY WAR, Michael Redgrave as Sir Henry Wilson and Laurence Olivier as Sir John French.*

and a warning, an overwhelming experience, with possibly the most moving and poignant conclusion in the history of British cinema.

BATTLE OF BRITAIN. Script: James Kennaway, Wilfred Greatorex, based partly on *The Narrow Margin* by Derek Wood and Derek Dempster. Direction: Guy Hamilton. Photography: Freddie Young (Technicolor, Panavision). Editing: Bert Bates. Music: William Walton, Ron Goodwin. Players: Laurence Olivier, Robert Shaw, Christopher Plummer, Susannah York, Michael Caine, Kenneth More, Trevor Howard, Michael Redgrave, Curt Jurgens. Production: Harry Saltzman, S. Benjamin Fisz. 131 mins.

*Battle of Britain's* treatment of a war of thirty years ago makes interesting comparison with *Oh! What a Lovely War's* treatment of one after fifty-five years. The former is a wholly factual reconstruction, striving after scrupulous accuracy, yet oddly enough conveying less of the true feeling of the time than does the latter film of its earlier events. It is a stirring picture of the only form of virtually single combat left—plenty of battles for the boys—though after a while one dogfight tends to look very like another, and the sight of swirling, dodging, zooming planes conveys little of the human emotions within. Down below things are less successful, except for Olivier's authoritative and often moving portrait of Dowding. The film's blitz is not the blitz London knew, neither in atmosphere nor, strangely, in appearance. Nor is the full sense of the battle's importance brought out. Of its kind, however, this is a finely made war spectacle. It bends over backwards in its attempts to be fair to both sides—a very different attitude to that encouraged while the events depicted were actually taking place: it thus interestingly implies that the "All Germans are villains" propaganda was utterly indefensible and false. This is, perhaps, the first step towards an *Oh! What a Lovely World War Two.*

WOMEN IN LOVE. Script: Larry Kramer, from D. H. Lawrence's novel. Direction: Ken Russell. Photography: Billy Williams (DeLuxe Colour). Editing: Michael Bradsell. Music: Georges Delerue. Art Direction: Ken Jones. Players: Oliver Reed, Alan Bates, Glenda Jackson, Jennie Linden, Eleanor Bron. Production: Brandywine (Larry Kramer). 130 mins.

Lawrence was a great, or at any rate a very influential writer, but he could also be, in the words of a contemporary poet, "hot, soft and woolly." A film does him a disservice when it emphasises the hysterical, febrile side of his work. The use of such filmic *clichés* as slow-motion flower-love-scenes in vertical/horizontal positions suggest an equivalent purple-patched bathos in the original. The notorious nude wrestling match, a minor if significant incident in the novel and obviously less sensational when described than when seen, here stands out in all its absurdity, and few funnier scenes can have been filmed in recent years than that of Alan Bates and Oliver Reed—good actors both—sweating and straining against each other all a-dangle in the discreet firelight. The amount of publicity this comic turn has been given is presumably a measure of its supposed importance in drawing the public. Much of the social comment of the novel has gone but the tormented breast-baring, literally, remains. The photography is outstanding and the twenties period accurately rendered throughout. Settings are often most skilfully matched in quality of emotion to the events that occur in them and many scenes, such as the Zermatt death, are very strikingly done.

A MIDSUMMER NIGHT'S DREAM. Script: the play by William Shakespeare. Direction: Peter Hall. Photography: Peter Suschitzky (Eastmancolor). Editing: Jack Harris. Music: Guy Woolfenden. Art Direction: John Bury. Players: Judi Dench, Paul Rogers, David Warner, Diana Rigg, Helen Mirren, Michael Jayston, Ian Richardson, Derek Godfrey, Barbara Jefford. Production: Michael Birkett. 124 mins.

Made with American television in mind, this transfers quite well to the larger screen. Peter Hall has paid his author the compliment of accepting that he meant what he said when he has Titania remark that her quarrel with Oberon has upset the order of the seasons. The film was shot, therefore, logically, in a period of rain. It opens with a pleasantly impudent, and equally logical, joke— the *façade* of an English country mansion superimposed with the title ATHENS. The handheld camera becomes somewhat obstrusively wavering at times, and the post-synchronisation is inclined to flatten the voices, but the whole treatment is

*1969: Paul Rogers as Bottom and Judi Dench as Titania in Peter Hall's A MIDSUMMER NIGHT'S DREAM.*

*Christopher Plummer, as Atahuallpa in THE ROYAL HUNT OF THE SUN.*

full of wit and imagination, while remaining Shakespeare's play rather than a producer's idea of what he could do to improve it. As is to be expected, full value is given to the verse, skilfully matched with, and counterpointed against, the cutting.

## THE ROYAL HUNT OF THE SUN.

Script: Philip Yordan, from Peter Shaffer's play. Direction: Irving Lerner. Photography: Roger Barlow (Technicolor). Editing: Peter Parasheles. Music: Marc Wilkinson. Art Direction: Eugène Lourié. Players: Christopher Plummer, Robert Shaw, Nigel Davenport, Michael Craig, Leonard Whiting. Production: Eugene Frenke, Philip Yordan. 121 mins.

The magnificence of the Inca kingdom was, paradoxically, more impressively suggested on the bare stage of the theatre than by all the resources of the camera—budget stringency doubtless proving a confining factor. The epic quality of the confrontation between the doomed king and his destroyer also is perhaps better suited to a stylised setting. Nevertheless there is a very great deal to admire in this inexpensively made film version—notably the astonishing performance of Christopher Plummer as Atahuallpa—an award-deserving piece of acting if ever there was one. This is one more interesting production which flashed across the screen and then vanished.

## SECRET CEREMONY.

Script: George Tabori, from a short story by Marco Denevi. Direction: Joseph Losey. Photography: Gerry Fisher (Eastmancolor). Editing: Reginald Beck. Music: Richard Rodney Bennett. Art Direction: John Clark. Players: Elizabeth Taylor, Mia Farrow, Robert Mitchum, Pamela Brown, Peggy Ashcroft. Production: John Heyman, Norman Priggen. 109 mins.

Losey's *Secret Ceremony* has had an unfortunate history—meeting with a very mixed reception, disappearing almost immediately from the cinema screens, and apparently suffering grievous mutilation in the television torture chamber. This last version has not so far been seen in Britain. Yet it is a strange and haunting film, concerned with the desperate need of human beings to replace that which is lost: a mother, a daughter, a house—hinting at the Stevensonian dualism of personality—shifting, ambiguous, extravagant, melodramatic, with a relentless hold. No small part of its fascina-

tion is the wonderful (and typical) use Losey makes of the extraordinary baroque house (an actual folly to be found in Kensington) in which nearly all the action takes place. If the story had not originally come from the Argentine, one could have believed that the house itself had told it.

*1969: Joseph Losey's SECRET CEREMONY, Elizabeth Taylor and a black-wigged Mia Farrow.*

## THE PRIME OF MISS JEAN BRODIE.

Script: Jay Presson Allen, from her own play based on Muriel Spark's novel. Direction: Ronald Neame. Photography: Ted Moore (DeLuxe Colour). Editing: Norman Savage. Music: Rod McKuen. Art Direction: Brian Herbert. Players: Maggie Smith, Robert Stephens, Pamela Franklin, Gordon Jackson, Celia Johnson, Rona Anderson. Production: Twentieth Century-Fox (Robert Fryer). 116 mins.

Jean Brodie, an unmarried teacher at an Edinburgh girls' school during the thirties, has a small group of pupils whom she outrageously favours: she ignores the timetable in order to enlarge to her class on the admiration she feels for Mussolini and Franco, entangles her girls in her own com-

*1969: THE PRIME OF MISS JEAN BRODIE, Maggie
Smith and her class.*

*1969: Vanessa Redgrave in ISADORA, directed by
Karel Reisz; she gives a bravura performance in a
patchy and overlong, but often entertaining film, the
extravagances of which match the extravagances of
its subject.*

plicated situations with members of the male staff, and generally behaves in a way calculated not to uphold the honour of the academy. Very late in the day, it seems, she is sacked. The main interest would appear to lie in how much of this frightful woman's influence remains with her girls in after-life, but this is not developed. Maggie Smith presents her in full horror, and Celia Johnson's performance dominates the film more forcibly than her character dominates the school of which she is head.

## 1969: Facts of Interest

Bryan Forbes is appointed head of production at A.B.P.C.

Cinecenta, a four-in-one house, opens in Panton Street, London, W.

Between January and November 81 cinemas throughout the country close, leaving a total of 1,636.

The Film Production Board of the British Film Institute, in a record year, secures four international prizes, completes fourteen short films, and has two features in the making.

# 1970

RYAN'S DAUGHTER. Script: Robert Bolt. Direction: David Lean (storm sequence: Roy Stevens). Photography: Freddie Young (2nd unit; Denys Coop, Bob Huke) (Metrocolor, Super Panavision 70). Editing: Norman Savage. Music: Maurice Jarre. Art Direction: Roy Walker. Players: Sarah Miles, Robert Mitchum, Trevor Howard, John Mills, Christopher Jones, Leo McKern, Barry Foster. Production: Anthony Havelock-Allan. 206 mins.

David Lean has applied epic values to a fragile and delicate love story, and the result is ninety-nine percent successful. Far from swamping or dwarfing the characters, the huge vistas of sea and sky set them in a perspective which gives both a universal reference and an individual intimacy to the human problems so sensitively presented by his outstanding cast. An enormous amount of thought went to the selection of a suitable location, and eventually an entire village was erected on the Irish coast. Here Freddie Young (with Denys Coop and Bob Huke as second units making up a notable trinity) entrances the eye with great sweeps of sea, sand, cliff, sunset and cloud— and Roy Stevens builds up the most shattering storm yet achieved on film. At only two points does the hold slacken: the first, a too abruptly timed kiss-and-scuffle between the girl and the officer which comes dangerously near to jerking out the unwanted laugh; the second, the obligatory copulation on the ground, mercifully implicit but moving into *cliché* symbolism of sun-dappling trees and mother nature. Apart from these relatively minor points there is nothing to cavil at in this beautiful, moving, exciting, superbly acted and photographed production.

*1970: After the storm, Leo McKern and Sarah Miles in RYAN'S DAUGHTER.*

KES. Script: Barry Hines, Ken Loach, Tony Garnett, based on a novel by Barry Hines. Direction: Ken Loach. Photography: Chris Menges (Technicolor). Editing: Roy Watts. Music: John Cameron. Art Direction: William McCrow. Players: David Bradley, Colin Welland, Lynne Perrie, Freddie Fletcher. Production: Woodfall (Tony Garnett). 113 mins.

In his second feature film Ken Loach has shaken

*1970: Boy and bird, David Bradley in Ken Loach's*
*KES.*

himself free of the over-emphasis that weighed down his first (*Poor Cow*) and offers a simple, touching, bitter little tale of a boy's taste of honey —in the form of a kestrel hawk he adopts and cares for. Though caustic in its picture of a cold, futile, dispiriting educational system, the film is mercifully free from hysterical over-statement—indeed, the one person who comes nearest to understanding the boy's emotions regarding his hawk is a well-meaning master from the school. The boy himself is no downtrodden angel—he is already, in fact, on the way to achieving proficiency as a petty thief—and this makes the destruction of the means by which he might have been liberated all the more deplorable. Though occasionally the comedy tips over into burlesque (e.g. the football scene), the result is so hilarious that the discrepancy of style is easily accepted. *Kes* had considerable difficulty in reaching a wide audience, partly because of fears that the North country dialect might prove unintelligible to alien ears: its subsequent success is a heartening indication that, in the end, occasionally, merit receives its deserts.

THE VIRGIN AND THE GYPSY. Script: Alan Plater, based on D. H. Lawrence's novella. Direction: Christopher Miles. Photography: Bob Huke (in colour). Editing: Paul Davies. Music: Patrick Gowers. Art Direction: David Brockhurst. Players: Joanna Shimkus, Franco Nero, Honor Blackman, Mark Burns, Maurice Denham, Fay Compton, Kay Walsh. Production: Dimitri de Grunwald. 95 mins.

In the best of Lawrence-based films to date, the story of a young girl's emancipation from her bleak

*1970: Franco Nero and Joanna Shimkus in THE VIRGIN AND THE GYPSY.*

and frigid rectory life through encounters with a gypsy, a free-living couple and a symbolic flood, is told with commendable sensitivity and restraint. Only in the case of the malicious Aunt Cissie is character blown into caricature. The girl's show groping towards a life and personality of her own is convincingly subtly portrayed by the excellent Joanna Shimkus—though Franco Nero's gypsy seems a rather half-hearted awakener. The Derby countryside and the gaunt grim house are put to beautiful atmospheric use, but the dam is so casually and briefly glimpsed that the climactic arrival of the waters appears too conveniently contrived. The flooding of the house itself, however, and the death of Grandma (Fay Compton at her snapping best) are terrifying—enough to drive any healthy young woman with a swarthy swain to hand to make the most of the short time apparently left to her.

HAMLET. Script: the play by William Shakespeare. Direction: Tony Richardson. Photography: Gerry Fisher (Technicolor). Editing: Charles Rees. Music: Patrick Gowers. Art Direction: Jocelyn Herbert. Players: Nicol Williamson, Anthony Hopkins, Judy Parfitt, Marianne Faithfull, Mark Dignam, Michael Pennington, Gordon Jackson. Production: Woodfall. 117 mins.

A red-brick *Hamlet*, shot entirely in an ex-railway turntable building, giving Elsinore a decidedly grimy look. It is, essentially, a reproduction of Tony Richardson's stage version, though the action appears to have been moved around into the corridors of the building. The characters are generally isolated against a very dark background, which gains in immediacy but destroys the epic qualities. The ghost does not appear—which seems strange in this medium—but is nevertheless most effectively suggested. Hamlet's mother looks as if she must have given him birth when she was around the age of ten—if not, indeed, before she was born herself. Nicol Williamson's Hamlet is powerful and often moving, though too determinedly un-princely and marred at times by some extraordinary vowel distortions. Anthony Hopkins gives an interesting and subtle performance as Claudius: but the unexpected pleasure is Marianne Faithfull's lovely Ophelia, youthful and yet avoiding the fey girlishness sometimes found, so that her loss of sanity wrings the heart. The textual

adaptation is generally acceptable, but once again, unhappily, the vital entrance of Fortinbras is cut.

THE ADDING MACHINE. Script: Jerome Epstein, from Elmer Rice's play. Direction: Jerome Epstein. Photography: Walter Lassally (Technicolor). Editing: Gerry Hambling. Music: Mike Leander, Lambert Wilkinson. Art Direction: Jack Shampan, John Lagen. Players: Milo O'Shea, Phyllis Diller, Billie Whitelaw, Sidney Chaplin, Julian Glover, Raymond Huntley. Production: Jacob Epstein. 99 mins.

The difficult task of adapting Rice's expressionist play for the screen has been most successfully accomplished with the exact mixture of the natural and the stylised. Much of the film is visually exciting, the beach sequence is ravishing, the cross-fading between sepia and colour to contrast theatrical aside and direct dialogue is very effective, the performances of O'Shea, Billie Whitelaw and Phyllis Diller could hardly be bettered. Some of the bite as well as the immediate relevance of the original has inevitably gone, a few ill-advised gags have been inserted, the beginning is better than the end: even so, the virtual disappearance of this film after a truncated showing in London, before the public had even had a chance to stay away, was a matter for—to put it mildly—regret.

*1970: THE ADDING MACHINE, Milo O'Shea and Phyllis Diller as Mr. and Mrs. Zero in an underrated film.*

BRONCO BULLFROG. Script, Direction: Barney Platts-Mills. Photography: Adam Barker-Mill. Edit-

*1970: Michele Dotrice contemplates her mysteriously wrecked bicycle in AND SOON THE DARKNESS, directed by Robert Fuest. Had this film carried the name of the Master of Suspense it would have been recognised as one of his minor works, perhaps, but still a first-class study of mounting and undefined terror, with an atmosphere of claustrophobic menace in wide-open spaces, of imprisonment in a world of barely understood language, of encroaching darkness both actual and metaphorical, unerringly sustained.*

ing: Jonathan Gili. Music: Howard Werth. Players: Del Walker, Anne Gooding, Sam Shepherd. Production: Maya (Andrew St. John). 86 mins.

There is always a chance that a first feature made on a miniscule budget, with an amateur cast, a low-class location, inexperienced photography and editing, and a theme of youthful frustration, will be overpraised simply because it has had a struggle to reach the commercial screen at all.

*Bronco Bullfrog,* however, deserves its ultimate success, taking a truthful, humorous, quirky, friendly but unbiased look at its shiftless but likeable characters and their dull, frustrating lives. The "generation gap" is treated from the inevitable point of view (a film on what parents think of their offspring and friends will be an interesting novelty one day), but it is not overplayed. For most of the way the film is refreshingly candid and

*1970: Anne Boleyn at her execution. Geneviève Bujold in ANNE OF THE THOUSAND DAYS, romantic history from the woman's angle, produced by Hal Wallis, directed by Charles Jarrott, a box-office success notable for its performances rather than its text. Richard Burton is Henry VIII.*

*1970: Peter Sellers in HOFFMAN, giving one of his very best performances in a wholly delightful British comedy of a mild man who suddenly finds himself in a position to blackmail a pretty typist, for whom he has yearned for months, into spending a week in his apartment. Alvin Rakoff's direction develops human relationships with considerable subtlety, with Sinead Cusack wholly captivating in support.*

clear-eyed; for all the way it is highly entertaining and pointed.

## 1970: Facts of Interest

E.M.I. and M-G-M. form a partnership for the operation of Elstree studios, and the former M-G-M. lot at Boreham Wood is closed down. Associated British Pictures Corporation changes its name to E.M.I. Film and Theatre Corporation but the cinemas are still known as A.B.C.

A new category system is drawn up by the British Board of Film Censors, consisting of "U" (suitable for general exhibition); "A" (general exhibition, but parents of under-fourteens are advised to be careful); "AA" (restricted to fourteen and over); "X" (restricted to eighteen and over).

Rank opens what is claimed to be the largest triple cinema complex in Europe—at Glasgow.

National Film Theatre Two is opened, and the number of B.F.I. regional theatres reaches thirty-three.

Death of William Beaudine—American director of a number of British films, including several starring Will Hay.

# 1971

THE GO-BETWEEN. Script: Harold Pinter, from L. P. Hartley's novel. Direction: Joseph Losey. Photography: Gerry Fisher (Technicolor). Editing: Reginald Beck. Music: Michel Legrand. Art Direction: Carmen Dillon. Players: Julie Christie, Dominic Guard. Alan Bates, Margaret Leighton, Michael Redgrave, Michael Gough, Edward Fox. Production: John Heyman, Norman Priggen. 116 mins.

One of the oldest of all dramatic themes is the gradual disintegration of an apparently ordered and placidly permanent pattern—whether of a character, a life, a society, a world, whether from within or without, or—as here—from both simultaneously. Rarely has the theme been more subtly developed or more thoroughly explored than in this dazzlingly beautiful film. Into the enclosed, serenely unassailable and leisured Edwardian world comes the external influence in the shape of the young son's schoolboy friend, bearing his seeds of destruction in his willingness to act as postman: but the canker, symbolised by the deadly nightshade in the neglected corner of the garden, is already there—and all that the intruder does is to nurture its growth. The long hot summer ends (with perhaps too pat a symbol) in the first storm as the final catastrophe occurs. Through the film are threaded flashforwards to the car moving through the cold, wet countryside as the elderly "go-between" revisits the place, to be sent on his last intermediary message. What was a seemingly pointless, temporal mystification in *Accident* is justified here as a vital part of and reference to the whole significance of the film. The reconstruction of a lost period, filtered through memory but essentially true, is masterly. Outstandingly acted by a flawless cast (including Michael Redgrave almost miraculously conveying a whole lifetime in a few close-ups and half-a-dozen words), and photographed with heartbreaking loveliness, this film alone would be sufficient to place Losey in the very forefront of directors in British cinema.

*1971: Dominic Guard as the "postman" and Alan Bates as the farmer in Joseph Losey's masterpiece THE GO-BETWEEN.*

THE RAGING MOON (LONG AGO, TOMORROW). Script: Bryan Forbes, from Peter Marshall's novel. Direction: Bryan Forbes. Photography: Tony Imi (Technicolor). Editing: Timothy Gee. Music: Stanley Myers. Art Direction: Robert

*1971: THE RAGING MOON (LONG AGO, TOMOR-*
*ROW), Malcolm McDowell reads the poem to Nanette*
*Newman by the seashore.*

Jones. Players: Malcolm McDowell, Nanette Newman, Georgia Brown, Barry Jackson, Gerald Sim, Michael Flanders. Production: E.M.I. (Bruce Cohn Curtis). 111 mins.

In this study of a young working-class man's gradual coming to terms with sudden physical disability which will confine him to a wheelchair for the rest of his life, Forbes triumphantly avoids the obvious pitfalls, in particular that of arousing the viewer's suspicions that his emotions are being unfairly manipulated, and produces one of the most moving and inspiring films for many a long month. Far from lapsing into easy sentimentality, he treats his characters and their situation with a toughness and resilience that make the moments of tenderness all the more effective—aided by superb performances from Malcolm McDowell and Nanette Newman; and from Georgia Brown and Barry Jackson in two beautifully drawn supporting parts. The opening wedding sequence is somewhat protracted and even veers briefly towards farce, but all else rings true: those who have criticised the portrayals of the Nursing Home officials as caricatures must have been fortunate, so far, in their own experiences.

TALES OF BEATRIX POTTER. Script: Richard Goodwin, Christine Edzard, based on Beatrix Potter's characters and stories. Photography: Austin Dempster (Technicolor). Editing: John Rushton. Music: John Lanchbery, based on various Victorian composers. Choreography: Frederick Ashton. Art Direction: John Howell. Masks: Rotislav Doboujinsky. Players: Carole Ainsworth, Frederick Ashton, Sally Ashby, Avril Bergen, Michael Coleman, Lesley Collier, Leslie Edwards, Erin Geraghty. Production: E.M.I. (Richard Goodwin). 90 mins.

This enchanting ballet film will obviously have particular appeal to those familiar with Beatrix Potter's mice, rabbits, squirrels, pigs, foxes and other inhabitants of the Lakeland countryside; but its attraction need be in no way conditional on knowledge of the stories. The opening vista of wide green fields across which bobs a small white dot that turns out to be Mrs. Tiggy-Winkle the hedgehog, sets the scene for the nature-based fantasy which is to follow, the several episodes culminating in a brilliantly staged picnic in which all the characters are gathered together. Particu-

larly ingenious is the use of proportion in the settings by which we are completely convinced of the relative size of the little creatures moving within them. The music is both fitting to its subject and pleasant to hear on its own, and the masks, vibrant with life, are little miracles. The brief scenes of the young Beatrix, drawing her small animals in the gloomy house, are done in complete silence save for the ticking of an old clock, admirably conveying the solitary introspection from which her fantastic world was created.

1971: Michael Coleman as Jeremy Fisher the frog, in the ballet film TALES OF BEATRIX POTTER.

SUNDAY, BLOODY SUNDAY. Script: Penelope Gilliatt. Direction: John Schlesinger. Photography: Billy Williams (DeLuxe Colour). Editing: Richard Marden. Music: Ron Geesin; the Trio from Mozart's Cosi Fan Tutte. Art Direction: Norman Dorme. Players: Glenda Jackson, Peter Finch, Murray Head, Peggy Ashcroft, Maurice Denham. Production: Vectia (Joseph Janni). 110 mins.

Sunday, Bloody Sunday opens cleverly with shots of a telephone exchange—the telephone being so important a part of the story that follows as almost to emerge as a character in its own right —symbolising both the complexity and the frailty of human communication, as well as the twisted, writhing nerves that both draw the characters together and hold them apart. Unfortunately, these characters themselves are less interesting than the machinery so necessary to them. It is difficult to work up much feeling for or involvement with the three abnormal and egotistical people (a homosexual Jewish doctor, a divorced woman business consultant, both sharing the same young hetero-homo-lover), whose tangled web is tortuously put before us. The young man escapes in the end, and one can't blame him—though he seemed to do quite well while it lasted. The deep, unsentimental pity of *Midnight Cowboy* is missing here, perhaps because of the worthlessness of two sides of the triangle. As the third side Peter Finch arouses, by his restrained and thoughtful playing, a certain sympathy.

THE RAILWAY CHILDREN. Script: Lionel Jeffries, from E. Nesbit's novel. Direction: Lionel Jeffries. Photography: Arthur Ibbetson (Technicolor). Editing: Teddy Darvas. Music: Johnny Douglas. Art Direction: John Clark. Players: Dinah Sheridan, Bernard Cribbins, William Mervyn, Jenny Agutter, Sally Thomsett, Gary Warren. Production: A.B.P. (Robert Lynn). 108 mins.

Telling E. Nesbit's well-known story absolutely straight, Lionel Jeffries in his directorial *début* has brought off an almost perfect grown-ups' children's film. There are no patronising concessions to presumed young tastes, and very little exaggeration of character or incident. The movie, as the book, relates a perfectly "possible" (and very exciting) tale which happens to be about three children—and some trains. The period is charmingly but unobtrusively re-created—serving as a background to the events rather than dwelt on for its own quaint qualities. The highest praise that can be given to the youthful trio of players is that they more than hold their own against the fascinating and photogenic old railway. It is interesting to compare this film with those of the Children's Film Foundation (of which one of the very best examples is noted this year)—each fulfilling their slightly different purpose to perfection and together representing one of the brightest sides of the British cinema.

UNMAN, WITTERING AND ZIGO. Script: Simon Raven, from Giles Cooper's television play. Direction: John Mackenzie. Photography: Geoffrey Unsworth (Eastmancolor). Editing: Fergus McDonell. Music: Michael J. Lewis. Art Direction: William MacCrow. Players: David Hemmings, Carolyn Seymour, Douglas Wilmer, Anthony Haygarth, Donald Gee, David Jackson, Colin Barrie. Production: Paramount/Mediarts (with David Hemmings). 102 mins.

John Ebony arrives at a small public school by the sea to take over from a master who has been found dead at the bottom of the cliffs. His form is composed of unruly teenagers with outlandish names—the last on the list, indeed, the invisible Zigo, never becomes more than a name. When Ebony attempts to impose a little discipline, they inform him that they may kill him as they did his predecessor, countering his initial total disbelief with item after item of proof. On this *Blackboard Jungle* variation has been constructed a parable of present-day menace in which the incredibly horrible becomes horribly credible. Only the ending of this unnervingly gripping film loses its power to chill, a last-minute routine hit at the System rationalising and thus weakening the terror. One might also perhaps question whether the master's wife could have escaped quite so easily from the attempted mass rape by some score of stalwart youths in the fives-court.

THE ABOMINABLE DOCTOR PHIBES. Script: James Whiton, William Goldstein. Director: Robert Fuest. Photography: Norman Warwick (Movielab Color). Editing: Tristam Cones. Music: Basil Kirchen, Jack Nathan. Art Direction: Brian Eatwell, Bernard Reeves. Players: Vincent Price, Joseph Cotten, Hugh Griffiths, Terry-Thomas, Virginia North, Aubrey Woods, Peter Jeffrey. Production: Louis M. Heyward, Ron Dunas. 94 mins.

This highly enjoyable essay in Gothic horror-comic concerns an obviously artificial-faced ex-music hall-musical-magician who revenges his wife's death during an operation by visiting the curses of Pharaoh—one by one—on the doctors he considers responsible. Amid settings of marvellously flamboyant absurdity a voiceless Vincent Price imbibes whiskey through a gurgling tube in his throat, utters metallic sentiments by means of a sucker-attached microphone, and commits a non-stop series of murders with unparalleled ingenuity and complexity. Most sinister touch of all: in the coffin he eventually enters to go to his rest (after self-embalming) is a telephone—ready, no doubt, for a call from his agent when the sequel script is prepared. (As this book goes to press news arrives that the telephone has rung).

*1971: UNMAN, WITTERING AND ZIGO, David Hemmings attempts to retain control of his class.*

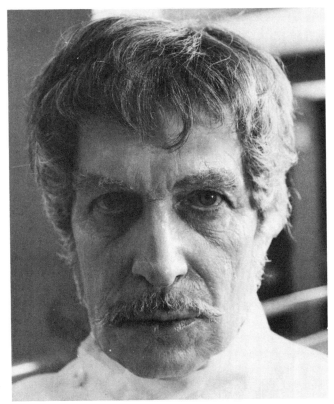

*1971: Vincent Price, wearing his "artificial face" as THE ABOMINABLE DR. PHIBES.*

## Short Films and Documentaries

KAMA SUTRA RIDES AGAIN. Script: Stan Hayward. Direction: Bob Godfrey. Photography: Paul Whibley. Editing: Tony Fish. Music: Johnny Hawksworth. Production: Ron Inkpen. 9 mins.

A little suburban sexologist and his wife, Stanley and Ethel Icarus, try to relieve their boredom by experimenting with increasingly original and complex sexual techniques—until Mr. Icarus, like his namesake before him—flies too close to the sun. Godfrey's sharp wit and humour is equalled only by his ingenuity and erudition in the subject of his hilarious and beautifully timed animation film.

## 1971: Facts of Interest

Bryan Forbes retires from his post of head of production of E.M.I./M-G-M. but remains on the board of the E.M.I. Film and Theatre Corporation as an advisory director.

John Trevelyan leaves the British Board of Film

*1971: Mr. Icarus tries out a novel technique in Bob Godfrey's animated short, KAMA SUTRA RIDES AGAIN.*

Censors after twenty years, for twelve of which he was Secretary.

Death of Basil Dearden, in a motor accident, and Seth Holt.

*1971: THE DEVILS. Vanessa Redgrave in one of the
striking compositions from Ken Russell's overheated,
anything-to-shock but often visually impressive film
about the "possessed" nuns of Loudun.*

# Index

*Figures in italics signify illustrations*